Beyond Blood

Beyond Blood

RETHINKING INDIGENOUS IDENTITY

Pamela D. Palmater

PURICH
PUBLISHING
LIMITED
SASKATOON, SK. CANADA

Purich Publishing Ltd.
Box 23032, Market Mall Post Office, Saskatoon, SK, Canada, S7J 5H3
Phone: (306) 373-5311 Fax: (306) 373-5315 Email: purich@sasktel.net
www.purichpublishing.com

Library and Archives Canada Cataloguing in Publication

Palmater, Pamela D. (Pamela Doris), 1970-
    Beyond blood : rethinking indigenous identity / Pamela D. Palmater.

Includes index.
Originally presented as the author's thesis (Ph.D. – Dalhousie) under the title: Beyond blood : rethinking aboriginal identity and belonging.
ISBN 978-1-895830-60-6

1. Indians of North America – Legal status, laws, etc. – Canada. 2. Indians of North America – Canada – Band membership. 3. Canada. Indian Act. I. Title.

KE7709.P35 2011   342.7108'72   C2011-901387-8
KF8205.P35 2011

Edited, designed, and typeset by Donald Ward.
Cover design by Jamie Olson.
Index by Ursula Acton.
Cover image: Istock.
Printed and bound in Canada at Houghton Boston Printers and Lithographers, Saskatoon.

Purich Publishing gratefully acknowledges the assistance of the Government of Canada through the Canada Book Fund, and the Creative Industry Growth and Sustainability Program made possible through funding provided to the Saskatchewan Arts Board by the Government of Saskatchewan through the Ministry of Tourism, Parks, Culture and Sport for its publishing program.

Printed on 100 per cent post-consumer, recycled, ancient-forest-friendly paper.

Contents

I DEDICATE THIS BOOK to my father, Frank Palmater, who passed away after living a life of contradictions — having fought for his country while his country abandoned him; having loved learning so much, but having been denied access to education; and having encouraged us to fight for our Mi'kmaq identity, despite being raised in a world that saw him as less than human.

I also dedicate this book to my two children, Mitchell and Jeremy, on whose behalf we have to continue this battle so they can enjoy the identity of our ancestors and that which most eluded my father — acceptance.

Forewords

WE, AS HUMAN BEINGS, are constantly developing our identity, from birth to the end of our lives. We build our identities based on our relationships to relatives, friends, community, geography, language, and other social factors. Those identities play a key role in our lives. When a child feels a sense of belonging to family, community, and peers, he or she is better able to deal with adversity. Most people are able to take their cultural identities for granted. Generally, people know they are Dutch, German, Italian, or Chinese, for example. In Canada, however, the federal government controls the identities of Indigenous peoples through its laws and policies. Specifically, it controls whether or not Indigenous people may identify themselves as "Indian," which in turn affects their ability to be a member in a local community or a citizen of their Indigenous nation.

The legal concept of "Indian" is based on the federal legislation known as the *Indian Act*. Canada has assumed that its responsibility for "Indians and Lands reserved for the Indians" under section 91(24) of the *British North America Act, 1867* extends to determining our identities. To be an "Indian" in Canada is not only a legal category, but for some, it has become a government-controlled criterion to access our Aboriginal and treaty rights. Canada, rather than Indigenous communities themselves, legislate who is an Indian — a power it had hoped would eventually lead to the assimilation of Indians.

Prior to contact, we, the First Nations of this country, had our own methods of determining our identity. We had matriarchal, patriarchal, clan, and kinship systems for transmitting our identities to our children. Before Europeans came to North America, First Nations were sovereign nations, and remain so today. We have never lost our right to be self-determining. Our oral history is supported by the work of countless anthropologists and historians, which shows that we had complex systems of governance, which included political alliances for the protection of our traditional territories, and extensive trading networks. We also had our own constitutions, laws, and systems of justice which were respected by our people. Our systems were characterized by oral teachings, histories, traditions, and the overall collective good. Most of our decisions were based on consensus. Our future as Indigenous Nations compels us to re-assert our sovereignty and go back to our laws and traditions to make citizenship determinations work for our nations.

From 1986-1991, I served as chair of the Chief's Committee on Citizenship for the Assembly of First Nations. During this time, we debated many issues, including the right of Indigenous nations to determine their own citizenship. There was a lot of frustration among participants that there was no respect for the right of First Nation governments to determine their own citizenship. My own feeling was one of anger against the fact that the federal government wanted to control who we are as peoples with no respect for our cultures and history.

Dr. Palmater's book provides a much-needed perspective on how we must identify the colonial origins of our current legal identities so that we can take back our traditional national identities. Her discussion of our inherent rights, the importance of our traditional laws, and our responsibility to protect our sovereignty will contribute significantly to the dialogue for Canadian politicians, the Canadian public, the academic world, and First Nation communities. Canada's control over our legal identity has resulted in the exclusion of thousands of Indigenous women and their children from our communities. Despite several legal determinations of discrimination, Canada has been slow to stem the tide of assimilation. Dr. Palmater's own family history is a living testimony to the wrongs of a legislated identity, and how we can't wait any longer to stand up for our future generations.

It is my hope that those who read this book will start to understand the inherent right of First Nations to protect their nationhood and the determining of our own citizenship. The reader must understand that our people have endured forced relocations of entire nations, and we have had our children kidnapped and placed in residential schools by the church and the state to remove the "Indian" from the child. Even today we are forced to spend huge amounts of time and money to have the Supreme Court of Canada bring the Canadian government to task to honour our constitutionally protected rights. Section 35 of the *Constitution Act, 1982* was a promise to First Nations to protect our rights and identities from further erosion by the state. Now, the *United Nations Declaration on the Rights of Indigenous Peoples* says that Canada has a positive, legal obligation not only to refrain from interfering with our right to determine our own identities, but to take steps to restore the identities that have been lost.

I am very proud of Dr. Palmater for having had the courage to engage in such a complicated and personal issue for the benefit of all Indigenous peoples.

Chief Bill Montour
Six Nations of the Grand River

As an Aboriginal woman and a leader in my community, I see this book as a valuable tool to ensure that our fight to regain and maintain our rights is kept in the forefront of national politics. The future of our children is dependent upon our refusal to allow government policy to determine entitlement to what is inherent by virtue of who we are as a nation. We must stand strong in the wake of continued attempts by government to assimilate us using blood quantum to water down the bloodline and with it our entitlement, our rich culture, and our heritage.

For hundreds of years, we have struggled to survive amid a patrilineal system of government. Attempts to weaken us have failed. If anything, they have made us stronger and more determined to move forward and take our rightful place as citizens of this country. We will not continue to allow government policy to manage our affairs, decide who is Aboriginal or not based on blood quantum, or gradually erode and eventually eradicate altogether that which is inherently ours. We will not be silenced.

Chief Candice Paul
St. Mary's First Nation

The federal government's 1969 White Paper and its objective of assimilating First Nations into Canadian society was defeated by the unanimous voices of First Nations across this country. Yet the *Indian Act* continues to do the very same thing through the registration (status) provisions in section 6 of the *Act*. The 'bleeding' out of our citizens through the ¼ blood rule in the status provisions means the eventual legislative extinction of our communities. In modern liberal democracies, there is no room for cultural intolerance, gender discrimination, or laws and policies designed to assimilate entire peoples. It is time that the *Indian Act* was revised, section by section, in full consultation with First Nations so that we can keep the sections which benefit our communities and finally eliminate those sections which threaten our very existence. Dr. Palmater's book raises these very important issues that need to be addressed for the benefit of our future generations.

Chief Lawrence Paul
Millbrook First Nation

A POWERFUL UNDERCURRENT of Indigenous justice is rapidly shaping this country. Whether traditional legal systems or political structures recognize this very important paradigm shift or choose to ignore it, change is inevitable. We are seeing a closing-in and shattering of old political ideologies and archaic laws that have alienated Canada from other jurisdictions in the world that have corrected tattered and tarnished histories with original peoples over the past 30 years.

Our women and children of our respective Indigenous nations in Canada continue to be discriminated against by the current *Indian Act* system. The continued reliance on Supreme Court rulings that do nothing more than narrow the scope of "Indian Status" rights, blatantly avoids the truth: our right to choose our own citizens has never been given away to any government. Geography, culture, kinship, and social and political order predating European contact scream for righteous considerations in the current political and legal debates on this important subject.

This work by Dr. Pamela Palmater is an important discourse that looks at a judicial anomaly that continues to perplex the integrity of the Canadian legal system and sheds glaring contradictions on an ever-weakening honour of the crown.

Chief Isadore Day
Serpent River First Nation

Acknowledgements

THE COMPLETION OF THIS BOOK would not have been possible without the help and support of all my friends, family, community members, and fellow activists. I am incredibly thankful to my children and my large extended family who have supported me throughout the entire process. They provided me with no shortage of opinions and views, many of which became the subject of protracted, Palmater-style, no-holds-barred debates. While Frankie, Nelson, and Phil often challenged me to think outside of the current legal context, Patsy, Glenda, and Phebe offered words of encouragement when I needed it most. Many times I thought I would not finish this project, but Mitchell and Jeremy reminded me of how important it was to keep going. After I had emerged from what felt like years of total academic seclusion, my loyal friend Sonia Milliea was also there to celebrate my success.

Thank you to my doctoral thesis committee whose incredible expertise challenged me to do better. A special thank you to Karen and Don at Purich Publishing for taking a chance on me and my book, and for having the special skill it takes to ever so gently convince a lawyer that not every single word of her manuscript is necessary for a book to convey an important message. There are also other special people who contributed to my book in different ways and they all know who they are — thank you.

A Mi'kmaq Woman

I AM A MI'KMAQ WOMAN. In the Mi'kmaq tradition, a large part of what makes me who I am relates to where I came from and the connections I share in common with other Mi'kmaq people: connections to our ancestors, my extended family, my children, our traditional territories, our shared histories, languages, customs and practices, our relations with other Indigenous nations, and my home community. While all these factors have contributed to my sense of identity, other factors have challenged both my identity and my sense of belonging. In particular, the *Indian Act* and its membership provisions have kept me from enjoying both the legal identity of "Indian" and membership in my band. As a result, I have not had the same access to elders and cultural practices as those who have been legally recognized as Mi'kmaq. I have been denied the opportunity to learn my language, to learn about gathering traditional medicines (for which my grandmother was well known), and to participate in cultural activities specific to my community.

I have done my best to compensate for the negative effects of the *Indian Act* by working with other non-recognized Indigenous peoples to advocate for change. Through these activities I have become close to various groups of Indigenous people who live off reserve but who very much identify with their traditional Indigenous nations. These people have suffered the same losses as I. Canada remains in control of our individual legal identities, a fact that continues to affect our communal and national identities. The same injustices I have suffered have been passed on to my children. If we do not find solutions, future generations will also be affected.

The ongoing challenges that my children and I share with Indigenous peoples all over Canada is the primary reason I have written this book. My views will be welcomed and criticized by Indigenous peoples, and I look forward to the debate, for it is only when we work toward practical solutions that respect our traditions and our responsibilities as nations that we can change the future for our children and grandchildren. My goal is to highlight the legal, political, and cultural challenges caused by Canada's control over our identities and suggest practical solutions that are just and fair. We owe it to future generations to reflect the traditional principles on which our nations were based, not those that have been modified to suit political ends.

The injustices forced on Indigenous peoples by colonial and modern governments have caused the worst kind of sickness: our own people are now perpetuating the same injustices imposed by governments. How is it that the most inclusive of Indigenous nations can now have exclusive communities? How is it that we can fight against residential schools but allow the *Indian Act* to achieve the same results? How can we celebrate individual success in the face of communal poverty and disease? How is it that Indigenous nations that have traditionally provided for their citizens have come to create groups of haves and have-nots — citizens who have a political voice and citizens who haven't? Worst of all, how have we allowed individual aspirations to power, wealth, and influence to supersede the good of the nation? Some individual Indigenous people now work alongside governments and bureaucrats to promote assimilatory legislation and policies. If we continue in this way, our cultures and traditions will be lost, and our nations may be irrevocably weakened.

I am the mother of two boys. I come from a huge family whose home community is the Eel River Bar First Nation. The Eel River Bar Reserve #3 was established by Order-in-Council on February 28, 1807.[1] It is a tiny reserve located on the Bay of Chaleur on the northern tip of New Brunswick, a few kilometres outside the town of Dalhousie. The band's current population of 608 is divided into 326 band members on reserve and 282 off.[2]

Historically, the Mi'kmaq people were the first to inhabit the area now known as Dalhousie, New Brunswick. During the summers, they lived close to the shore where they ate salmon, shellfish, and other seasonal fish and fowl. In the winters they lived in the forest for shelter, where they would hunt and trap fur-bearing animals. They had close relations with the rest of their nation, which was spread out over other parts of what is now New Brunswick, Nova Scotia, Prince Edward Island, and parts of Quebec and the United States. They were especially close with the Mi'kmaq community at Restigouche, known as Listuguj.

Many Indigenous communities were relocated during the colonial period to meet the settlement requirements of the colonists. The Eel River Bar community used to be located in the New Mills area of northern New Brunswick where they held thousands of acres of land. They were relocated to the current reserve, which many of the residents have described as swamp land. The Mi'kmaq name for Eel River Bar is Oqpi'kanjik. While the community itself is one of the smaller ones, it makes up for its size with a rich oral history, and passionate community members who pass it on.

One of the first families to have lived in the relocated community was headed by my great grandfather, Louis Jerome, and my great grandmother, Susan Hamilton. Louis Jerome was one of the first chiefs of Eel River Bar and was well known for his frequent travels to maintain relations with other Mi'kmaq communities. "Large in stature, clothed in deerskin, decorated with porcupine quills, this Christian man travelled the North American Continent by foot," according to a family genealogy. "He would journey every summer to the Miramichi with his family to meet other Mic-Macs and celebrate in the Indian festivities."[3]

Susan Hamilton was much younger, and the affection between her and Louis was apparently a forbidden one, as her family did not approve. As the story goes, Louis decided that he had to have Susan for his wife, so he paddled across the Bay of Chaleur to what is now Quebec and "stole" her from her family. They were married on June 22, 1875, at St. John Baptist church in Dalhousie, New Brunswick. They went on to have many children, one of whom was my grandmother, Margaret Jerome.

Margaret Jerome was born October 5, 1888, according to the family history, or October 19, 1889, according to early census records. She grew up on the reserve and had close connections in Listuguj, where she visited often. She married William Palmater on June 7, 1910, and later gave birth to my father, Frank Palmater, on April 8, 1914. When the reserve was first established, there were only a handful of large families, but by 1930 the population had grown to over 30 extended families, including the Jeromes, the Labillois, the Martins, and the Caplans.

Chief Jerome's daughter Margaret lived on the Eel River Bar reserve for many years. She had many connections to various Mi'kmaq communities, and was often sought by community members for her detailed knowledge of the healing properties of local plants and herbs. She tended to the wounds of her family and other community members without the need for doctors or nurses. I have heard many stories about my father and his brothers having their heads or noses stitched up by her right in their kitchen. According to family history, many years ago there was a serious illness that spread through the communities on the north shore of New Brunswick, but few of the people my grandmother Margaret treated died from it. Large numbers of people from the non-Indigenous community were dying from the illness, despite being attended by the local doctor. When he asked my grandmother to attend with him to treat his non-Indigenous patients, it was the first time in her life she had been permitted into their homes. She successfully treated many of his patients, without pay, but when the illness was over, she was no longer permitted through their front doors. This story has been passed down to me from my siblings and to them from Margaret Labillois and other community elders who knew my grandmother well.

Margaret Jerome was raised in a traditional Mi'kmaq family and could therefore speak her language fluently. Outside her community, however, she did not speak the Mi'kmaq language, as it was not approved of in the non-Mi'kmaq community.

Margaret later married William Palmater, a non-Indigenous man with whom she had five children, one of whom was my father, Francis (Frank) Xavier Palmater.[4] Despite my grandmother's ability to speak the language fluently, she told her children that speaking Mi'kmaq would only cause them harm in the outside world. She did not feel free to pass on her language to her children and grandchildren. She passed away in 1965 at the age of 76.

Frank Palmater, my father, was Margaret's eldest son. He had a difficult life growing up. He was made to feel ashamed of his heritage and was not welcome in many public establishments. At a young age, his father, William, abandoned the family. Frank had to leave school around Grade 3 to work to support the family. He used to tell us that he missed going to school, and when his brothers and sister would get home from school he would read their school books and try to teach himself as much as he could. His brothers and sister looked up to him. One of them, my uncle Guy Palmater, used to say that his brother Frank was more like a father to them than a brother.

Frank was extremely intelligent. He owned his own electrical company at one point, and was well known for his artistic hand, but there was a part of him that suffered in silence — in that in-between world of knowing his roots and having close communal and familial ties, but not allowed to be part of the community because of the strictures of the *Indian Act*. He was not welcome in the non-Indigenous community, either.

Frank's coming-of-age coincided with the Second World War, and he jumped at the chance to serve his country and find his place in the world. He and his brothers and sister enlisted in the army, which forever changed their lives. After seeing the many atrocities of war, Frank and his siblings were all affected emotionally in significant ways. On their return, they were not recognized for their efforts. Indigenous veterans did not receive the same benefits as non-Indigenous veterans, and, in some instances, reserve lands were taken up to provide land to non-Indigenous veterans. My father received a small settlement after he had passed away. As Indigenous veterans, my uncles and aunts received far less than others, and were treated with the same distain as they had previously been treated as Mi'kmaq people.[5]

Even so, Frank Palmater always felt lucky that he made it back from the war, and was able to get married and have sons and daughters of his own. When his first wife, Betty, died, he and my mother, who had several children from a previous marriage, met and had several more children together, including me. We all lived in one house; the older siblings would leave home and return as necessary. With all the difficulties associated with a large family living in a poor region and battling racism daily, our family did its best to stay together and deal with the hardships that ensued.

One of the ways my father thought we could all have better lives than he did was to get an education, and not just a high school diploma; he wanted us to get the highest level of education possible. He encouraged me to become a scientist so that I would have the training necessary to explain the mysteries of the world. Instead of the usual presents children receive on birthdays, Christmas, and other special occasions, my father would find used books at flea markets, yard sales, and church events. He gave me many books about the Lost City of Atlantis, the secrets of the pyramids, the Loch Ness Monster, the Sasquatch, UFOs, and others dealing with subjects like ghosts, haunted houses, or the powers of the mind. Other books would be related to math, science, and nature.

Each time my father gave me a new book, he would show me news clippings and reviews he had saved in relation to that particular book and we would talk for hours about the credibility of the evidence and how one would go about researching these subjects. Most exciting were our conversations about the many discoveries one could make if one had an open mind. Conversations with him were always enlightening. If we weren't discussing science, he was telling stories about his life, including his time in the war. His stories were never negative, and he always found a way to inject humour into them. It was only when I grew up and my older siblings and relatives filled in the missing details that I realized how much he had edited for my benefit. He wanted me to see the positive side of life and not to know about his suffering.

Overlaid on this family history was the *Indian Act* and other federal policies relating to Indians.[6] My great-grandfather, Chief Louis Jerome, had every reason to believe in the text of the sacred treaties and that the rights of his heirs would be protected. He had no idea that the future would be so different from what he had fought for.[7] He could never have known that Canada would impose the *Indian Act* on his descendents in such a way as to deny them not only their treaty rights but their identity and communal membership as well.[8] My grandmother Margaret lived a long life, enduring her own pain while she tried to cure everyone else's, but she had no way of knowing that the identity she held on to so tightly, albeit behind closed doors, could be taken from her simply by marrying a non-Indian. My father Frank also had no way of knowing that fighting for his country would result in such inequitable treatment on his return. Near the end of his life, he was finally granted status as an Indian, but by then he could no longer access benefits such as post-secondary education, his lifelong dream.

My great-grandfather, my grandmother, and my father would never have expected that I would be denied my Mi'kmaq identity by the *Indian Act*, which would also mean exclusion from membership in our own home community of Eel River Bar First Nation. My father was heartbroken when Indian and Northern Affairs Canada (INAC) sent him a letter after the 1985 Bill C-31 amendments to the *Indian Act* telling him that, although he was a status Indian, none of his children would be so recognized.[9] This kind of unilateral exclusion was unforeseen in my great-grandfather's time, and it was never negotiated in our treaties. Collectively as a nation, or as individual Mi'kmaq communities, we never surrendered our rights to determine who we are as a people.

I know who I am as a Mi'kmaq woman, and I know where I come from, but I have suffered a great deal of exclusion based on my lack of Indian status. My history, ancestry, and territory are the same as that of my family who live on reserve; the only difference between us is that I am barred from living on the reserve. However, for the majority of my life, I have lived in traditional Mi'kmaq territory. I may be an off-reserve, non-status Indian, but I am an on-territory Mi'kmaq person. I have come to learn many of our traditions and beliefs, but I have also missed out on access to our community based elders to seek clarity, inspiration, and further teachings. I have familial, social, and cultural connections to my traditional community and other Mi'kmaq communities, but I cannot become a member of any of these communities because I do not have Indian status. None of this is part of our traditional culture; it has been imposed by discriminatory laws.

I have done my best to ensure that my children maintain our cultural connections, but they, too, are limited in accessing our elders' teachings. They feel hurt and shame at not being able to speak their language, at not knowing our practices and not being able to take part in all of them. While they danced at powwows when they were younger, they have not been officially allowed to register as dancers at most powwows because they lack status as Indians. They know that on the reserve there are elders who teach children their traditional language and dances, but they are barred from taking part. My children and I have to skulk around like criminals if we want to hunt or fish, not because we are not the rightful descendants of Mi'kmaq treaty signatories, but because Canada has assumed the power to determine who is an Indian, and therefore who is a Mi'kmaq. The same shame my grandmother felt for speaking her language has been passed on to my father, then to me, and now to my children.

These personal experiences are made worse by jurisdictional debates over whether the federal or provincial governments have responsibility for non-status Indians. Jurisdictional questions have led to litigation, funding gaps, and poor socio-economic indicators for non-status Indians. I am keenly aware of the political, social, and cultural background to this legal issue because my whole family has lived it. I am passionate about it because my brothers and sisters worked hard in partnership with similarly situated families in New Brunswick to ensure that we were not forgotten. It has been a long, hard struggle, and were it not for the work of my brothers and sisters and people like Sharon McIvor, these issues would still be unknown.

Sharon McIvor started her legal case over 20 years ago when her application for status on behalf of herself and her children was denied. She was successful both at trial and at appeal in proving that section 6 of the *Indian Act* determines status in a discriminatory manner against Indian women and their descendants. As the appeal court offered a decision that limited the remedy available, she filed an application to have the case heard at the Supreme Court of Canada, which was subsequently denied. As Canada's legislative response was also limited, McIvor has filed her complaint with the United Nations.[10]

I feel the need to address this complex issue because generations keep being negatively affected by their legislated exclusion from their individual identities as Indians, their communal identities through band membership, and, therefore, their national identities as Mi'kmaq. All of us — status and non-status, on reserve and off — have a responsibility to fix it. Status or non-status, we are all affected by the second generation cut-off rule in the *Indian Act*. If we do not act now, there will be no status Indians left to maintain our communities and culture into the future.

My family's experience with the exclusionary provisions of the *Indian Act* applies equally to thousands of other families across Canada. There are many different ways in which the *Indian Act* has discriminated against non-status Indians. My grandmother and her direct descendants, from my father, to me, and to my children, all suffer what is known as "cousins" discrimination, which is a form of gender discrimination. The *Indian Act* gives lesser status to the descendants of Indian women who "married out" — married or parented with a non-registered man — compared to the descendants of Indian men who married out. We also experience the second generation cut-off rule, which stipulates that two successive generations of an Indian parenting with a non-Indian will result in no status for their descendants. This kind of discrimination is based on a kind of notional blood quantum allocation or descent-based criteria for determining who is really an Indian that is not reflective of actual blood quantum, descent, or culture.

There are many more Indigenous peoples who have suffered other types of *Indian Act* discrimination, such as the double mother clause, unstated paternity, and siblings discrimination. Registration as an Indian has become a significant part of Indigenous identity on an individual and communal level, despite our best efforts at maintaining our cultural identities. An individual's proof of Indian status more often than not equates with that individual's acceptance by others as being truly Indigenous. Status affects band membership for the majority of bands in Canada whose membership is determined by the *Indian Act*. Status also affects one's ability to be included on treaty beneficiary lists, land claim rolls, and self-government citizenship enrollee lists.

While status under the *Act* is controlled solely by Canada, some bands have enacted their own membership codes that are just as exclusionary as the rules provided under the *Act*. They exclude people based on lack of Indian status, choice of spouse, lack of residency on a reserve, ill health, poor finances, and/or inadequate blood quantum. While membership codes offer bands the opportunity to rid themselves of outdated or racist concepts of themselves as Mi'kmaq, Mohawk, or Cree, for example, many of them have incorporated those concepts.

Non-status Indians all over Canada have banded together to raise awareness about these inequities and seek solutions to the divisions imposed on our communities. Together with the work of Indigenous women, this is how the original changes to the *Indian Act* (Bill C-31) came about.[11] These controversial amendments remedied some of the discrimination, but not all of it. This political activity also led to the birth of various provincial political organizations across Canada, set up to protect, promote, and assert the rights of non-status Indians.

I grew up knowing I was a Mi'kmaq person, but that my situation in life was that of a non-status Indian. My family made sure I knew it was not my fault that I was not included in reserve-based activities, but the many negative consequences of that lack of status affected me nonetheless. I was barred from running for elected office. I could not live on the reserve, nor could I exercise treaty rights off reserve. My family has been routinely harassed by provincial enforcement officers for exercising Aboriginal and treaty rights, but have yet to lose a case when challenged in court.[12] I was one of the lucky ones who had a politically active family. They made sure I understood that the discrimination in the *Indian Act* was the cause of the divisions among our people, and that we did not have to settle for this state of affairs.

My brothers and sisters, aunts, uncles, cousins, and friends, many of whom are non-status Indians, worked hard to fight for equality for us, the children of status Indians, who were really the children of Mi'kmaq people. They knew that differential treatment based on sex, marital status, residence, or blood quantum/descent in the *Indian Act's* registration provisions was the reason for the substantial population of non-status Indians and the corresponding erosion of status Indians. Bill C-31 was passed in 1985 to address the discrimination faced by Indian women who married out under the former section 12(1)(b) of the *Indian Act*. However, it did not address all the inequality and discrimination. As a result, we are left with a growing population of non-status Indians and a future where status Indian populations will continue to decline. While McIvor spent 25 years trying to remedy this, Canada has once again legislated inequality.

In 1985, the federal government tried to detach registration from membership by allowing bands the option of creating their own membership codes. Even so, these remain, for the most part, tied together both legally and practically, as individual Indigenous identity and communal belonging go hand in hand. Even the legitimacy of current and future self-government agreements is questionable, given that some are based on unconstitutional or discriminatory citizenship codes. Citizenship codes that merely carry on the status quo will not satisfy the constitutional promises made to Indigenous peoples to protect their identities and cultures for future generations.

Section 35 of the *Constitution Act, 1982* promises to protect the distinct cultures of Aboriginal peoples so that they can survive into the future, but through its control of Indian status, Canada has ensured the legislative extinction of Indians.[13] The world of non-status Indians is unlike other groups who fall outside the *Indian Act*, despite some obvious commonalities. The three groups of Aboriginal people who currently find themselves outside the *Act* are non-status Indians, Métis, and Inuit. Each of these groups has its own special relationship to the *Indian Act* and the *Constitution Acts, 1867* and *1982*.[14] The Inuit are outside the *Indian Act* by virtue of section 4 of the *Act*.[15] The Métis, as a group, are not specifically mentioned in the *Indian Act*, but "scrip takers" are excluded in previous *Indian Acts* and were not reinstated with the Bill C-31 amendments. Litigation involving all these groups is winding its way through the courts. Unless agreement can be reached on these issues, questions of identity will be resolved by the courts instead of by Aboriginal peoples. Non-status Indians, by virtue of their "non-registration" under the *Act*, are only covered by the *Act* in limited circumstances.[16]

Similarly, section 91(24) of the *Constitution Act, 1867* provides that the federal government has jurisdiction to legislate with regard to "Indians and Lands reserved for the Indians." The federal government's position is that this means they have jurisdiction over status Indians, but not non-status Indians or Métis.[17] The Supreme Court of Canada had previously decided that the Inuit were included in section 91 (24), but Canada amended the *Indian Act* specifically to exclude them from its application.[18] On the other hand, section 35 of the *Constitution Act, 1982,* includes Indians, Inuit, and Métis, but the question is whether section 35 includes non-status Indians in the term "Indian."[19] Layered on top of these legal questions of recognized identity and legislative authority are questions of individual identity and communal belonging, and where these concepts fit within the broader legalized definitions.

Many Indigenous people feel they have both an individual and a communal right to define themselves and their communities, based on their inherent Aboriginal rights and treaty rights.[20] The federal government has assumed the authority to define Indigenous individuals and communities by virtue of section 91(24) of the *Constitution Act, 1867*, but this authority is questionable.[21] Although the relevant case law is only starting to make its way to the higher courts, it becomes obvious in reading the submissions made in *McIvor v. Canada* [2009] by the appellants (Canada), the respondents (McIvor), and the seven interveners that financial considerations are the main reason Canada maintains such a tight grip on Indigenous identity.[22] The federal government appears to find itself stuck in a complex web of costing exercises, out-dated assimilatory policies, *Charter* litigation, and self-government negotiations that are moving faster than the bureaucratic decision-makers can keep up.

The issue of individual identity is inherently tied to that of communal identity and belonging (band membership and nation citizenship). While my experience has been one of rejection from communal identity on the basis of my lack of status, others have had a different experience. There are Mohawks in Kahnawake, for example, who are status Indians, but who do not meet the blood quantum set in their community's band membership code and have therefore been stripped of their band membership. In the same community, there are women who have been stripped of their band membership and their right to live in the community for marrying non-Mohawks, despite the fact that they are status Indians. These band membership rules were enacted long after Bill C-31 came into effect, long after the international community clearly stated that this kind of exclusion was discriminatory.[23] Therefore, while non-status Indians experience rejection, discrimination, and lack of recognition, so do some band members who may also be status Indians. The recent publicity around Kahnawake's residency by-law mandating that non-band members leave the reserve will have the effect of splitting families and creating hardships based on the same discriminatory rules as those once promoted by Canada. Those who are considered "non-band members" can include Mohawk people who don't meet blood quantum requirements. The issue of Indigenous identity and belonging is far more complex than simply drawing lines between Indigenous and non-Indigenous people, but involves rules that sometimes discriminate against or privilege various members within a community.

Even band membership does not guarantee equal rights. In some communities, some band members are more "equal" than others. The Supreme Court of Canada in *Corbiere*[24] noted that band members who live off reserve have just as important an interest in maintaining relations with their communities as those who live on reserve. It is for this reason that non-status Indians, non-band members, and off-reserve band members — many of whom are status Indians — often join together to advocate for equality and recognition. The federal government has empowered, and arguably encouraged, status Indians who live on reserve to exclude over 50 per cent of the Indigenous population from full legal recognition and full participation in their communities and governments.[25] The exclusion of non-status Indians from legal recognition as Indians due to the second generation cut-off rule is but one form of discrimination. However, this usually results in exclusion from band membership and subsequent exclusions from self-government agreements, land claims, and treaty benefits. Even some status Indians are excluded on the basis of their type of status — 6(1) or 6(2) Indians — their blood quantum, or whether they live on or off reserve.

One of the goals of this book is to highlight some of the current legal challenges with regard to the determination of individual and communal Indigenous identity and belonging. While I have alluded to some of these issues in this introduction, they will be explored in more detail in the chapters that follow. Chapter

I will undertake a review of the legislative treatment of Indigenous peoples by colonial governments, and examine how the definition of Indian and community have changed over time. While the definitions may have changed, the rules for determining Indigenous identity and belonging did not necessarily improve. In fact, the definitions became more restrictive over time on the principle that Indigenous peoples should be assimilated. This legislative context is important in understanding the current political and social relationships that divide Indigenous peoples, their communities and nations. The divide between traditional ways of determining identity and belonging have been twisted to meet legislated rules in order to satisfy unrelated factors, such as Canada's funding restrictions or a band's own financial predicaments. Concern over money has come to outweigh concerns about future existence.

The current demographic studies related to the different legal categories of Indigenous peoples also highlight the dangers in maintaining the legislative status quo. The problem is that Indigenous identity and, in most cases, community membership, are determined through an artificial "Indian filter" over which Indigenous peoples have no control. Identity is tied to Indian status, and this legal recognition is often the only accepted criterion for Indigenous identity. In 1985, with the Bill C-31 amendments to the *Indian Act*, the federal government tried to separate status from membership, and therefore individual identity from communal identity and belonging. It appears that Canada hopes that, by separating individual identity from communal identity, it can avoid claims that its actions adversely affect culture, while at the same time maintaining enough jurisdiction over identity to control costs. It is imperative that the implications of these legislative changes are fully explored.

Some may ask whether preserving an Indigenous identity in a modern liberal democracy is a necessary or desirable goal. Chapter 2 attempts to answer this question, providing an analysis of the theory behind the assertion of Indigenous identity and what it means to cultural survival. The term "Indian" lumps all the different Indigenous individuals and nations into one group, and ignores the fact that they all have their own cultures, histories, languages, traditions, customs, and practices. The issue of why Indigenous identity is important explains why Indigenous people don't simply give up and assimilate into the majority culture, as some academics like Tom Flanagan promote. The core principles which underlie the liberal democracies in the western world also provide the basis upon which Indigenous cultures can and should be protected. Access to culture and a secure identity in a liberal democracy is reflected in every aspect of public life for the majority population, and, as a result, it is often taken for granted. Yet, access to culture and a secure identity for Indigenous peoples has turned into a race against legislative extinction imposed by that same majority. In liberal democracies, individuals are supposed to be free from arbitrary interference from the state, but

Indigenous peoples have suffered direct and arbitrary interference in virtually every aspect of their lives.

While it is important for Indigenous peoples to maintain their cultural and communal boundaries as a way of rejecting colonization and protecting their identities, they must do so in a way that is flexible, contextual, and which incorporates the various ways of being Indigenous, so as to ensure the survival of their cultures for future generations. Chapter 2 also considers the various principles which underlie Indigenous identity and belonging, and highlights key differences between criteria such as ancestry and blood quantum, as well as the importance of modern connections to one's identity and community as opposed to freezing traditions in time. This discussion is built upon by the argument that there is an obligation on liberal democracies to take positive actions to protect vulnerable groups within Indigenous nations and the nations themselves.

In Chapter 3, I argue that the Indigenous nations in Canada have a section 35 right to determine their own citizenship. I build on this argument by explaining that the current *Van der Peet* test for determining section 35 Aboriginal rights may have to be adjusted to accommodate this unique right, because the foundation of the right to determine citizenship is based on survival of the culture into the future. Canada, through section 35 of the *Constitution Act, 1982,* made a constitutional promise to all Aboriginal peoples to protect their distinctive cultures so that they can survive into the future. However, as with all constitutional or other rights, there are limits on the right of Indigenous nations to determine their own citizenship. Governments all over the world are subject to limits on their power, and Indigenous governments are no exception. The question considered in Chapter 3 is, what kinds of limits should be placed on the right to determine citizenship? The debate whether the *Charter* applies to Indigenous peoples and their governments is also considered. I acknowledge that the question of whether the *Charter* applies to Indigenous peoples will inform the apparent tension between the right of Indigenous nations to determine their own citizenship and the right of individual Indigenous peoples to belong to those nations.

This tension is often framed as a question of individual versus group rights, or Indigenous women's rights versus the rights of their communities. The assumption by many has been that any viewpoint or concern raised by any particular sub-group of an Indigenous community or nation that is not in keeping with the position or positions asserted by the leadership of that community or nation must necessarily be in conflict with it, given the communal nature of Aboriginal rights. Chapter 3 considers whether polarized positions cause the decision-makers to overlook the fact that the community of each Indigenous nation is made up of individuals and their own identities, viewpoints, and interpretations of their traditions, values, beliefs, customs, inter-relationships with others, and ideas about the "good life." This mischaracterization of the issue as individual or women's rights versus group or community rights has led to the discrimination claims that are reviewed in the next chapter.

In Chapter 4, I briefly review some of the legal claims relating to residual discrimination in the *Indian Act* that were not addressed by Bill C-31, and some new forms of discrimination that may have been created by the newly enacted Bill C-3. Most, if not all, of these types of discrimination are currently being litigated by affected individuals across the country. The first case to deal with the constitutionality of the registration provisions of the *Indian Act* was the Sharon McIvor case which was successful both at trial and appeal levels, but was denied leave to be heard at the Supreme Court of Canada. The Court of Appeal decision in *McIvor* will therefore have a significant impact on the cases that follow it, such as Brenda Sanderson, Lynn Gehl, Connie Perron, and others. In this chapter, I also review the current case law related to *Charter* discrimination claims with a view to focusing on a theoretical claim based on my personal situation of exclusion from status based on the second generation cut-off rule. The claim raised in *McIvor* was known as the "cousins rule," which is tied to my own situation. I also consider the policy and legislative reaction to the *McIvor* case. It is in this context that I propose interim solutions to address second generation cut-off discrimination, as well as the longer term consequences of not doing so.

Chapter 5 puts all the history, statistics, law, and theory reviewed in the preceding chapters into the current political context of band membership codes, self-government agreements, and citizenship codes. The Royal Commission on Aboriginal Peoples (RCAP) offered numerous recommendations related to Indian bands in Canada, and how they might "reconstitute" themselves into their traditional nations in order to exercise their rights of self-government and jurisdiction over their citizens. While the RCAP offered many good suggestions on how to address the inequities faced by those who fall inside and outside the purview of the *Indian Act*, some have criticized their solutions as being too idealistic and unable to be practically applied. Comprehensive land claim agreements, modern treaties, and self-government negotiations can take upwards of 20 years to finalize. Many bands do not have the capacity to participate in such long-term negotiations. The question considered in this chapter is how to address the identity issues faced by those, such as non-status Indians, who are currently excluded by Canada and their own bands from legal recognition and membership. The RCAP suggested that long-term solutions lie with self-government agreements, but the question remains as to what should be done in the interim, given that those kinds of negotiations can take decades.

Even if self-government agreements were available for all First Nation communities or collective Indigenous nations in the near future, it is unlikely that these agreements would address the current inequities and discrimination found in the *Indian Act*, if one takes the current self-government agreements and federal policies related to status as any indication of what is to come. In Chapter 5, I argue that there must also be shorter-term and medium-term solutions that address Indigenous identity and belonging, so that the rights of future generations are protected when and if self-government agreements are negotiated. All Indigenous nations have their own traditions, values, and long-term nation-building priorities, and it is unlikely that a pan-Aboriginal approach would be either acceptable or practical. Even so, it is arguable that there are fundamental human rights which are inherent in all peoples and must be protected regardless of one's particular nation. Similarly, so long as there is an *Indian Act* with registration criteria, it must be in keeping with the constitutional promises made to all Aboriginal peoples. Finally, I argue that any system, whether maintained by the Crown, bands, or self-governing nations, will fail to meet the basic principles of equality if they rely on criteria such as blood quantum, genetics, gender, or race-based criteria to include or exclude people from recognition, membership, or citizenship, or from partaking in the benefits and responsibilities of their heritage passed down to them by their ancestors.

Finally, in Chapter 6, I review the key legal, political, and cultural factors affecting Indigenous identity and belonging, and I propose solutions to the current discrimination faced by non-status Indians and others regarding their Indigenous identity and membership. Any solutions that are proposed in the future, either by Canada or the Indigenous communities and nations, will have to account for the intervening history of contact, colonization, forced assimilation policies, Canada's unilateral control over both our identity and belonging, and the long-term negative impact this has had on our views about what makes us Indigenous — or Mi'kmaq, for example.

Prime Minister Stephen Harper publicly apologized on behalf of all Canadians for the assimilatory attitudes upon which government policies like residential schools were built. As a result of these harms, Canada agreed to compensate the victims of residential schools. Yet the *Indian Act* is based on those very same attitudes, and the status and membership provisions of the *Act* have had the same effects on Indigenous peoples, especially Indigenous women and their descendants. Canadians would not allow the re-institution of residential schools to assimilate Indigenous peoples. How, then, can they allow the continued assimilation of Indigenous peoples through the registration and membership provisions of the *Indian Act*?

The survivors of residential schools are commencing a process of telling their stories. They speak of the loss of connection to their families, friends, and communities, as well as the loss of knowledge about their traditions, customs, practices, and languages. Few would blame them for having lost some of their culture, language, or communal connections. How, then, could one blame non-status Indians, or status Indian women, for their loss of status, identity, and membership? The severe harms that were suffered by Indian women and their descendants, as well as other Indigenous peoples, because of the exclusionary provisions of the *Indian Act* should not be minimized.

I conclude the book by emphasizing that the severity and intergenerational effects of this discrimination must be acknowledged so that individuals, communities, governments, nations, and the public can truly understand the potential consequences of any proposed solutions.

CHAPTER ONE

Legislated Identity:
Control, Division, and Assimilation

The Honour of the Crown

Indigenous peoples in Canada have been subjected to varying degrees of government control over their individual and collective· identities, including divisive membership rules based on the goal of assimilation. The ways in which individual Indigenous peoples have been controlled and divided have furthered Canada's original aim of eliminating the "Indian problem." As Duncan Campbell Scott famously wrote, "Our objective is to continue until there is not a single Indian in Canada that has not been absorbed into the body politic and there is no Indian question, and no Indian Department. . . ."[1]

Despite Canada's apology for the foundation upon which its Indian policies were created,[2] the country continues to defend numerous assimilatory laws and policies, including the *Indian Act*'s registration provisions. The *Indian Act* and its previous incarnations have resulted in many groups and individuals being excluded from legal recognition as Indians or band members based on grounds of gender, marital status, family status, race, age, and blood quantum or descent.[3] As my band relies on Indian status to determine membership, this has precluded my children and me from membership in our home community of Eel River Bar First Nation. With Bill C-3 I will be entitled to both status and membership, but it will exclude my children. While my band has the power to amend its membership code to include non-status Indians, the band has chosen not to do so. The reasons for this are varied and complex, but they always lead back to some form of federal interference. My children will continue to be excluded from their individual and communal identities as "Indians" and therefore as Mi'kmaq peoples because Canada determines who qualifies.

In addition to using my own family as an example, in this chapter I will cite Sharon McIvor's decades-long legal battle to illustrate the current debates around registration.[4] McIvor's case deals primarily with gender discrimination in the registration (status) provisions of the *Indian Act*, as between the descendants of

Indian women who married out and Indian men who married out. My grandmother Margaret married a non-Indian man. As a result, her children, including my father, were registered as section 6(2) Indians. Had Margaret been a man who married a non-Indian woman, both the non-Indian woman and the children would have been section 6(1)(a) Indians. The grandchildren of Indian women who married out do not have status, whereas the grandchildren of Indian men who married out do. While Bill C-3 will grant status for some grandchildren, many will be excluded.

Registration under the *Indian Act* is complex, with many confusing and illogical rules that give preference to Indian men. The overall formulas, on the other hand, are quite simple, and reflect a basic concept of blood quantum or descent-based rules designed to assimilate all Indians through legislative extinction. I argue that the *Act* discriminates against my family on the basis of blood quantum because the registration provisions incorporate what amounts to a second generation cut-off rule that is based on racist concepts of blood purity. These criteria are not only discriminatory, but counter to modern democratic principles and notions about identity and human dignity. While the *Indian Act* does not use the term "blood quantum" in the registration provisions, through its reliance on specific degrees of birth descent, Canada has, in effect, incorporated a type of blood quantum by birth descent for status Indians born after April 17, 1985, when Bill C-31 amended the *Indian Act*. In other words, one generation of marrying out equals 50 per cent notional Indian blood quantum, two generations equals 25 per cent, and so on. I refer to this kind of discrimination as blood quantum for ease of reference.

Canada makes the presumption that blood quantum or remoteness of descent from one's Indian ancestor equates with one's level of connection to both an individual and a communal Indigenous identity and culture. My children and I are excluded from status on the basis of the sex of our grandmother and the blood quantum rules assessed against us by Indian and Northern Affairs Canada (INAC). This lack of status and membership means that we cannot live on the reserve, nor can we participate in our band's governance activities. We cannot run for elected office on reserve, vote in elections, or have a say in referendums affecting our reserve and title lands or our treaty rights. We are excluded from land claim negotiations and benefits, treaty entitlements, and regular access to our elders and community-based mentors. We are excluded because our band has a membership code that allows only status Indians to be members. Our band likely has this code because Canada's funding formulas are often based on status Indian population numbers, not membership or "citizenship" numbers. Our band is not the only one with these types of membership provisions; the majority of bands in the country rely on Canada to determine their membership or they have codes that rely on *Indian Act* status provisions to determine membership.[5]

While the goal of Indigenous Nations, however constructed, is to have their inherent jurisdiction to determine their own citizenship rules recognized, and while few may assert their inherent jurisdiction, practically speaking this will likely only come about in negotiated self-government agreements or modern treaties. In the meantime, communal identity will equate to band membership in individual First Nations or bands, and the registration provisions determined by Canada will determine membership.[6] I explore these discrimination arguments in more detail in Chapter 4 and review some of the band membership codes and self-government citizenship codes in Chapter 5. The purpose of this chapter is to examine the historical and legislative context in which Canada has asserted jurisdiction over Indian identity and belonging. I also look at some of the key amendments to the *Act's* registration provisions, and how they have affected traditional concepts of identity, with legally recognized identity (status) and belonging (membership) as a result. To demonstrate the impact of the status and membership provisions, I include a review of some of the demographic studies that have been done on both status and membership, and discuss what the future holds for First Nations if we continue on our current path. Canada may have backed away from publicly supporting assimilatory policies, but its defence of this registration system over the years is evidence that assimilation continues.

The majority of the traditional territories in which the Mi'kmaq, Maliseet, Mohawk, and other Indigenous Nations lived and hunted, and the seas and lakes on which they fished and travelled for trade, were taken up by colonial governments in the name of settlement. Their customs and languages were considered inferior, and in some cases were outlawed by colonial governments. The Crown eventually assumed some form of control over most aspects of their individual and communal lives. The majority of the land, natural resources, and power in Canada is in the hands of the federal government or non-Indigenous settlers. Indigenous nations have been denied the use of their lands and resources and their traditional means of subsistence, and are criticized for failing to prosper in the same ways and at the same level as the settlers. Federal and provincial governments have assumed control over economic levers through legislation, regulations, policies, and enforcement measures so as to maximize economic benefits to the settler populations while leaving Indigenous nations in Third World conditions.

The *Report of the Royal Commission on Aboriginal Peoples* (RCAP) was a comprehensive research undertaking that examined all facets of Aboriginal history and conditions in Canada. The RCAP explained that it was Canada's assimilatory laws and policies which have been the cause of weakening of First Nations:

Policies of domination and assimilation battered Aboriginal institutions, sometimes to the point of collapse. Poverty, ill health and social disorganization grew worse. Aboriginal people struggled for survival as individuals, their nationhood erased from the public mind and almost forgotten by themselves.[7]

Not only has Canada denied Indigenous peoples their traditional lands and resources, it has further denied them reasonable access to mechanisms to address outstanding treaty, land, and other obligations. This has had a devastating effect on their cultures, identities, and well-being.[8]

In recent decades, Indigenous peoples have started to use Canadian laws and adjudication processes to address their grievances, but these mechanisms often require that they bring forward each issue separately, and usually in isolation from the larger context from which the issue stems. Sharon McIvor was thus forced to litigate the narrow issue of gender discrimination in one sub-section of the *Indian Act*, instead of addressing all the discrimination on a once-and-for-all basis. Despite the fact that McIvor won her case at trial and on appeal — the Supreme Court of Canada refused to hear a further appeal — Canada's response has been to limit the potential legislative remedy to a narrow interpretation of the *McIvor* appeal case.[9] At trial, the British Columbia Supreme Court found that there was gender discrimination between the descendants of Indian women who married out (now registered under section 6(1)(c) of the *Indian Act, 1985*) as compared to the descendants of Indian men who married out (now registered under section 6(1)(a) of the *Act*).[10] On appeal, the court reduced the finding of discrimination to one that was not even argued at trial: discrimination between the descendants of section 12(1)(b) women (Indian women who lost status by marrying out) and descendants of section 12(1)(a)(iv) men (Indian men who lost status due to the double mother clause).[11] Equality rights are worth little without timely access to justice, and McIvor's case shows that, for Indian women and their children, court mechanisms are delayed at best and offer hollow remedies at worst. McIvor's long struggle has not yet resulted in full equality for Indian women and their descendants, and if the current legislative response (Bill C-3: *Gender Equity in Indian Registration Act*) is any indication, other individuals will be forced to go through the court system for many decades in order to have nearly identical concerns heard, because Bill C-3 does not even address the limited discrimination found in the appeal decision.[12]

Even if Canada had addressed the limited gender discrimination issue addressed in *McIvor*, or if it had gone further and addressed all gender discrimination in the registration provisions of the *Indian Act*, there would still be other discriminatory provisions, such as those based on blood quantum criteria, that would divide communities and discriminate against individuals. For example, under Bill C-3, my father will be registered as a section 6(1)(c.1) Indian as opposed to a section 6(2) Indian. Had his mother been his father, he would have always been registered under section 6(1)(a), as would his wife and children. Additionally, Bill C-3 will make me a section 6(2) Indian, but it will not address the fact that my children will remain non-status Indians because of the second generation cut-off rule in the *Act*.[13] Yet, had my grandmother been my grandfather, my children would be section 6(2) Indians. This differential treatment between categories of status Indians is based on a notional allocation of blood quantum that Canada has determined is required to prove descent from an Indigenous community. Descent from a single Indian ancestor can be no more than two generations (or no less than one-quarter blood quantum) in order to be recognized. This determination is arbitrary and has little to do with actual identity, citizenship, or nationhood. This kind of discrimination is based on ideologies about what makes a "race" and is clearly a violation of section 15 of the *Canadian Charter of Rights and Freedoms*.[14] Even a complete remedy in *McIvor* does not address other forms of discrimination. Litigating each of the issues separately makes for a painfully slow way to address ongoing inequalities caused by the registration and membership provisions of the *Indian Act*. The honour of the Crown requires that Canada do better.

Labels and Politics

The recurring theme here is control, division, and assimilation — the crux of the problem being Canada's jurisdiction over the individual and communal identities of Indigenous peoples. The *Indian Act* has had a profound influence on Indigenous identity, especially since the introduction of the registry in 1951.[15] No single factor has had a more profound effect on the determination of Indigenous political, cultural, social, and legal identity as the *Indian Acts* and related policies.[16] While not every act was intended to define who was or was not an Indian, most of the colonial legislation had provisions that defined Indigenous individuals and their communities. The effect is still felt today, as Indigenous people are judged in terms of where they fit on the "Indianness" scale.[17] The whole concept of Indianness was based on the idea that there was one Indian people who existed at a point frozen in time, and that they should either be civilized or assimilated to free up lands for settlement. Some of the tools used by Canada to this end were forced relocations, residential schools, and legislative disenfranchisement.

Canada has acknowledged that its policies were wrong. On June 11, 2008, the Prime Minister offered an apology on behalf of Canada to former students of Indian residential schools. He stated, in part,

> Two primary objectives of the residential school system were to remove and isolate children from the influence of their homes, families, traditions and cultures, and to assimilate them into the dominant culture.

These objectives were based on the assumption that aboriginal cultures and spiritual beliefs were inferior and unequal. Indeed, some sought, as was infamously said, "to kill the Indian in the child."

Today, we recognize that this policy of assimilation was wrong, has caused great harm, and has no place in our country.[18]

It is hard to imagine that an official assimilation policy designed to legislatively eliminate a people would be acceptable in a liberal democracy after such an apology, but the registration system that divided Indigenous peoples and diminished access to their cultures decades ago was just as destructive as the residential schools, and it is still active — recognizing, of course, that residential schools and the severe abuse suffered there make them the worst of Canada's assimilation policies, and some argue they cannot be compared for that reason.

The political context is important for understanding how complex the issue of Indigenous identity has become. The words used to describe the various groupings of Indigenous peoples reflect their current political and social divisions. To understand the politics, one must understand the terminology, the origins of these terms, and what they mean, legally and politically. The legal and political uncertainties related to Indian identity issues spill out into other Aboriginal groups such the Métis, who now have their own rules about whether to accept status and non-status Indians as members.[19] Indigenous nations were not just divided socially and culturally by the definitions of the *Indian Act*; they are now divided politically, forming complex groups that often overlap.

Local, provincial, regional, territorial, and national Aboriginal organizations must work with hundreds of communities to articulate the goals and aspirations of their constituents. In a highly charged political atmosphere, the divisions created fall along lines that do not always represent traditional affiliations, and terminology is not always consistent; many of the terms used in this book may have different meanings to different people. For example, I use the word "Indigenous" to refer to First Peoples, such as the Mi'kmaq, Mohawk, and Maliseet. Although "Aboriginal" is a constitutional term, it includes Métis and Inuit, who are not the subject of this book.

The definition of "aboriginal peoples" found in the *Constitution Act, 1982* is likely the one with which most people are familiar.[20] Section 35(2) states: "In this Act, 'aboriginal peoples of Canada' includes the Indian, Inuit and Métis peoples of Canada." The term "Indian" is found in section 91(24) of the *Constitution Act, 1867*, which provides the federal government with the exclusive legislative authority for "Indians, and Lands reserved for the Indians,"[21] although it does not define the term.

Section 2(1) of the *Indian Act* defines an Indian as "a person who pursuant to this *Act* is registered as an Indian or is entitled to be registered as an Indian."[22] Indigenous people who are registered as Indians today are divided into which section of the *Act* they are (or are not) registered under, section 6(1) or 6(2). Aboriginal people who are barred from registration, or who never applied, are called non-status Indians.[23] The major difference between those registered under sections 6(1) and those registered under 6(2) is the latter's inability to pass on their Indian status to their children in their own right. Even within the 6(1) category of status Indians, divisions were created among Bill C-31 reinstatees[24] who are registered under section 6(1)(c) of the *Act* and those who are registered pursuant to section 6(1)(a), often referred to as the "acquired rights" group. Section 6(1) registrants are considered to have full status, while those under section 6(2) are considered to have half status.[25] The fact that one cannot transmit one's status to one's children in one's own right is the reason most people do not want to be a section 6(2) Indian.

A term often used to describe a status Indian in Western Canada is "Treaty Indian." The term is associated with a person who is registered under the *Indian Act* and is affiliated with a First Nation that has a treaty with the Crown. In other parts of the country, a Treaty Indian may refer to an Indigenous person who is affiliated with or descended from a First Nation which has treaties with the Crown, regardless of status under the *Act*. Associating treaty status with Indian status allows Canada to dictate treaty terms that were not part of the original treaty.

INAC defines the term "Indian" as including status, non-status, and Treaty Indians:

> The term "Indian" collectively describes all the indigenous people in Canada who are not Inuit or Métis. Indian people are one of three peoples recognized as Aboriginal in the Constitution Act, 1982: Indian, Inuit, and Métis. In addition, three categories apply to Indians in Canada: Status Indians, Non-Status Indians, and Treaty Indians. Some people may fit into more than one of those categories.[26]

Some non-status Indians are also deemed to be status Indians under certain provisions of the *Indian Act*, but are largely excluded from federal programs and benefits for Indians and some band programs.[27] The Métis have their own definitions as well as those that have been developed by the courts. In the past, many off-reserve Aboriginal organizations advocated on behalf of both Métis and non-status Indians as one group, and some still use the terms as if they were synonymous, but this is not the case politically or legally.

INAC defines the Métis as "People of mixed First Nation and European ancestry who identify themselves as Métis, as distinct from First Nations people, Inuit or non-Aboriginal people."[28] Dickason notes that "there is considerable variation in both the use of the term and in material culture; there is no nationally agreed-upon definition."[29] The Métis National Council (MNC) defines a Métis as "a person who self-identifies as Métis, is of historic Métis Nation Ancestry, is distinct from other Aboriginal Peoples and is accepted by the Métis Nation."[30] Other Métis groups not affiliated with the MNC, such as the Métis Settlements in Alberta, define Métis as "a person of Aboriginal ancestry who identifies with Métis history and culture."[31] The Supreme Court of Canada has also provided guidance on how to identify Métis peoples for the purposes of adjudicating Aboriginal rights: "In particular, we would look to three broad factors as indicia of Métis identity for the purpose of claiming Métis rights under section 35: self-identification, ancestral connection, and community acceptance."[32]

Definitional issues as they relate to the Inuit have not been as controversial as they have been for the Métis, or as regulated as they have been for Indians. Although the term "Inuit" appears in section 35(2) of the *Constitution Act, 1982,* it is not defined further. INAC defines the term as "[a]n Aboriginal people in Northern Canada, who live in Nunavut, Northwest Territories, Northern Quebec and Northern Labrador."[33]

While the Inuit are excluded from the application of the *Indian Act* by virtue of section 4, they are included in the definition of "Indian" for the purposes of section 91(24) of the *Constitution Act, 1867.* The Supreme Court of Canada held that the term "Eskimo" was just a type or category of Indian, based on the historical usage of the term "Eskimo" (now "Inuit") as well as contemporary understandings.[34] The Inuit Tapiriisit Kanatami (ITK) provides clarity: "The term 'Inuit' replaces the term 'Eskimo'; Inuit are not 'Indians'; Inuit are 'Aboriginal' or 'First Peoples'; Inuit are not 'First Nations'; and Inuit are not Innu, as the Innu are a First Nations group."[35]

There are other, more generic terms used to describe the collective of Aboriginal groups in Canada. Dickason explains:

> Although the term "Indian" is recognized as originating in a case of mistaken identity, it has come to be widely accepted, particularly by the Aboriginal peoples themselves. The trouble with that term, of course, is that it is also used for the people of India. . . . In Canada, with its substantial population from India, this ambiguity is particularly obvious. Francophones have solved the problem by using "amerindien," which is specific to the Americas, or "autochtone," which translates as Aboriginal. Anglophones have not reached such an accord; in Canada, "Native" has come to be widely used, but it is not accepted in the United States on the grounds that anyone born in that country is native, regardless of racial origin; their accepted form is "native American." In Canada, "Aboriginal" is becoming widely used by Indians as well as non-Indians. "Amerindian" has not received popular acceptance in English language Canada and has even less in the United States.[36]

The RCAP defines "Aboriginal peoples" as the "organic, political and cultural entities that stem historically from the original peoples of North America, (not collections of individuals united by so-called racial characteristics)."[37] The terminology used to refer to the collective does not reflect the special place that Indigenous peoples or their nations have in this country. Since the term "Indian" was legislatively imposed and does not reflect the diverse cultural differences among Indigenous nations, there has been some rejection of it among those nations. Many Indigenous peoples refer to themselves according to their traditional nations, clans, families, and communities, which more properly reflect their languages and cultures.

The RCAP describes an Aboriginal nation — what I call an Indigenous nation — as "a sizeable body of Aboriginal people who possess a shared sense of national identity and constitute the predominant population in a certain territory or collection of territories."[38] The term "First Nation" is often used to refer to an Indigenous nation, but it is also frequently used to refer to a band, defined in the *Indian Act, 1985* as a body of Indians:

(a) for whose use and benefit in common, lands, the legal title to which is vested in Her Majesty, have been set apart before, on or after September 4, 1951,
(b) for whose use and benefit in common, moneys are held by Her Majesty, or
(c) declared by the Governor in Council to be a band for the purposes of this Act.[39]

INAC further explains the terms:

Although the term First Nation is widely used, no legal definition of it exists. Among its uses, the terms "First Nations people" refers to the Indian people in Canada, both Status and Non-Status. Some Indian people also use the term First Nation to replace the word "band" in the name of their community.[40]

Terminology and definitions applicable to Indigenous peoples can cause confusion for non-Indigenous peoples, but even within Indigenous communities there can be significant differences in how people self-identify or organize themselves politically. While some identify as Indians, others detest that term. On the other hand, some find the term Aboriginal offensive and prefer the terms Indigenous, First Nation, or Native. I have chosen to use the term Indigenous in this book because it better reflects the specific peoples to whom the *Indian Act* applies, but many organizations that advocate on behalf of Aboriginal groups use these terms interchangeably.

There is a growing movement among Indigenous peoples toward using the traditional names for their nations and communities, as well as individually identifying by other signifiers, such as clans, houses, or other hereditary groupings. This crucial link between individuals and their communities is not available in legislative categories such as those found in the *Indian Act* or the *Constitution Act*. At the same time, it is important to understand that factions may develop within a community around allegiances to different Aboriginal organizations that represent themselves along political lines.

There are Indigenous political groups at the national, provincial, regional, and local levels. Some are organized around legal divisions such as status and non-status, some around constitutional status such as Indian, Inuit, and Métis, while others are based on treaty areas, province or territory, residence, or gender. These divisions have served to reduce the representative numbers of Indigenous peoples in any given group, with the result that their power to pressure governments on issues related to their rights has been diminished.

Given that there is a renewed focus on nation-building, the natural question is whether these political organizations should continue to hold as much influence. Multiple organizations that compete to represent overlapping categories of constituents can result in a duplication of efforts and a waste of resources. Legal divisions created by the *Indian Act* can create significant differences in power structures, resources, and political influence. Even court cases have the power to affect political organizations, to the extent that one legal decision can lead to a number of organizations brought together by the ramifications of that decision. However, the biggest impact the *Indian Act* has had is in changing the relationship from one between the Crown and Indigenous nations to one between Canada and individual Indians.

From Peoples to Indians

Basic concepts about who we are as Canadians and how our society should work are still largely based on outdated assumptions about the proper place of Indigenous peoples in Canadian society. Non-Indigenous Canadians who divide themselves into francophone and anglophone have often referred to themselves as the "founding peoples" of Canada. It is the reason Canada was officially structured as bilingual.[41] There are Canadians who feel today that the country only came about through the industry of the settlers, ignoring the alliances, treaties, and cultural contributions, not to mention the land and natural resources, of Indigenous peoples.[42]

The history books have left Indigenous people out of the spotlight, and their rightful place in this country has been greatly under-appreciated. Instead, Indigenous peoples have been forced into the debate over "racialized" legal and political rights — a discourse invented by colonial governments based on anachronistic ideologies about race and cultural superiority.[43] Instead of a place of respect as the First Nations of this country, Indigenous people are often portrayed as burdens on society.[44] The context of how Indigenous people came to live in deplorable conditions is not always provided, nor is reference made to how current injustices contribute to their ongoing struggle. More importantly, little reference is ever made to the economic contributions of Indigenous peoples in the early years. "Their contributions in economic terms alone were substantial and can probably never be properly assessed," writes Thomas Flanagan. In the most profound sense of the term, they are Canada's founding peoples.[45] From contact to present day, Indigenous peoples have had to adapt to the complex relationship between their nations and the Canadian nation.

The Royal Commission on Aboriginal Peoples provided a detailed history of Aboriginal-colonial relations, and summarized the four stages of this relationship between the Aboriginal and non-Aboriginal nations from pre-contact times.[46] Stage 1 was that of "Separate Worlds" since both groups lived on opposite sides of the Atlantic Ocean. The point made by the RCAP was that both societies, Aboriginal and non-Aboriginal peoples alike, had organized themselves "into different social and political forms according to their traditions and the needs imposed by their environments," and were self-governing "national groups."[47] Stage 2 was "Contact and Co-operation," which the RCAP describes as the beginning of increased contact between Europeans and Aboriginal Nations and the establishment of trade and military alliances between the two groups. In this period, there was intermarriage, mutual cultural adaptation, conflict, tolerance, respect, and large Aboriginal death tolls from diseases. Most importantly, the RCAP stressed that the European nations and the Aboriginal nations were each "regarded as distinct and autonomous, left to govern its own internal affairs but co-operating in areas of mutual interest and, occasionally and increasingly, linked in various trading relationships and other forms of nation-to-nation alliances."[48]

The third stage was referred to as "Displacement and Assimilation," a time when settler populations and governments were "no longer willing to respect the distinctiveness of Aboriginal societies."[49] Non-Aboriginal people wanted Aboriginal peoples to conform to the majority's view of Canadian society and were willing to force this upon Aboriginal peoples through relocations, residential schools, and the various *Indian Acts*, some of which outlawed cultural practices.[50] The fourth stage, called "Negotiation and Renewal," which leads up to modern times, "is characterized by non-Aboriginal society's admission of the manifest failure of its interventionist and assimilationist approach."[51] The RCAP goes on to explain the present situation:

From the perspective of Aboriginal groups, the primary objective is to gain more control over their own affairs by reducing unilateral interventions by non-Aboriginal society and regaining a relationship of mutual recognition and respect for differences. However, Aboriginal people also appear to realize that, at the same time, they must take steps to re-establish their own societies and to heal wounds caused by the many years of dominance by non-Aboriginal people.[52]

Most Aboriginal groups supported the findings of the *RCAP report* and still cite its conclusions and recommendations.

Stage three of Canada's historical relations with Aboriginal peoples was characterized by federal control over their identity, the division of people from their bands and nations, and their assimilation through the *Indian Act* and related policies such as residential schools. Without input from Aboriginal nations, the federal and provincial governments divided jurisdiction over key governance areas in the *Constitution Act, 1867*; through section 91(24), Canada assumed the power to legislate the identity of individual Aboriginal people.[53] Federal control over Indianness and membership has become the primary filter through which government, society, and even some Aboriginal groups have come to view Aboriginal peoples. With regard to accessing programs and services, land, natural resources, and seats at self-government negotiating tables, the real question is not whether one is a citizen of the Mi'kmaq, Cree, or Mohawk, but whether one is an Indian and a band member. Indian policy has been renamed Aboriginal policy so as to be consistent with the *Constitution Act, 1982,* and presumably to include Métis and Inuit, but the real criterion which determines whether one accesses legal, political, and cultural rights as a Mi'kmaq, for example, is whether one meets Canada's definition of an Indian, which Canada alone controls.

Although Indian registration, as we know it today, was only introduced in 1951, definitions of who was an Indian can be found in legislation pre-dating confederation.[54] In 1850, *An Act for the better protection of the Lands and Property of the Indians in Lower Canada* was enacted to protect encroachments by settlers on Indian lands.[55] Section V of that *Act* defined Indians in relation to whether they belonged to a tribe that had an interest in lands that had been appropriated for them. This early definition included those with Indian blood who were reputed to belong to a body or tribe of Indians and their descendants. This also included those intermarried among or adopted by the Indians. This definition was amended in 1851 to include those with an interest in Indian lands and their "immoveable property."[56] In 1857, *An Act to encourage the gradual Civilization of the Indian tribes in this Province, and to amend the Laws respecting Indians* was enacted with a view to removing all legal distinctions between "Indian Tribes" and "Her Majesty's other Canadian Subjects." The method by which the Crown proposed to do this was through assimilation, which was to be effected, in turn, through a process of voluntary enfranchisement whereby individual Indians, without the consent or involvement of their tribes, could apply to be enfranchised, take a first and last name, and obtain up to fifty acres of land from their tribe's allotment as well as a share of the tribe's annuities.[57]

Grievances brought by individuals and tribes mandated that subsequent acts provide protection for the lands set apart for the tribes. In 1861, *An Act respecting Indians and Indian Lands* made it an offence for settlers to reside in Indian villages or in Indian country without a license.[58] It also confirmed that lands set apart for Indians would be protected for the exclusive use of tribes, together with an annual grant.[59] Indians were still defined as those with Indian blood reputed to belong to a tribe, all those intermarried among them, and their descendants.[60]

The assimilatory underpinnings of pre-confederation legislation would be carried through to the modern *Indian Act*, albeit in different ways. The common thread was that Indians were defined by whether or not they had Indian blood and were affiliated with a tribe or body of Indians who lived on lands over which they had an interest. It was a combination of racial attributes and connection with one's community that equated with Indian identity for legislative purposes.

Post-confederation legislation continued with the goal of assimilation and racial definitions. In 1868, *An Act providing for the organization of the Department of the Secretary of State of Canada, and for the management of Indian and Ordnance Lands* provided the following definition of "Indians belonging to the tribe" for the purposes of who could use tribal lands and property:

> Firstly. All persons of Indian blood, reputed to belong to the particular tribe, band or body of Indians interested in such lands or immoveable property, and their descendants;
>
> Secondly. All persons residing among such Indians, whose parents were or are, or either of them was or is, descended on either side from Indians or an Indian reputed to belong to the particular tribe, band or body of Indians interested in such lands or immoveable property, and the descendants of all such persons; And
>
> Thirdly. All women lawfully married to any of the persons included in the several classes hereinbefore designated; the children issue of such marriages, and their descendants.[61]

This definition imported some of the criteria found in pre-confederation legislation. While descent from an Indian ancestor was part of the definition, it was possible for women to marry into this group, and so "Indian blood" was not necessary in all cases. In this way, the definition had some characteristics of a kinship model, rather than one based exclusively on blood, but the power to make this determination rested with government. Similarly, in 1869, *An Act for the gradual enfranchisement of Indians* incorporated previous provisions related to land and the prohibition of intoxicants, but also included new provisions related to the distribution of Indian property upon death, the election of chiefs, and by-law making power for tribes.[62] The Superintendent General of Indian Affairs had the power to decide whether Indians — i.e., "persons claiming to be of Indian blood" or persons "intermarried with an Indian family" — were lawfully in possession of land in certain townships.[63] While this *Act* was consistent with previous definitions based on blood or intermarriage, it did not completely displace traditional forms of individual identification and communal belonging. The focus of the legislation was on individual identification; it did not provide rules for how tribes could determine who was a member.

At the same time, it was obvious that the government viewed Indigenous peoples as a race; it therefore developed administrative criteria based on biological conceptions of who formed part of that race.[64] Blood quantum often determined not only their identity, but also their legal rights and entitlements. Section 4 of the *Act* provided as follows:

> In the division among the members of any tribe, band, or body of Indians, of any annuity money, interest, money or rents, no person of less than one-fourth Indian blood, born after the passing of this Act, shall be deemed entitled to share in any annuity, interest or rents, after a certificate to that effect is given by the Chief or Chiefs of the band or tribe in Council, and sanctioned by the Superintendent General of Indian affairs.[65]

The amount of Indian blood one was thought to have was therefore directly tied to one's entitlements, and with this *Act* the government directly involved the chiefs in the exclusion of their citizens in sharing the resources provided by Canada. It is not hard to make the link from this *Act* to what happens today with some band membership codes, where Indian identity becomes associated with monetary and other entitlements.

The first *Indian Act* that consolidated previous legislation and created detailed provisions for the management of Indian Affairs was enacted in 1876. Entitled *An Act to amend and consolidate the laws respecting Indians*, its short title was *The Indian Act, 1876*.[66] The term "Indian" was redefined to include:

> *First.* Any male person of Indian blood reputed to belong to a particular band;

Secondly. Any child of such person;

Thirdly. Any woman who is or was lawfully married to such person.[67]

This section was a much-abbreviated version of previous provisions, the major difference being that the *Indian Act, 1876* had a more detailed list of individuals that could be excluded from membership in the band. For example, illegitimate children, Indians who resided in foreign countries for more than five years, Indian women marrying other than an Indian or non-treaty Indian, and some "half-breeds" could now be excluded. A non-treaty Indian was defined as a person of Indian blood who was reputed to belong to an irregular band (a band without reserve lands, money appropriated by Canada, or treaty relations with the Crown), or someone who followed an Indian mode of life.[68] The *Act* further made it illegal for anyone other than a member of a band to reside on the reserve. It provided for the election of chief and council, and tax protections for Indians.[69] These latter provisions have been carried through to the modern *Indian Act, 1985*.

Section 86 of the *Indian Act, 1876* also provided for the enfranchisement of Indians who reached the age of 21 and who demonstrated a "degree of civilization," integrity, morality, and sobriety, so long as a competent person vouched for that person. Similarly, anyone who had a university degree, became a lawyer, or entered holy orders would also become enfranchised.[70] There have been numerous amendments to the *Indian Act* since 1876, but the key provisions that defined Indians, bands, and those who would be enfranchised remained a staple of the *Act* until 1985. The *Indian Act, 1906* kept certain provisions that excluded illegitimate children from band membership and enfranchised Indian women who married non-Indians.[71] The *Indian Act, 1927* also excluded from recognition as an Indian any "half-breed" in Manitoba who took half-breed lands.[72]

The *Indian Act, 1951* included several amendments that increased Canada's role in administering the identities of Indians and their bands. It also created the Indian Register, in which those entitled to both registration and band membership were recorded on a band list, and those entitled to be registered but not entitled to band membership were recorded on the General List.[73] This was to be administered by the Registrar, who had the power to add and delete names. The charter list was whatever lists existed in the department prior to the *Act* coming into effect.[74] This *Act* solidified the privileged position of male Indians in regard to registration and band membership.[75] Even if women married Indians from other bands and did not lose their status, their band membership was automatically transferred to their husbands' bands.[76]

These provisions stayed the same until 1985 when the *Act* was amended owing to an international human rights case involving an Indian woman who lost her status by marrying out.[77] While the 1985 amendments (also known as Bill C-31 amendments) were supposed to deal with discrimination under the *Act*, they fell far short of that objective. Similarly, the recent Bill C-3 amendments fell short of addressing even the limited gender discrimination found in the *McIvor* case. With both amendments, the federal government retains control over the determination of Indian status and even band membership for the majority of bands in Canada.

The Future of a People

Many status Indians are further divided between those who are considered to be the "original" group (often referred to as full status Indians), and "new" Indians (new registrants or reinstatees and who are referred to as half-status or half-Indians). The difference between the two basic groups is that 6(1) Indians can transmit their status to their children in their own right, whereas 6(2) Indians have to partner with another registered Indian in order to transmit their Indian status to their children. While the Bill C-31 amendments were meant to address discrimination against Indian women under the *Indian Act, 1951*, all they did was delay the disenfranchisement process by one generation.[78] It also preserved the preferential entitlement for the descendants of male Indians over female Indians and created new discrimination between the descendants of the double mother clause and section 12(1)(b) reinstatees. All this has resulted in a plethora of litigation against the federal government, alleging that there is both residual and new discrimination in the current *Indian Act* that was not addressed by the amendments. The different claims include:

- Cousins (gender) discrimination: descendants of male Indians who married out have better status than the descendants of female Indians who married out;
- Siblings discrimination: illegitimate male Indians are often entitled to section 6(1)(a) status whereas illegitimate female Indians are only entitled to section 6(2) status, meaning that males are automatic band members and females may or may not have band membership and their children won't have status where the children of male Indians would;
- Unstated paternity: while previous *Indian Acts* contained a legal presumption of Indian paternity for the children of unwed Indian women, the current *Act* removed this presumption and now INAC administers the *Act* with a policy presumption of non-Indian paternity for the children of unwed Indian women, which leads to lesser or no status for these children; and

- Second generation cut-off rule: two generations of out-marriage (parenting between Indians and non-Indians) results in children without status, a form of discrimination based on race, family status, and an anlogous ground of blood quantum.[79]

While other claims have also been made, this represents the main groupings of discrimination that can also be found in ongoing litigation claims.

The Bill C-31 amendments have had a profound impact on the eligibility of Indigenous peoples being registered as Indians. Not only does the *Indian Act, 1985* not eliminate gender discrimination, its residual and new forms of gender discrimination result in the exclusion of thousands of descendants of Indian women.[80] After studying the population implications of Bill C-31 and these new changes to the *Indian Act*, Clatworthy, a demographic expert used by Canada in *McIvor* and other cases, concluded:

> The Indian Act was amended in 1985 to remedy the unequal treatment of Indian men and women who married non-Indians. However, the amendments passed in 1985 do not create equality among Indians. Rather they create inequality that is gender neutral. Before 1985 the Act penalized Indian women for marrying out. After 1985 it penalizes both Indian men and women who marry out by making their children unequal to other Indian children.[81]

Clatworthy refers here to the differences between section 6(1) and 6(2) Indians generally. However, the claim that the *Indian Act* is "gender neutral" on a go-forward basis is false.[82] When added to the discriminatory provisions of some band membership codes, Indian women and their descendants can be dually disadvantaged in relation to both status and membership. Regardless of the membership codes, the federal government still retains control over how status is determined. Clatworthy argues that, without significant amendments to the *Act*, there can be no true equality in First Nations communities:

> C-31 thus lays the groundwork for social inequality in First Nations communities. It establishes an ongoing distinction between two "classes" of Indians, 6(1) and 6(2) registrants. In First Nations whose membership is controlled by the Act, these two classes are unequal in one important respect: the ability to transmit Indian status to their children. In time, as awareness of this distinction increases, it is likely to enter the political and social lives of the First Nations as the distinction between "full" and "half" Indians. C-31 is the gateway for the First Nations to a world in which some are more equal than others.[83]

Pam Paul (now Paul-Montour) analyzed Bill C-31's effects within First Nations. She argued that, while Bill C-31 was designed to eliminate discrimination against Indian women, what resulted was additional discrimination against them and their children:

> Women fought against discrimination within the old Indian Act because it alienated women and their children from their families and communities and created false divisions between native people. Yet Bill C-31 has brought with it two new varieties of discrimination, one based on generation, the other based on labelling. It has also brought with it a number of economic issues which have served to divide native organizations and communities. Problems attributed to Bill C-31 extend far beyond the parameters of programs and administrative confusion. The end result is that Indian women and their families are once again victims of bureaucratic structures, both by band councils and the federal government.[84]

She goes on to review the history of Bill C-31, how it was implemented and its effects on First Nations, concluding that its sole purpose was to assimilate Indigenous peoples:

> Although the implementation and interpretation of Bill C-31 has divided Indian communities, there is one common unifying thread across the country. It is a commonly held view that Bill C-31 policies serve no other purpose that [sic] to further advance the federal government's crusade to assimilate native people into the mainstream Euro-Canadian society.[85]

The Royal Commission on Aboriginal Peoples came to a similar conclusion:

> Although the current *Indian Act* contains no enfranchisement provisions, the status rules, as modified in 1985 by Bill C-31, are still highly problematic. Not only are they extremely complex, but like their historical predecessors, they appear to continue the policy of assimilation in disguised but strengthened form. This is because of the distinctions drawn between the two classes of Indians under the post-1985 rules.[86]

The RCAP also pointed out that the children of an Indian who is registered under section 6(2) of the *Act* are "penalized" if that parent "marries out." At the same time, the child of an Indian who is registered under section 6(1) will be registered regardless of the status of the other parent.[87] The RCAP further highlighted the historical underpinnings of the federal government's self-interest in the *Act*'s changing definition of "Indian":

During the 1946-48 parliamentary hearings on revising the *Indian Act*, federal officials were unable to explain whether or to what extent they planned remedial action. As it turned out, the response of federal officials dealt with the situation of these women, but also served to confirm the continuing assimilative thrust of federal Indian policy. In a letter to the joint committee examining the issues, Indian affairs officials were candid regarding their motivations in the case of Indian women who married non-Indian men:

"by the alteration of the definition of Indian by the Statute of 1876 the Dominion very substantially reduced the number of people for whose welfare it was responsible and by that action passed the responsibility on to the provinces for thousands of people, who, but for the statute of 1876, would have been federal responsibility for all time."[88]

This historical evolution of the *Indian Act* has shown that various amendments to the registration provisions have had a significant impact on Indigenous identity and have changed the way many Indigenous individuals, families, communities and nations define themselves and inter-relate with one another. What is most disturbing about the registration provisions of the *Act* is the impact they will have on future generations and what that means for the internal composition and legal existence of Indigenous nations into the future. The RCAP clearly warned of what is in store for Indigenous peoples should Canada continue to use the *Indian Act* to control and define Indigenous identity:

Thus, it can be predicted that in future there may be bands on reserves with no status Indian members. They will have effectively been assimilated for legal purposes into provincial populations. Historical assimilation goals will have been reached, and the federal government will have been relieved of its constitutional obligation of protection, since there will no longer be any legal "Indians" left to protect.[89]

While Canada acknowledges that "once there has [sic] been two consecutive generations of a person entitled to registration parenting with a non-Indian, the resulting descendants will not be entitled to registration," it defends this formula despite the analyses by its own experts on how it will negatively affect Indian population numbers and create inequalities.[90] Canada wants to ensure that individuals registered under the *Act* are "sufficiently connected to the historical population that the federal government treated with or for whom reserves were set aside."[91] It is hard to see how this objective is met by a registration formula that ensures there will be no "legal" Indians left to protect. The only other way to read this is that Canada wants to ensure that those registered have sufficient Indian blood. However, Canada's relationship with Indigenous peoples is not with their "historical population," frozen in time; it is with current Indigenous populations who are the natural descendants of these traditional nations.

A review of current population figures, together with future indicators, shows that the continued use of the *Indian Act, 1985* and certain membership provisions to determine Indigenous identity in Canada will have drastic effects on Indigenous communities now and into the future. Disease, relocation, residential schools, adoption, warfare, and other colonial activities have reduced Indigenous populations both pre- and post-contact. What is happening now is a legislated form of population reduction based on the previous goal of assimilation. The ultimate effect of the legislation, despite changes in official policy with regard to assimilation, is to reduce the number of people the government must be accountable to in terms of protection, treaty obligations, land rights, self-government, and other Aboriginal rights, including a whole series of culturally specific programs and services that are provided today. While Canada points to various objectives behind their defence of the discriminatory registration provisions, the historical record shows clearly that cost reduction is the ultimate objective.[92] Canada's positions in court are countered by internal documents that specifically state that the object of Bill C-31 was to figure out "how some form of reinstatement could be implemented at reduced cost" and that the "final policy decision on reinstatement will be shaped by financial more than any other considerations."[93]

The Indigenous people who are most at risk right now are those who are being legislatively excluded: non-status Indians. Indian women who married out and their descendants are disproportionately represented in this group. But eventually, according to current demographic studies, all Indians will be legislated out of existence, as will their communities.[94] Bill C-3 will only delay this process by one generation, and only for a limited group of reinstatees. In some cases, as self-government agreements move forward, even those who enjoy status as Indians but are non-band members may be excluded if citizenship codes in self-governing Indigenous nations continue to be based on *Indian Act* provisions. Clatworthy explains:

> The descent rules that now govern the inheritance of Indian status appear unsatisfactory as a basis for defining citizenship in self-governing First Nations. In the long run these rules will lead to the extinction of First Nations. In the shorter term, they will involve the denial of citizenship to many children and grandchildren.[95]

Thus, there are short-term and long-term implications to the *Indian Act, 1985,* and problems that must be resolved regardless of whether the future is moving toward self-government agreements or not. If self-government citizenship codes rely on the inequities found in the status or membership provisions of the current

Act, then those agreements are equally suspect. The forecast population figures for status Indians reveal certain extinction if the current issues of inequality, discrimination, and lack of control over Indigenous identity by Indigenous peoples are not soon addressed. A closer look at these population forecasts is necessary to fully appreciate the long-term effects of this legislation.

There is no way of knowing with certainty how many Indigenous people were living in North America prior to contact. Dickason has reviewed the historical data and estimates the population could have been as high as 112.5 million for the entire hemisphere in the 15th century, and as high as 18 million for North America north of the Rio Grande for the beginning of the 16th century. While she does not suggest that the numbers were in fact this high, she does point out that the importation of diseases by the Europeans likely destroyed as much as 93 per cent of the Indigenous population.[96] The RCAP adds that several experts using different methodologies have arrived at estimates of two million people at contact, while other figures put it as low as 500,000.[97] Today, the Indigenous population in Canada seems to be growing, yet the actual number of Indigenous people in Canada varies, depending on which figures one uses. Census data reveal that, according to ancestry, Aboriginal people (Indian, Inuit, Métis) make up 4.5 per cent (1,319,895) of the population.[98] According to identity, however, they make up only 3.3 per cent (976,310).[99] In the 1990s, when the RCAP carried out its mandate, it chose to use the identity figures. However, constitutional lawyer Joe Magnet asserts that the Indian identity question in the Census is faulty, and therefore, reliance on that data as opposed to the ancestry data is compromised:

> It seems unlikely that people would exaggerate their Aboriginality on the census form by a positive identification as Aboriginal when there are so many negative stereotypes associated with Aboriginal people and no benefit to be gained. It is possible that respondents interpret the next question (question 18), which asks about identity, as a question about Indian registration, not as an opportunity for self-identification as Aboriginal. This seems plausible given the close correlation between registration and those who respond positively to the identity question (a stunning 92 percent of those who respond positively to question 18 about identity are registered Indians).[100]

Perhaps, then, excluding the ancestry data on the assumption that it was not a form of Aboriginal self-identification may indicate inaccurate numbers with regard to the actual self-identifying population. That being said, there is ample demographic data to make reliable population predictions based on current trends.

Numerous demographic studies present a clear picture of how the various *Indian Acts* have not only divided Indigenous nations in Canada, but have also ensured their legislated extinction. Pam Paul noted the situation in the Atlantic region:

Without a doubt Section 6(2) of the *Indian Act* poses the greatest concern for First Nations as a whole, but in the Atlantic Provinces where the numbers are small it poses an even greater concern. As more and more people are registered under Section 6(2), more and more of the population base is lost when these people chose non-natives or non-status for partners. When these people reach childbearing age, and, if they do not partner with a status Indian person, Indian status will be lost in the next generation.[101]

If nothing is done to address the current problem, the numbers of non-status Indians and section 6(2) Indians will continue to increase. Together with varying rates of out-marriage, this means that the 630-plus Indian bands in Canada will be legally extinct at calculable dates in the future.[102]

Clatworthy reviewed the different types of membership codes that each band had in place at the time of his study as well as the population figures for registered Indians held at INAC. Taking this information in conjunction with the Bill C-31 amendments to the *Indian Act,* he concluded:

> The resulting projections suggest a declining Indian Register population beginning in roughly fifty years or two generations. We anticipate that some First Nations, whose out-marriage rates are significantly higher than the national norms, would cease to exist at the end of the 100 [year] projection period.[103]

Though many First Nations are looking at self-government agreements and their own citizenship codes as a way of moving forward, some are considering using the same principles or criteria embedded in the *Indian Act, 1985* as the basis for their citizenship codes. The *Indian Act* therefore has the potential to cause problems for First Nations long after self-government agreements have been signed. The problem will only continue to get worse for status and non-status Indians as the effects of the *Act* will continue to shrink the population entitled to registration. The effects will begin to compound and could make the legal extinction rates even faster than previously thought. Clatworthy explains:

> In addition to these factors, the process of out-marriage itself can be expected to promote further out-marriage by altering the registry [i.e. 6(1)/ 6(2)] mix of the population. This will occur as the effects of the Act's rules and out-marriage begin to reduce the share of the population entitled to Indian registration. Over time, the opportunity for in-marriage will shrink as fewer and fewer individuals in the community qualify for registration under the Act. This process may be particularly important in many reserve communities where small population size and close kinship ties already

limit the number of potential marriage partners. The combined effect of the factors outlined above may well be to increase rates of out-marriage much higher and much more quickly than the models developed for this study have assumed.[104]

The projection period of Clatworthy's study was 1991 - 2091 and it looked at four types of membership codes: (1) one-parent rules; (2) two-parent rules; (3) blood quantum rules; and (4) *Indian Act* rules. Clatworthy explains how each rule is applied:

One-parent rules: A one-parent descent rule declares a person to be eligible for membership based on the eligibility or membership of *one* of that person's parents. One-parent descent rules are found in 90 First Nations or 38 percent of the 236 that adopted membership codes.

Two-parent rules: A two-parent descent rule establishes a person's eligibility based on the eligibility or membership of *both* of that person's parents. Rules of this type are found in 67 First Nations, 28 percent of the 236 with codes.

Blood Quantum Rules: A blood quantum rule establishes eligibility based on the "amount of Indian blood" a person possesses. In effect, a blood quantum measures the number of Indian ancestors a person has and sets the criterion for membership based on an amount of ancestry. Thirty (30) First Nations (13 percent of the 236) have adopted blood quantum rules. A typical criterion is 50 percent Indian blood, a standard set by 21 of the 30, though there are examples of codes that set higher and lower criteria. The "arithmetic" of blood quantum codes measures a person's quantum by adding the quantum of each parent and dividing by two. The child of parents who are 100 percent and 0 percent Indian is 50 percent, as is the child of two parents who are 50 percent Indian.

Indian Act rules: These rules are embodied in the Act's Sections 6(1) and 6(2). . . . Forty-nine (49) First Nations, or 21 percent of the 236 that have adopted codes, implicitly rely on the Indian Act rules to determine eligibility for membership. Indian Act rules also pertain to the 360 First Nations that have *not* adopted membership codes and whose membership is, therefore, still regulated by the Act.[105]

The study compared each type of membership code with current birth rates, death rates, and rates of out-marriage, and determined that only the one-parent descent rule showed a significant increase in band membership in the future, and then levelled off in growth. The other types of band membership codes all had small increases in band member populations and then declined significantly over time.[106] Clatworthy concluded:

> It should be noted that all of the membership rules with the exception of unlimited one parent descent rules, are expected to eventually result in decreases in the size of the population eligible for membership. The consequences of the rules in the long term will be the eventual elimination of the member population.[107]

Given the grim outlook for all but one-parent rules, could a one-parent code for status also help prevent legislated extinction? Should the solution involve amending the *Act* or replacing it? How would amendments to the *Act* affect communities and individuals, and what would this mean in terms of numbers? These are all important questions when considering the complex relationship between status and band membership as well as between band membership and self-government citizenship.

Clatworthy updated his work in 2004 in a study entitled *Re-Assessing the Population Impacts of* Bill-C31.[108] In this study, the question asked was what would happen if the rules of Bill C-31 were applied similarly for the Bill C-31 reinstatees and the pre-Bill C-31 populations? For example, what would the population forecasts be for First Nations if the Bill C-31 amendments had applied equally as between Indian men and Indian women who married out, and their descendants. The major findings of the report are that those not entitled to registration are expected to outnumber those entitled to registration within three generations, and within five generations no further children born will be entitled to registration. If the rules were applied similarly for both groups, there would be incremental growth for two generations only.[109] So, while the elimination of gender discrimination is important, the issue of the second generation cut-off will still lead to extinction.

This study also looked at other scenarios and how they might affect population numbers, and all of them had the same result. There would be initial growth, but as long as the *Indian Act, 1985* stays in place, there would be an eventual decline in registrations.[110] As Bill C-3 keeps the second generation cut-off in place, Clatworthy's studies are still relevant as future predictors of population declines. A further study updated the types of membership codes that bands were using and which bands were even using their own codes.[111] The four types of membership codes were expanded and reclassified:

1. *Indian Act* or *Act* Equivalent descent rules which also extend initial membership to all registered individuals (413 First Nations);
2. *Act* Equivalent (Limited One Parent) descent rules which restrict initial

membership to those with acquired rights as of June 27, 1987 (6 First Nations);

3. Unlimited One Parent descent rules which also extend initial membership to all registered individuals (72 First Nations);
4. Unlimited One Parent descent rules which restrict initial membership to those with acquired rights as of June 27, 1987 (12 First Nations);
5. Two Parent descent rules which restrict initial membership to those with acquired rights as of June 27, 1987 (64 First Nations);
6. 50% Blood Quantum rules (22 First Nations); and
7. 25% Blood Quantum rules (4 First Nations).[112]

Clatworthy looked at the usage of membership codes among First Nations bands and found that the majority of First Nations who had adopted codes were still using them to determine membership.

Only 18 (8.5 per cent) of the 212 First Nations with codes reported that they were not using their own codes to determine membership.[113] Some of the reasons given for not applying their codes were: "no reason"; "never implemented"; "under review"; "legal challenges"; or "administrative burden to apply the rules."[114] Instead, these First Nations were using the following to determine membership: "would not say"; "*Indian Act, 1985*"; "Chief and Council"; "moratorium on membership"; or membership was based on family or community sponsorship.[115] Clatworthy also noted that 86 (40.5 per cent) of the 212 First Nations with codes were actively considering changes to their membership rules and many of them reported that their changes would affect large numbers of individuals.[116] The rate of out-marriage or exogamous parenting (parenting between a registered Indian and a non-registered person) significantly affects the levels of Indian registration and membership in First Nations communities. The majority of First Nations have a moderate to high level of exogamous parenting within their communities.

Clatworthy further explains that it is mainly Aboriginal women and children who continue to be treated unequally in their communities, and even excluded from them: "At the present time, nearly all of those who lack eligibility for First Nations membership are the descendants of women who lost their registration as a consequence of the prior *Indian Act*'s rules concerning mixed marriages."[117]

Whether it is the federal government enforcing discriminatory legislation or First Nations' governments implementing discriminatory band membership codes, it has to stop in order to prevent further loss of membership in Indigenous communities and future loss of citizens for self-governing Indigenous nations. The problem arose because Canada created the *Indian Act* and the rules of the relationship between the Crown and Indigenous peoples for the past century. This has not yielded positive results for either the relationship or the identity of Indigenous peoples. Now, instead of the baseline population of the Mi'kmaq being comprised of the Mi'kmaq people, their heirs, and heirs forever, like any other nation, the baseline populations of the Mi'kmaq Nation are comprised of the following individuals who are further divided by community:

(1) s.6(1)(a-f) band members;
(2) s.6(1)(a-f) non-band members;
(3) s.6(2) band members;
(4) s.6(2) non-band members;
(5) non-registered band members; and
(6) non-registered non-band members.[118]

Within those groups, there are those who live on and off reserve, and those who live on and off traditional territory.

Bill C-31 was hailed as an amendment that would remedy gender discrimination and at the same time give more power to the bands to control their own membership. It was an illusion of equality. It reinstated Indian women who married out and some of their descendants, but reinstated them to a lesser position than that of Indian men who married out and their descendants. Bill C-3 is also an empty shell of a legal remedy. Regardless of how First Nations write their codes, the underlying base is unequal registration, which is guaranteed to cause community division. Even communities who accept non-status Indians as members may be faced with funding shortages for programs and services in cases where the federal government only provides funding for status Indians.[119] Meanwhile, bands that use the other codes may face a different scenario where conflict will arise from caste-like social structures.

An important first step is the recognition of the depth of the *Indian Act* principles that are embedded within band membership codes and the damage this causes to Indigenous communities. One of the most important long-term implications of the continued use of unequal registration under the *Indian Act, 1985* and exclusionary band membership codes will be to alienate rightful members from reserve-based political structures. Exclusion from reserve-based communities can equate to future exclusion from nation-based activities. Political structures that are based on inequality and exclusion will likely have "little credibility among people they exclude."[120] This will have a domino effect, as the provincial, regional, and even national organizations that represent these bands will lose their representative authority from the growing number of people who are excluded at the community level. This will ultimately mean that "[c]ompeting organisations whose electoral processes enfranchise those excluded by First Nations' electoral processes will grow and prosper."[121]

Many status Indians who are band members today were once non-status Indian members of off-reserve Aboriginal groups fighting for their rights to be included. Now, the next generation is doing the same thing, and hoping that the previous generation has not forgotten what they were fighting for. It concerns all Indigenous people because the path to legislated extinction leads to the same place for on- and off-reserve, status and non-status. These divisions will be a significant hurdle in future discussions with Indigenous Nations about reconstructing their citizenship principles for the purposes of self-government and other self-identifying exercises. While there may be legal and political challenges to First Nations taking back their power to define themselves and their citizens, the necessary task of sorting out how many of us have internalized Canada's racialization of our peoples may be just as challenging. While the early years saw colonial governments and churches assimilating our people, today many Indigenous people are helping to assimilate themselves. Leaders can help their people acknowledge the damage that has been done to our communities and our self-esteem, and overcome assimilatory attitudes and rebuild our nations by welcoming home our citizens. While there may appear to be a tension between the right of Indigenous nations to determine their own citizenship and the right of individuals to belong to their Nations, the next two chapters lay the basis for the argument that in fact one right is inherently tied to the other. There can be no rebuilding of our Nations without loyal citizens to carry forward our identity, culture, practices, traditions, beliefs, laws, and customs for future generations.

CHAPTER TWO

The Right to Determine Citizenship

IN CHAPTER 1, I EXPLAINED that the current political and social divisions affecting Indigenous peoples in Canada stem largely from colonial interference with their traditional ways of life and identities. Despite Canada's condemnation of assimilatory policies, it has maintained the discriminatory registration system within the *Indian Act*, knowing that this will eventually mean legislative extinction for First Nations. In the meantime, continued legislative control over both individual and communal identities means social, cultural, political, and legal divisions within First Nations which hamper their nation-building exercises.

In this chapter, I argue that Indigenous nations have the right to be self-defining — i.e., to determine their own communal identities. This translates into the right to determine who can be citizens in their nations without interference from Canada. This right is supported by the constitutional promise that Canada will protect their cultures for the benefit of future generations. While this right is a core element of Indigenous jurisdiction and the inherent right of self-government, like other rights in Canada, it can be limited by the rights of others. As a result, the applicability of the *Charter* is also addressed. This chapter sets out the fundamental issue of who gets to decide who is an Indian.

Legal issues related to Indigenous identity and belonging for both status and non-status Indians represent a growing trend in litigation, and may continue to grow for some time unless workable solutions can be negotiated. It is because of Canada's conflicting policy and litigation positions, together with its continued failure to respect its legal and moral obligations to consult with and accommodate the legitimate interests of Indigenous peoples, that Indigenous peoples are forced into litigation. The Crown's "winner take all" approach in litigation has replaced negotiations in many instances, and in others has forced First Nations to abandon costly litigation or agree to settlements that do not reflect the fair resolution of their interests.[1] The recent land claim agreement of the Mississaugas of New Credit which settled for a little over $145 million for the city of Toronto is one example. Courts are left with little choice but to address singular issues such as Indian registration outside of the larger context of identity and membership and try to fashion decisions or remedies with limited consideration of the laws and traditions of the Indigenous nations affected. While litigation may resolve singular issues, such as whether the Maliseet have a right to harvest timber, it does not settle the numerous underlying issues of title to land, the harvest of other natural resources, the right to be self-determining, or treaty beneficiary status.[2] Similarly, the *McIvor* case was able to prove that the *Indian Act* still contains gender discrimination, but the courts did not resolve the underlying cause of the litigation: Canada's jurisdiction over Indigenous identity and belonging, and the broken constitutional promise to Indigenous peoples to protect their identities and cultures for future generations.[3] This means that there will be continued litigation on the same subject matter as *McIvor* to try to deal with discrimination under the *Indian Act* regarding the determination of status and band membership on a case-by-case basis.[4]

Indigenous Identity in a Liberal Democracy

Canada is a democracy, and Canadians enjoy the rights and freedoms that western liberals think are essential for individuals to live the "good life." According to liberalism, all humans are valued as individuals, each as an "autonomous, rational, self-interested entity, possessed with a number of unspecified natural or inherent rights."[5] While many philosophers and academics debate the specific content of liberalism, it can be summarized briefly:

> Liberals believe that every individual has a special dimension, a uniqueness that cries out to be realized. The purpose of life is to realize that potential, to become whatever it is one is capable of becoming. As a free agent, man is able to define and pursue his own definition of happiness, his own version of the good, his own set of values. The role of the state is to produce the conditions under which individuals have the broadest possible choice in deciding upon their definition of the good. Society, meanwhile, should relish this diversity while dispensing equal treatment regardless of one's origins, colour, sex or status in life.[6]

Despite the specific focus on individualism, liberals also believe that one cannot equally pursue happiness if one is not of equal capacity to do so, and so the redistribution of wealth and obligations to address these inequalities also form part of liberalism. One of the rights central to western liberalism is being free from arbitrary interference from the state. Canada's assumption of jurisdiction over Indigenous identity, and the legislative imposition of Indian registration criteria for Indigenous peoples would appear, then, to be both illiberal and undemocratic.

The denial of such an important aspect of the good life for Indigenous peoples is not in keeping with a modern liberal democracy. The *Indian Act*'s blood quantum definitions of Indians, its exclusion of non-status Indians from registration, and the assignment of different types of status and rights among Indians do not conform to the standards of liberal tolerance and respect for basic human rights. The question of how liberal democracies can both accommodate and support the identity and communal aspirations of Indigenous peoples raises additional questions as to why identity should matter, and whether it is an individual or communal identity that should be protected, or both.

Protecting "Difference"

How many blonde, blue-eyed Indigenous people have had their Indian "credentials" questioned, not only by non-Indigenous people but by friends and family? The same identity insecurity has been experienced by non-status Indians, Métis people, status Indians who have had their band membership rejected, status Indians who were once band members but now lack the requisite blood quantum to maintain membership, and status Indians who either choose to or have no choice but to live off reserve. This group is bigger still when one includes Bill C-31 reinstatees who were rejected by their communities, "non-traditional" Indigenous people, educated Indigenous people who were rejected because of their education, and anyone who has been rejected for having spoken out against their chief and council. Do "real" Indians only include those who: (1) live on reserve, (2) are considered "traditional," (3) have 50 to 100 per cent Indian blood quantum, (4) have never had their status taken away, (5) do not question band politics, and (6) do not want an education? If so, this represents far less than a third of the Indigenous population.[7] Many chiefs of First Nations claim to represent only their band members on reserve, which *de facto* leaves off-reserve political organizations to represent band members who live off reserve, status Indians who are not band members (on the General List) and who live off reserve, and non-status Indians.

This plethora of divisions has led to what some have described as "cultural trauma" in Indigenous individuals.[8] Yet some Indigenous people have come to judge, discriminate, and exclude each other in the very same fashion that non-Indigenous people and governments have. Is this an inevitable part of asserting and protecting Indigenous identity in Canada, or are more complex issues at play? Even some of the Indigenous nations that assert their identities more strenuously have fallen victim to the demoralizing powers of the *Indian Act's* registration and band membership provisions, and struggle to find solutions from within their nations.[9] From the most populous, politically astute, sovereignty-asserting First Nations to the smallest, remote, rural First Nations — each is plagued by the legacy of the *Indian Act*.

Patrick Macklem asserts that the Indigenous peoples of Canada belong to distinctive cultures that "have been and continue to be threatened by assimilative forces."[10] He argues that "Indigenous difference" includes more than cultural differences between Indigenous and non-Indigenous peoples:

> Aboriginal cultural difference exists by virtue of the distinctive content of the cultures in which Aboriginal people participate. Some aspects of Aboriginal cultures, including practices that Aboriginal people have engaged in before contact with Europeans as well as ways in which Aboriginal people have resisted, responded to, adapted, and incorporated non-Aboriginal ways of life into their collective identities, are unique to Aboriginal people. It is in this sense that Aboriginal cultural difference is exclusive to Aboriginal people and . . . merits constitutional protection.[11]

The danger is that defining Indigenous peoples solely by their cultural identities — i.e. their practices in pre-contact times — serves to stereotype them and ignores the importance of their current identities.[12] For Macklem, Indigenous difference should be protected in the *Constitution Act, 1982,* but that difference should reflect more than just culture; it should reflect the whole of their identities, which includes territory, sovereignty, and treaties.[13] He justifies why each element of Indigenous difference should be protected: (1) international law supports the protection of Indigenous cultural integrity within sovereign states;[14] (2) Indigenous peoples occupied and had a special relationship to the land prior to state creation;[15] (3) Indigenous peoples would have continued sovereignty but for the inequality of the law at state creation;[16] and (4) unlike immigrant minorities, Indigenous people have treaties with Canada and are the only groups in Canada who have the right to treat with the state.[17] Some of these factors have already been recognized by the Supreme Court of Canada as justifying the special constitutional protection of Aboriginal and treaty rights.[18]

That being the case, the difference between Indigenous peoples and non-Indigenous peoples in Canada amounts to more than pre-contact hunting practices and traditional ceremonies, but includes the many ways in which Indigenous peoples have resisted assimilation and protected the future of their cultures and communities — such as recognizing their descendants from mixed marriages as citizens. Taiaike Alfred notes that between the 1950s and the 1970s anthropologists studying Indigenous communities were concerned with the acculturation of Indigenous peoples, and that any kind of change in those communities automatically equated with a loss of culture. This resulted in a situation where, as Macklem writes, "[a]rchetypal Indian and monolithic White cultures were paired off as poles between which individuals navigated in constructing their identities."[19] This has led to the courts protecting only the "difference" between Indigenous and non-Indigenous peoples, and laws and policies which affect the views of Indigenous and non-Indigenous peoples alike as to who and what is "Indigenous."

Any future solutions require a discussion within First Nations communities that includes an analysis of how colonial worldviews, objectives, laws, and policies applied over generations have negatively affected how Indigenous peoples view themselves, and how to undo the damage that has been done.[20]

Contrary to an identity based on "difference," Schouls argues that focusing on what makes Aboriginal people different puts them at risk of losing the rights associated with that difference, regardless of what is included.[21] According to Schouls, if one equates Aboriginal identity only with cultural or political sources and highlights those differences between Aboriginal and non-Aboriginal peoples, then any sort of identity transformation that does occur within Aboriginal groups over time becomes an end to that group, as opposed to merely a change in the group.[22] As opposed to maintaining strict identity boundaries between Aboriginal and non-Aboriginal peoples based on race, culture, or other criteria, Schouls suggests that peaceful co-existence between the two is more likely to be achieved when "political agreement, cooperation, and mutual cultural influence are featured as central to the relationship rather than cultural and political incompatibilities."[23] That is not to say that boundaries are not important. Indeed, Schouls maintains that boundaries are the "antidote to colonialism."[24] Maintaining such boundaries is an exercise of the Aboriginal right to be self-defining in Canada, which Schouls considers to be a central criterion for just relations between Aboriginal nations and Canada.[25] The key to these boundaries is not to lose sight of the fact that Aboriginal identity can incorporate more than one kind of identity, even within the same nation, community, or family. Therefore, the maintenance of the Aboriginal right to be self-defining in Canada flows all the way through to the Aboriginal individual, so that members can have "control over their own lives in ways which are consistent with their own aspirations," as opposed to being forced to follow a strict cultural, political, or racial code about what a community member should or should not be.[26] It is not the difference between Aboriginal people and non-Aboriginal people that is crucial to maintaining Aboriginal identity as much as protecting what makes up that Aboriginal identity.

Will Kymlicka examines the issue from the perspective of liberalism and notes that the "difference" in identity between citizens of a nation has been at odds with the views of most western political theorists, whose ideal of citizens involves a common descent, language, and culture. As history has demonstrated, many democratic nations have gone to great lengths to achieve the ideal of sameness by attempting to physically eliminate cultural minorities by means of genocide, forced assimilation or segregation, and large-scale institutional discrimination.[27] Canada has been no exception. National minorities, such as Indigenous nations, are different from both immigrant minorities and social movements within national groups, given their prior occupation, their pre-existing culture, laws and governments:

These groups have fought to retain their existence as distinct societal cultures, although not all have been accorded the language and self-government rights necessary to do so. . . . Yet they have persisted, and their status as self-governing "domestic dependent nations" is now more firmly recognized. The determination they have shown in maintaining their existence as distinct cultures, despite these enormous economic and political pressures, shows the value they attach to retaining their cultural membership.[28]

Indigenous individuals benefit by their identity being recognized through recognition of the collective.[29] Debates which have focused on separating the individual and communal aspects of identity have led academics away from solutions regarding how to address the current cultural trauma experienced by Indigenous peoples.[30]

Those engaged in the Aboriginal rights debate have often characterized the issue as individual rights versus collective rights. Liberal critics of collective rights cite apartheid for what can happen when minorities want protection from the majority, but this extreme example is not the automatic result of protecting the identity of collectives:

> However, external protections need not create such an injustice. Granting special representation rights, land claims, or language rights to a minority need not, and often does not, put it in a position to dominate other groups. On the contrary . . . such rights can be seen as putting the various groups on a more equal footing, by reducing the extent to which the smaller group is vulnerable to the larger.[31]

In Kymlicka's view, self-government rights act as protection for their culture, whereas special representation rights within dominant political institutions protect them from having their views ignored. The result is putting smaller cultural groups on a more even field with dominant cultures so as to protect them from assimilation.[32] "Such groups are concerned with ensuring that the larger society does not deprive them of the conditions necessary for their survival. . . ."[33] The very survival of Indigenous peoples around the world is dependent on the protection of their "difference," but this difference includes more than just cultural practices; it also includes their land base, laws, and government.[34] At the same time, the maintenance of boundaries between the groups is important both to protect the right of Indigenous peoples to be self-defining in Canada and to ensure their survival as a people into the future. Protecting the culture and identity of Indigenous peoples in Canada is not only a legitimate goal for Indigenous peoples; is also consistent with the values and goals of a modern liberal democracy.

Why Not Assimilate?

Aboriginal and treaty rights are specifically protected in the *Constitution Act, 1982* and the Supreme Court of Canada has explained that Canada has made a constitutional promise to Aboriginal peoples to protect their identities and cultures for future generations. The *Constitution Act, 1982* is the supreme law of the land — a fundamental aspect of liberal democracy in Canada. Yet, Indigenous peoples are forced to defend not only their rights but their very existence against right-wing academics, media, and government. The debate over whether Indigenous peoples should assimilate and be like other Canadians runs counter to Canada's constitutional commitment to ensure that that does not happen. It also runs counter to the Prime Minister's recent apology for the residential schools. Many Canadians are not familiar with the real history of Canada or its First Nations, and therefore the critics are easily able to influence the discussion.

Alan Cairns is one of those critics who sees Aboriginal claims for the protection of their difference as "sporadic," violent, and "pent-up."[35] He describes Aboriginal peoples as "penetrated societies"[36] owing to the high levels of intermarriage, and concludes that it should be Aboriginal peoples who accommodate and assume non-Aboriginal identities and influences.[37] In his view, Canada is an urban society and the survival of Aboriginal identity off reserve in urban settings is practically impossible. Thus, the assimilation of Aboriginal peoples and their identity is inevitable: "Several generations of off-reserve living, especially if accompanied by intermarriages, will weaken Aboriginal identity, and in some cases lead to its disappearance. This is unavoidable."[38] He also sees this weakening or loss of Aboriginal identity as an acceptable "cost" to produce successful urban Aboriginal people.[39] His overall premise is that there is no support for nation-to-nation relations in Canada, and even the use of the term "non-Aboriginal" creates a binary view of Canada as two societies.[40] At the same time, he maintains that Aboriginal peoples could still be viewed as "Citizens Plus" — a concept that originated from the 1966 *Hawthorn Report*, which envisioned Indians living in villages, not as nations, and those who did not make the trek to the city to become assimilated would be largely Europeanized by now, anyway. He argues that his plan for Aboriginal peoples should not be viewed as assimilation under a different guise.[41] One has to question what his definition of assimilation is if leaving one's home territory, working in the city, giving up identity for economic benefit, and forgoing all ties to one's community and identity as Aboriginal is not assimilation.[42]

While academics like Cairns stop short of openly supporting the assimilation of Indigenous peoples, there are others like Tom Flanagan who actually promote it.[43] Flanagan's view of Canada focuses on individualism, which he views as the basis of modern liberal democracies.[44] He contrasts this with the collective nature of nationhood claims made by Indigenous peoples:

The . . . aboriginal orthodoxy encourages aboriginal people to withdraw into themselves, into their own "First Nations," under their "self-governments," on their "traditional lands," within their own "aboriginal economies." Yet this is the wrong direction if the goal is widespread individual independence and prosperity for aboriginal people.[45]

Flanagan believes that people who receive benefits on the basis of who their ancestors were is unfair.[46] He argues: "Once we are citizens, we will both have the same legal rights, which will also be the same rights of all other citizens, both natural born and naturalized."[47] Flanagan has close ties to the current prime minister, Stephen Harper, and has served as his campaign manager.[48] He is also associated with the Fraser Institute, a conservative research and educational organization.

There has been support for Flanagan's views in the non-Indigenous community. A book entitled *A New Look at Canadian Indian Policy* by Gordon Gibson is really a review of the not-so-new assimilation and individualist views of Flanagan and Cairns.[49] *Disrobing the Aboriginal Industry* by Frances Widdowson and Albert Howard offers the same views regarding Indigenous peoples.[50] Both books see Indigenous peoples as a race, and their criticisms focus on what they perceive as race-based rights.[51] While at times appearing to criticize racist views of Indigenous people, they construct their own arguments around racist concepts, stereotypes, and generalizations which detract from their main arguments rather than bolster them. Widdowson describes the empowering of Aboriginal communities through the devolution of powers as having resulted in "a large amount of corruption where powerful families siphon off most of the resources while the majority remain mired in poverty and social dysfunction."[52] She does not provide any empirical evidence for these claims.

Kymlicka answers these claims by explaining that countries such as Canada and the United States are justified in working toward the voluntary assimilation of immigrants into the values and norms of the host country. What is not acceptable is the coërced assimilation of national minorities such as Indigenous peoples which pre-date the nation-state.[53] The forced assimilation of national minorities in an attempt to create a common citizenship will only cause further division and alienation of Indigenous groups from the nation-state, as their bonds with their culture are usually too deep to give up.[54] While some liberal theorists may assert that Indigenous peoples would not make nationalist claims if they had the same "opportunities" as immigrants, Kymlicka explains that history has proven this to be false:

Indeed, this is completely at odds with the history of Indian tribes in America or Canada. Indians have often been pressured to become "just another ethnic group," but they have resisted that pressure and fought to protect their distinct status. As I noted earlier, Indians are indeed subject to racism, but the racism they are most concerned with is the racist denial that they are distinct peoples with their own cultures and communities.[55]

Kymlicka also points out that the positive protection of minority rights has long been an important part of the liberal tradition.[56] While some liberals like John Stuart Mill argued the need for a common national identity, others like Lord Acton argued the opposite: "[T]he divisions between national groups and their desire for an internal life of their own serves as a check against the aggrandizement and abuse of state power."[57] To academics like Cairns, the maintenance of any kind of difference between Aboriginal peoples and non-Aboriginal peoples is harmful to the goal of citizenship in Canada.[58]

Restitution for past harms, recognition of current rights, and title and protection for individual and communal identities form the very basis of most Indigenous claims and grievances in Canada. Addressing the basis of these claims could only serve to foster bonds between Canada and Indigenous peoples. Is the issue really one of loss of identity, or is it about different standards among majority and minority cultures? Are Indigenous people bound to assimilate into the majority culture, or is their culture naturally evolving and adapting to different circumstances over time? The majority culture in Canada has been allowed to evolve over time. Why must Indigenous peoples choose between assimilation and protecting their cultures as they were pre-contact?

Is Cultural Change Forbidden for Indigenous Peoples?

The Supreme Court of Canada has specifically held that Indigenous peoples' rights do not have to be exercised as they were in pre-contact times.[59] The "frozen rights" concept in law has been rejected, but the ideas about what makes an Indigenous person have not. Macklem argues that all cultures transform significantly over time and that Indigenous peoples, while maintaining their own unique world views and cultural traits, are no exception:

Aboriginal cultures undergo dramatic transformations· in response to internal and external circumstances and developments. A frozen rights approach ignores the dynamic nature of cultural identity and the fact that cultures undergo deep transformations over time. It risks stereotyping Aboriginal people in terms of historical differences with non-Aboriginal people that may or may not have existed in the distant past and profoundly under-describes important aspects of contemporary Aboriginal cultural identities.[60]

To limit Indigenous people to pre-contact cultural practices not only locks them in a cultural time box, but sentences them to cultural death when change occurs over time.

Schouls argues that Indigenous communities can and do change their perceptions of community identity over time, and so do individual Indigenous peoples within those communities.[61] One can be Indigenous and also participate in the various social, political, and economic aspects of Canadian society without losing one's culture or identity: "Aboriginal structures should be seen, not as ends, but as community identity in process, made by ongoing choices of individual Aboriginal peoples."[62]

According to Kymlicka, it is natural for Indigenous cultures to change over time, and cultural evolution does not have to mean assimilation. "The process of modernization does not change the fact that these nations still form separate societal cultures, with their own institutions, using their own languages."[63] New ways of living, like living on a reserve, do not change the fact that Mi'kmaq are still Mi'kmaq, and, in the same vein, off-reserve living should not change the fact that Mohawks are still Mohawks.

No culture in the world that has existed for thousands of years has done so without changing. Sometimes change itself is a significant part of a culture. Change should not now be highlighted as a justification for the termination or assimilation of a culture. The key to the survival of Indigenous identity, therefore, is the acceptance by majority and minority cultures alike that both identity and culture can adapt and evolve and still maintain important connections with the past. Thus, cultural change does not have to mean assimilation. The fact that Indigenous peoples have fought so hard to maintain their identities and cultures stands as testament to their ability to survive. There are many negative aspects of Indigenous identity that have been imposed on their communities, such as discriminatory status and band membership rules, and the reduction of their traditional territories to small reserves where people are divided into on- and off-reserve categories. Since identity is a process, Indigenous peoples have the power to identify these negative aspects that were imposed on them, acknowledge their impacts on the community and individuals, and make informed decisions about future citizenship processes.

The question of whether an Indigenous identity should publicly matter has been answered in the affirmative by the majority of academics. Amy Gutmann argues that most people need a "secure cultural context to give meaning and guidance to their choices in life."[64] In this way, a secure cultural context and the identity that is derived from it would be considered a "primary good" in a liberal democracy. Gutmann explains that full public recognition of equal citizens in a liberal democracy can only occur when there are two forms of respect: "(1) respect for the unique identities of each individual, regardless of gender, race, or ethnicity, and (2) respect for those activities, practices, and ways of viewing the world that are particularly valued by, or associated with, members of disadvantaged groups, including . . . Native Americans. . . ."[65] This requires more than governments and institutions refraining from racism or discrimination; it requires them to act positively to "recognize the particular cultural identities of those they represent."[66] A lack of recognition of Indigenous identity causes harm to Indigenous individuals and communities, and the divisive labels imposed by the *Indian Act* have further compounded that harm. Charles Taylor explains that this kind of non-recognition and misrecognition can cause serious damage:

> The thesis is that our identity is partly shaped by recognition or its absence, often by the misrecognition of others, and so a person or group of people can suffer real damage, real distortion, if the people or society around them mirror back to them a confining or demeaning or contemptible picture of themselves. Nonrecognition or misrecognition can inflict harm, can be a form of oppression, imprisoning someone in a false, distorted, and reduced mode of living.[67]

Equal recognition therefore amounts to more than formal equality:

> Equal recognition is not just the appropriate mode for a healthy democratic society. Its refusal can inflict damage on those who are denied it. . . . The projection of an inferior or demeaning image on another can actually distort and oppress, to the extent that the image is internalized.[68]

The images created by Canada of different kinds of status and non-status Indians with differing sets of rights project inferior and demeaning images of categories of Indigenous peoples. This has had a negative effect on Indigenous identities. Legal divisions have been internalized by Indigenous peoples and are reflected in political, social, and communal structures. Further attempts at assimilation will not foster bonds, but run the risk of further alienating and dividing Indigenous peoples from Canada.

The policy choice for liberal democratic governments is whether to be neutral with regard to the identity of a minority group, or to accommodate that group. Martha Minow argues that "[g]overnment neutrality may be the best way to assure equality, yet governmental neutrality may also freeze in place the past consequences of difference."[69] While both aspects may have their difficulties, assimilation, or integration, causes the most damage to the cultures and identities of Aboriginal peoples:

Acknowledging and organizing around difference can perpetuate it, but so can assimilation. Separation may permit the assertion of minority group identity as a strength but not change the majority's larger power. Integration, however, offers no solution unless the majority itself changes by sharing power, accepting members of the minority as equal participants and resisting the temptation to attribute as personal inadequacies the legacy of disadvantage experienced by the group.[70]

A negative label such as "non-status Indian" can be so harmful that it should properly be understood as a deprivation of liberty.[71] The failure to acknowledge difference can leave children "scarred by silent nonrecognition and implicit rejection."[72] This kind of harm affects them in all aspects of life: "When their identities are devalued in the society, children know it, and that message damages their self-esteem and ability to succeed."[73] It is no wonder, then, that Indigenous peoples occupy the lowest ends of the socio-economic indicators. Simply educating Indigenous people or creating greater economic development opportunities will not address the underlying ills in First Nations.

The government's use of registration to determine who can and can not live on a reserve and have access to housing, education, and other federal programs and services necessary to ensure a basic quality of life has shifted the focus of identity from one of culture to one of economic and physical survival. Cultural membership is important to societal groups like First Nations, and many cultural theorists believe that "it is in the best interests of every person to be fully integrated in a cultural group."[74]

Indigenous people have a right to exist, both in terms of legal recognition and protection as well as culturally within their nations. Anything less causes real harm, and does not respect the liberal values of tolerance and the need for everyone to access what makes the "good life" for them.

Kymlicka argues that not only should liberal democracies recognize Indigenous cultural identities, but that they must be protected from extinction: "The survival of a culture is not guaranteed, and, where it is threatened with debasement or decay, we must act to protect it. Cultures are valuable, not in and of themselves, but because it is only through having access to a societal culture that people have access to a range of meaningful options."[75]

Indigenous peoples are concerned about preserving their cultures, traditions, and languages, and Canada has a responsibility to try to undo some of the damage it has done. Canada has a long history of imposing its own values, culture, and religion on Indigenous peoples in an effort to assimilate them and open up their traditional territories for settlement. As capacity is rebuilt and nation-building activities are renewed, litigation has also increased. If Canada refuses to see the moral and philosophical reasons why it should respect and protect Indigenous identities and cultures, then First Nations will likely continue to assert their constitutionally protected Aboriginal and treaty rights in this regard.

Aboriginal Rights in Canada

Aboriginal rights litigation has evolved significantly since earlier cases like *Sparrow*, and has presented more challenges for Aboriginal peoples to overcome.[76] Although *Sparrow* set out the test for determining Aboriginal rights, it was adjusted in the *Van der Peet* trilogy and then again in *Sappier and Gray*.[77] Those decisions should also be looked at in the context of other significant cases relating to treaty rights, such *Marshall 1* which was "revisited" in *Marshall 2*, and title cases like *Delgamuukw*.[78] Aboriginal rights litigation is constantly shifting and adjusting to new tests, and interpretations of old ones. For example, the Supreme Court of Canada in *Powley* amended the *Van der Peet* "integral to distinctive culture" test for Aboriginal rights specifically to suit the situation of Métis peoples.[79] Given that the law is constantly evolving in this area, it is hard to predict with any degree of certainty how a claim of Aboriginal right to a new activity, tradition, custom, or law will be received at the Supreme Court. This is especially so for non-gathering claims related to self-government or identity and citizenship/membership rights.[80] The Supreme Court of Canada has only provided glimpses of its position on these issues in cases like *Pamajewon, Corbiere*, and *Lovelace*, as it refused to hear the *McIvor* appeal and the *Sawridge* case has not gone forward.[81] That makes Aboriginal rights claims to determine citizenship somewhat uncertain.

Indigenous identity and communal belonging are important issues that affect the social, cultural, and even physical health and well-being of individuals and communities. Most, if not all First Nations bands in Canada assert an Aboriginal right to determine the membership of their communities.[82] These rights are recognized in their powers to determine membership in their communities under section 10 of the *Indian Act* and by virtue of the inherent right of their nations to be self-governing, which is included in section 35 of the *Constitution Act, 1982*. There may also be a free-standing Aboriginal right for Indigenous nations to determine their own individual and collective identities through citizenship rules.[83] At this point, it is necessary to point out the potential difference between the right of an Indian band to determine membership protected in section 10 of the *Indian Act* and an Aboriginal right of an Indigenous nation to determine citizenship as protected in section 35 of the *Constitution Act, 1982*. For some bands who decide to assert or negotiate self-government separately from their larger nation, band membership and citizenship may end up being one and the same. For this practical reason, the arguments relating to an Aboriginal right to determine citizenship are made generally so that all possibilities are left open.

As far as many First Nations are concerned, effective government can only occur when they have control over issues that are part of their core governance jurisdiction, such as identity and citizenship.[84] It is also arguable that the treaties between Indigenous nations and Canada were intended to protect not only the rights of the original signatories, but also their future generations. Many treaties included language that specifically protected the rights of "their heirs and the heirs of their heirs forever."[85] Given that their treaty rights are constitutionally protected, one should be able to assume that that their successive generations of heirs are also protected. Seeing as the treaties in no way surrendered the jurisdiction of Indigenous nations to determine their own heirs or citizens, then this power remains today.

Aboriginal rights in Canada are protected by section 35 of the *Constitution Act, 1982*.[86] Section 35(1) of the *Act* provides that the "existing aboriginal and treaty rights of the aboriginal peoples of Canada are hereby recognized and affirmed." That section goes on to define Aboriginal peoples as including "Indian, Inuit and Métis," and clarifies that Aboriginal rights are "guaranteed equally to male and female persons." An important point about section 35 is that, while it protects Aboriginal rights, it is not the source of those rights.[87] The Supreme Court of Canada in *Van der Peet* cited *Calder* with approval when it held, "In identifying the basis for the recognition and affirmation of aboriginal rights it must be remembered that s. 35(1) did not create the legal doctrine of aboriginal rights; aboriginal rights existed and were recognized under the common law."[88] The court went on to explain: "The pre-existence of aboriginal rights is relevant to the analysis of s. 35(1) because it indicates that aboriginal rights have a stature and existence prior to the constitutionalization of those rights and sheds light on the reasons for protecting those rights."[89] It provided the basis for why Aboriginal rights are protected in the constitution:

> In my view, the doctrine of aboriginal rights exists, and is recognized and affirmed by s. 35(1), because of one simple fact: when Europeans arrived in North America, aboriginal peoples were already here, living in communities on the land, and participating in distinctive cultures, as they had done for centuries. It is this fact, and this fact above all others, which separates aboriginal peoples from all other minority groups in Canadian society and which mandates their special legal, and now constitutional, status.[90]

The court in *Van der Peet* also explained the meaning of constitutional protection for Aboriginal rights:

> More specifically, what s. 35(1) does is provide the constitutional framework through which the fact that aboriginals lived on the land in distinctive so-

cieties, with their own practices, traditions and cultures, is acknowledged and reconciled with the sovereignty of the Crown. The substantive rights which fall within the provision must be defined in light of this purpose; the aboriginal rights recognized and affirmed by s. 35(1) must be directed towards the reconciliation of the pre-existence of aboriginal societies with the sovereignty of the Crown.[91]

This is the underlying reason why Aboriginal rights are protected, but how that plays out in litigation is the basis of an ever-evolving test for determining whether a specific Aboriginal right exists.

The "Integral to Distinctive Culture" Test

Any analysis of Aboriginal rights usually starts with the *Sparrow* case, as it was the case where the Supreme Court of Canada would "explore for the first time the scope of s.35 (1) of the Constitution Act, 1982, and to indicate its strength as a promise to the Aboriginal peoples of Canada."[92] The appellant in this case was a member of the Musqueam Indian Band. He was charged under the *Fisheries Act* for having a drift net longer than what is permitted under the Musqueam Band's Indian food fishing license. The appellant admitted the facts but defended his actions on the basis that he had exercised his Aboriginal right to fish and that the net restrictions were a violation of that right. He argued that, since his Aboriginal rights were protected under s.35 (1), the net length restrictions were invalid. Prior to setting out the test for determining Aboriginal rights, the Court addressed some interpretive issues within its analysis of section 35(1) for use in future Aboriginal rights cases. First, Chief Justice Dickson and Justice LaForest explained that the word "existing" in s.35 (1) meant that only those rights which were in existence when the *Constitution Act, 1982* came into effect would be protected.[93] The Court further explained that "existing aboriginal rights cannot be read so as to incorporate the specific manner in which it was regulated before 1982. The notion of freezing existing rights would incorporate into the Constitution a crazy patchwork of regulations."[94] Despite Canada's assertion that its obligations toward Aboriginal peoples were only political in nature, the court confirmed that the significance of section 35 was to provide Aboriginal peoples with constitutional protection against the Crown's legislative powers.[95]

Similarly, the "recognition and affirmation" of Aboriginal rights means that the power to legislate with regard to Indians pursuant to section 91(24) of the *Constitution Act, 1867*, is a limited power, such that the Crown's power must be reconciled with its obligations toward Aboriginal peoples.[96] Other interpretive principles to be used in applying section 35 include:

- the government must act in a trust-like capacity towards Aboriginal peoples; a fiduciary, which is not adversarial in nature;[97]
- treaties and statutes relating to Indians should be liberally construed and doubtful expressions are to be resolved in favour of the Indians;[98]
- the honour of the Crown is always at stake in its dealings with Aboriginal peoples and no appearance of sharp dealings will be sanctioned;[99]
- section 35 of the *Constitution Act, 1982* itself must be construed in a "purposive," "liberal," and "generous" way.[100]

This results in a priority for Aboriginal rights over rights which are not constitutionally protected. The test for Aboriginal rights in *Sparrow* asks, first, whether the legislation interferes with an existing Aboriginal right, the onus being on the Aboriginal claimant to prove the existence of the right.[101] If the answer is yes, then that constitutes a *prima facie* infringement. The kinds of questions asked to determine a *prima facie* infringement are whether the limitation is "unreasonable," whether the limitation imposes "undue hardship," or whether the limitation denies the rights holders "their preferred means" of exercising their Aboriginal rights.[102] Should the infringement be found, the burden then shifts to the Crown to answer a two-part justification test.[103] First, is there a valid legislative objective? If so, then the Crown's fiduciary relationship with Aboriginal peoples becomes the focus.[104] The questions to be asked in the second part of the justification analysis could include: whether there has been any consultation with the affected Aboriginal group on the matter of conservation, whether there has been as little infringement as possible of the Aboriginal right in question, and whether fair compensation has been offered in situations of expropriation.[105] This was the test for Aboriginal rights until the Supreme Court of Canada decisions were rendered in the *Van der Peet* trilogy.

The *Van der Peet* trilogy of decisions included *Van der Peet, Gladstone,* and *Smokehouse.*[106] In *Van der Peet,* the court explained that the trilogy of cases would address issues that were left unresolved in *Sparrow* — namely, how the specific Aboriginal rights protected in section 35 would be defined.[107] Chief Justice Lamer explained: "Until it is understood why aboriginal rights exist, and are constitutionally protected, no definition of those rights is possible."[108] The court further clarified that these rights are protected for Aboriginal peoples because they are Aboriginal and that these rights are equally as important as other constitutional rights.[109]

> The task of this Court is to define aboriginal rights in a manner which recognizes that aboriginal rights are rights but which does so without losing sight of the fact that they are rights held by aboriginal people because they are aboriginal. . . . The Court must define the scope of s.35 (1) in a way which captures both the aboriginal and the rights in aboriginal rights.[110]

It was on that basis that the Court explained the test: "In order to be an aboriginal right an activity must be an element of a practice, custom or tradition integral to the distinctive culture of the aboriginal group claiming the right."[111] The factors that must be taken into account in the "Application of the Integral to Distinctive Culture Test"[112] are as follows:

- Courts must take into account the perspective of aboriginal peoples themselves;[113]
- Courts must identify precisely the nature of the claim being made in determining whether an aboriginal claimant has demonstrated the existence of an aboriginal right;[114]
- In order to be integral a practice, custom or tradition must be of central significance to the aboriginal society in question;[115]
- The practices, customs and traditions which constitute aboriginal rights are those which have continuity with the traditions, customs and practices that existed prior to contact;[116]
- Courts must approach the rules of evidence in light of the evidentiary difficulties inherent in adjudicating aboriginal claims;[117]
- Claims to aboriginal rights must be adjudicated on a specific rather than general basis;[118]
- For a practice, tradition or custom to constitute an aboriginal right it must be of independent significance to the aboriginal culture in which it exists;[119]
- The integral to a distinctive culture test requires that a practice, custom or tradition be distinctive; it does not require that that practice, custom or tradition be distinct;[120]
- The influence of European culture will only be relevant to the inquiry if it is demonstrated that the practice, custom or tradition is only integral because of that influence;[121] and
- Courts must take into account both the relationship of aboriginal peoples to the land and the distinctive societies and cultures of aboriginal peoples.[122]

In *Van der Peet*, the Sto:lo were unable to prove that the practice of exchanging fish for money or goods was an Aboriginal right,[123] whereas in *Gladstone*, the matter of whether the Heiltsuk had an Aboriginal right to sell herring spawn on kelp was sent back to trial.[124]

Assuming that an Aboriginal group could prove they were exercising an Aboriginal right, the burden of proof would shift to the Crown to prove that the right had been extinguished, and, if not, whether the Crown had infringed that right, and finally, whether the infringement was justified.[125] After the *Van der Peet* trilogy, the basic *Sparrow* test remained, albeit the first part, relating to the identification of the actual Aboriginal right, has been substantially clarified or expanded. A key difference between *Sparrow* and the *Van der Peet* trilogy is the court's treatment of Aboriginal rights as depending on whether they were categorized as food, social, and ceremonial rights or whether they were considered commercial rights. In *Sparrow*, the Indian food fishery was recognized as the first priority after conservation.[126] However, in *Gladstone*, the Aboriginal right was categorized as a commercial right and was therefore assigned a lesser priority.[127] Specifically, it was described as "something less than exclusivity but which nonetheless gives priority to the aboriginal right."[128] While the clarifications made in the *Van der Peet* trilogy still form the basis of the test for defining Aboriginal rights, the Supreme Court of Canada in *Sappier and Gray* made some important clarifications to it.[129]

The case of *Sappier and Gray* involved two members of the Maliseet Nation (at the Woodstock First Nation) and one member of the Mi'kmaq Nation (at the Papineau First Nation). The Court found that all three claimants had proven their Aboriginal right to harvest wood for domestic purposes on Crown lands. However, exercise of the right was restricted to lands traditionally harvested by members of the Woodstock and Papineau First Nations.[130] In considering the claim, the court made some clarifications about the *Van der Peet* test for defining Aboriginal rights. How the resource was "harvested, extracted and utilized" by an Aboriginal group was considered necessary in order to understand the "aboriginal" aspect of Aboriginal rights.[131] The court also reworded the right from "harvesting wood" to the right to "harvest wood for domestic uses as a member of the aboriginal community."[132] Another important clarification in *Sappier and Gray* related to previous descriptions of the test for defining Aboriginal rights which has led to confusion in the lower courts. Specifically, the use of concepts such as "core identity" and "defining feature" to describe the integral aspect of traditions, customs, and practices was described by the Court as having created "artificial barriers to the recognition and affirmation of aboriginal rights," and should be discarded.[133] They also cited the appeal decision with approval and warned that "courts should be cautious in considering whether the particular aboriginal culture would have been fundamentally altered had the gathering activity in question not been pursued."[134] The court went on to emphasize that Aboriginal rights must be permitted to evolve and take on modern forms, otherwise they would become "utterly useless."[135]

While there are many other cases that inform an Aboriginal rights analysis, these are the main principles with which one can assess a possible Aboriginal right to determine citizenship. That being said, there has been much written about the *Van der Peet* test and its practical impact on the ability of Indigenous peoples to meet those tests. The following section reviews some of the academic interpretations of the test and how it may be amended to bring it more in line with the purpose of constitutional protection for Aboriginal rights.

Evolving Interpretations

The *Van der Peet* test has not been without criticism. In fact, the weight of academic authority seems to suggest that the "integral to distinctive culture test" severely limited the original test set out in *Sparrow* and, as a result, may even violate the *Constitution Act, 1982.* Dufraimont argues that Aboriginal rights cannot be assessed separately from the test for justification, and that the test for justification has gone from the stringent test in *Sparrow* to an "absurd extreme" in *Delgamuukw* which allows nearly any public interest to trump Aboriginal rights.[136] She cited McLachlin J., who argued in *Van der Peet* that no court has the ability to diminish the substance of Aboriginal rights in this way:

> How, without amending the Constitution, can the Crown cut down the aboriginal right? The exercise of the rights guaranteed by s. 35(1) is subject to reasonable limitation to ensure that they are used responsibly. But the rights themselves can be diminished only through treaty and constitutional amendment. To reallocate the benefit of the right from aboriginals to non-aboriginals would be to diminish the substance of the right that s. 35(1) of the Constitutional Act 1982 guarantees to the aboriginal people. This no court can do.[137]

She also argues that this concept of reconciliation is hardly different from those of the past which caused so many historical injustices for Aboriginal peoples.[138]

> Seen in its historical context, this redefinition of reconciliation has been both regressive and catastrophic. Consider the fact that, in the nineteenth and early twentieth centuries, subordinating Aboriginal rights to larger social demands was the very idea underlying a historical government strategy of "development relocation." Pursuant to this policy, governments in the nineteenth and early twentieth centuries dispossessed Aboriginal communities of their lands and "relocated" them to less valuable lands to make way for non-Aboriginal economic development.[139]

McNeil also argues that the justification test originally set out in *Sparrow* and later refined by *Van der Peet* and *Delgamuukw* amounts to a violation of the *Constitution Act, 1982.*[140]

McNeil argues that this violation stems from the use of public interest objectives to justify infringement on Aboriginal rights. The test for infringement has been so relaxed that it now allows for the interests of private third parties (e.g., large corporations) that do not have similar constitutional rights, to violate Aboriginal rights.[141] He also cites with approval Justice Vickers' lengthy decision in *Tsilhqot'in*, which criticized British Columbia and Canada's "impoverished" views about Aboriginal title.[142] Although speaking specifically about Aboriginal title, McNeil's views are equally applicable to other Aboriginal rights: "It would be highly discriminatory for aboriginal titleholders to be treated less favourably, especially when their lands were taken in violation of the Canadian Constitution. Given that these wrongs were committed by governments acting on behalf of Canadians and B.C. residents, we should all bear the costs."[143]

While he may have been critical of *Delgamuukw* and other cases for their limitation on the infringement of Aboriginal rights, he prefers the mixed Aboriginal-common law approach taken in *Delgamuukw* for establishing the right, versus the strictly common law approach taken later in *Marshall* and *Bernard*.[144] He also argues that the views of the current Chief Justice, McLachlin, are preferable to those of the former Chief Justice, Lamer.[145] McNeil reviewed Lamer's approach to Aboriginal rights:

In other words, past violations of Aboriginal rights by non-Aboriginal persons apparently can be used to justify continuing infringements of those rights today. The reason why this is permissible appears to be that "successful attainment" of reconciliation "may well depend" on this kind of balancing of rights and interests. In this context, reconciliation appears to relate more to the maintenance of established economic interests than to the protection of constitutional rights.[146]

Other academics such as Zalewski agree with McNeil and argue that the "invisible politics" that truly drive the courts are the need to accommodate non-Aboriginal interests.[147] The Supreme Court of Canada has modified the test in *Sparrow* so much that subsequent cases have adopted the very frozen rights approach they claimed to have rejected.[148]

Borrows and Rotman also argue that the very essence of Aboriginal rights is the bridge between two cultures.[149] Aboriginal rights are not only *sui generis* because they are held by Aboriginal peoples, but because they are based on Aboriginal laws, customs, and practices.[150] Their constitutional protection is to ensure the physical and cultural survival of Aboriginal peoples. "Clearly, if Aboriginal rights exist to secure physical and cultural survival, they cannot be ascertained exclusively by reference to pre-contact 'Aboriginality.' There are far more relevant aspects to the determination of Aboriginal rights."[151] They cite with approval McNeil, who argued that Aboriginal peoples are being denied the opportunity to "develop contemporary ways of life within their own communities on the basis of their Aboriginal rights."[152] Further, if this legal approach continues, then the result will be "the disappearance of the Aboriginal cultures which make those communities distinct, as the Aboriginal peoples will be obliged to assimilate into the dominant Canadian culture which surrounds them in order to survive."[153]

Slattery also criticizes the case law on Aboriginal rights, but takes a slightly different approach.[154] He argues that, in addition to Aboriginal rights held by specific First Nations living in specific territories, there are also Aboriginal rights which should be considered universal, such as the right to cultural integrity.[155] Slattery analyzes the test laid out in *Van der Peet* and explains that it makes several assumptions: (1) that "aboriginal rights are shaped entirely by factors particular to each indigenous group — that they are specific rather than generic rights";[156] (2) that the test "looks exclusively to conditions prevailing in the remote past";[157] and (3) that the test "makes no reference whatever to the extensive relations that developed between indigenous peoples and incoming Europeans in the post-contact period, or to the legal principles that informed those relations."[158] The result is that the court has rejected the notion that Aboriginal rights make up "a range of abstract legal categories with normative underpinnings," and instead has reduced them to an "exercise in historical ethnography."[159] Similarly, by focusing on the pre-contact era, the test excludes activities that became central to the lives of Aboriginal peoples, and does not allow Aboriginal peoples to meet modern needs.[160] Despite the fact that the court described Aboriginal rights as being grounded in "intersocietal law," the test is based on pre-contact times when there were no intersocietal relations between Aboriginal peoples and Europeans.[161] Therefore, the *Van der Peet* test does not adequately address the key foundational basis of Aboriginal rights that would allow findings to be relevant to Aboriginal communities today. Although a frozen rights approach was specifically rejected by the court, it appears as if this is the effect of what they have done.

That being said, the Supreme Court of Canada has confirmed that very purpose of section 35 protection is to protect the culture and identity of Aboriginal peoples for future generations. In *Delgamuukw* the court held that that special relationship between Aboriginal peoples and the land, which is an essential part of their identity, "should not be prevented from continuing into the future."[162] Similarly in *Sappier and Gray,* the court explained that the object of section 35 is to provide "cultural security and continuity for the particular aboriginal society."[163] Again, in *Powley,* it emphasized that the purpose of section 35 is to protect the distinctive cultures of the Métis so that they can survive for future generations, like all Aboriginal groups.[164] In order for Aboriginal nations to continue, the Supreme Court explained that "[t]he pre-contact test in Van der Peet is based on the constitutional affirmation that aboriginal communities are entitled to continue those practices, customs and traditions that are integral to their distinctive existence or relationship to the land."[165] An argument can therefore be made that the *Indian Act's* status and membership provisions which guarantee the legislative disappearance of both individual Indians and their communities are unconstitutional. Indigenous identity cannot remain distinctive so long as it is controlled by a different culture.

Making the Case

Indigenous nations have a constitutional right to protect their identities, distinctive cultures, and future existence as nations.[166] The Court in *Powley* explained that "[t]he inclusion of the Métis in s. 35 is based on a commitment to recognizing the Métis and enhancing their survival as distinctive communities."[167] This can be no less true for the Indigenous nations who were the original occupiers of Canada for many thousands of years before the Europeans came or the Métis evolved. How each Indigenous nation traditionally welcomed their citizens into the world, named them, and celebrated their unions, or what the traditional responsibilities of each citizen were, are matters for each Indigenous nation to determine. But the starting premise has to be that each Indigenous nation has the right to exist, the promise of which is now a constitutional protection. Whether addressed at the generic or specific level, the test for assessing Aboriginal rights must evolve to reflect a more workable application of the principle of the evolutionary nature of the constitution, the organic nature of the Aboriginal groups asserting their rights, and the very purpose of section 35 rights.

The first question is whether there is any legislation that interferes with an existing right. In the case of Indigenous identity, how this sort of case would be brought to court would obviously differ from how hunting and gathering cases are considered. With Indigenous identity issues, there is no arrest or charge for failing to comply with laws that allow a defendant to raise an Aboriginal right as a defence. The matter would likely arise in a challenge to Canada's determination of status or band membership. Another way that an Aboriginal right to determine citizenship might be heard is through a challenge in a regular court to a specific provision of a future Mi'kmaq citizenship code by an individual or government. In that instance, the Mi'kmaq might defend their use of specific criteria as based on their Aboriginal right to determine their own citizenship. Recent changes to the *Canadian Human Rights Act* (CHRA) allow individuals to bring discrimination complaints against Canada and First Nations to the Canadian Human Rights Commission (CHRC) in relation to decisions or actions taken pursuant to the *Indian Act, 1985*, which would be heard in the Canadian Human Rights Tribunal (CHRT).[168] For argument's sake, one could assume that the challenge would be against Canada for its imposition of the registration provisions in the *Indian Act* on an individual or First Nation. The legislation in question would therefore be the *Indian Act* and the specific offending provision(s) would likely be section 6.

Assuming that was the case, then the specific right that would be asserted would be the right of an Indigenous nation to determine its own citizenship either as a separate right or as part of its inherent right to self-government. The question would then be whether that right was an existing right — i.e. one that had not been extinguished. Canada has acknowledged that the inherent right of self-government for Aboriginal peoples is both recognized and protected in section 35(1) of the *Constitution Act, 1982*.[169] Specifically, Canada explained that Aboriginal jurisdiction over matters internal to their communities is integral to their culture and identities.

Matters that Canada considers integral to a First Nation's culture and identity include governance and selection of leaders, membership, adoption, and the enforcement of Indigenous laws.[170] While it would appear as though the right to determine citizenship is recognized by both Canada and First Nations as an Aboriginal right protected under s.35, if faced with this claim in court Canada's usual position is to deny the right. Therefore, it would still be necessary for the Indigenous claimant to introduce historical evidence that his or her nation was self-governing or had citizenship rules.

Assuming also that Canada would lead evidence of its regulation of Indigenous identity through the *Indian Act*, it might also argue that this regulation amounted to an extinguishment of the Aboriginal right to determine citizenship. However, the Supreme Court of Canada in *Sparrow* specifically addressed the issue of the impact of regulation on Aboriginal rights and held that "an existing aboriginal right cannot be read so as to incorporate the specific manner in which it was regulated before 1982. The notion of freezing existing rights would incorporate into the Constitution a crazy patchwork of regulations."[171] The court held that an express intention is necessary to effect an extinguishment of an Aboriginal right.[172] The fact that fisheries was "progressively restrictive" and detailed in its regulation was not sufficient to prove extinguishment.[173] Canada's position "confuses regulation with extinguishment. That the right is controlled in great detail by the regulations does not mean that the right is thereby extinguished."[174]

The same can be said with regard to the *Indian Act's* registration and band membership provisions, in that the determination of status may have become progressively restrictive from the time it was first imposed on Indigenous peoples, and the registration provisions themselves may be detailed and complex, but that is not evidence that the Aboriginal right to determine citizenship has been extinguished.

I would argue that the amendment of the *Indian Act* in 1985 to include section 10, which encouraged bands to develop their own membership codes, is support for their underlying right. The inherent right policy is further evidence that membership, culture, and identity are integral to Indigenous peoples and form part of their core jurisdiction with regard to self-government, and is far from an explicit extinguishment by Canada.

The right of an Indigenous nation to determine its own citizenship is a unique right that has not yet been specifically considered by the Supreme Court of Canada. The nature of the right to determine citizenship is so profoundly different in character from a right to hunt moose, for example, that the current legal tests for determining Aboriginal rights may have to be adjusted to accommodate that fact. The Supreme Court in *Powley* adjusted the test for Aboriginal rights in the unique context of the Métis, so there is precedent for doing so. Similarly, the court in *Powley* held that Métis peoples had the right to determine who their own people were, and were encouraged to continue to develop their own citizenship rules.[175] This would be no less true for First Nations, who pre-date Métis by thousands of years. Whether as a part of the larger inherent right of self-government, or as a stand-alone right, the Aboriginal right to determine citizenship is obviously a key aspect to maintaining the distinctive cultures of both Métis and First Nations. Even the Royal Commission on Aboriginal Peoples (RCAP) explained that one of the main or core "spheres" of Aboriginal jurisdiction for self-government would be Aboriginal control over their own "citizenship and membership."[176] Since it has not been expressly extinguished in the *Indian Act* prior to 1982, this right is now constitutionally protected and cannot be unilaterally extinguished by Canada, either directly or indirectly.

If, therefore, an Indigenous nation could show that the *Indian Act* has interfered with its right to determine citizenship, and that the right had not been extinguished, then the burden would shift to Canada to justify the infringement. Before this analysis can take place, a consideration of the integral to distinctive culture test in *Van der Peet* is required.[177] The first three parts of the *Van der Peet* test are inherently related. The perspective of Indigenous peoples, the nature of the claim, and its significance may be ascertained from similar evidence. Numerous political representatives of First Nations have repeatedly asserted their right to determine their own citizenship, and this right can include the right to determine status and membership, and the right is of central significance to their culture and identity.[178] The Assembly of First Nations (AFN) undertook a consultative process whereby they talked to members of First Nations all over Canada about governance.[179] From that process a broad consensus was obtained around citizenship and its central significance to First Nations' governance, specifically that "First Nations have to be in control of their membership/citizenship and electoral rules in order to start rebuilding their governments."[180] At various times, different First Nations have also asserted this right publicly. They did so during the 1980s when Bill C-31 was being debated and they have done so again during the Bill C-3 study and debate process. During the Bill C-3 process, the AFN asserted that

> long term solutions do not lie with further tinkering of the Indian Act. Our Nations have an inherent right to determine who is and who is not a citizen of our Nation in accordance with our own laws, customs and traditions.

This is fundamental to self-governance. The real and ultimate solution to addressing ongoing discrimination in the Indian Act lies with full recognition of First Nations' jurisdiction over our own citizenship.[181]

The Chiefs of Ontario also asserted an Aboriginal right to determine citizenship which includes the right of First Nations to determine their own identity and membership.[182] The Union of British Columbia Indian Chiefs made the same assertion.[183] In any future litigation, there would no scarcity of materials relating to the Indigenous perspective that this right is integral to their distinctive cultures and the nature of the claim, including the right to determine their own rules in relation to citizenship.

The central significance of an Aboriginal right to determine citizenship is closely related to other aspects of the *Van der Peet* test — namely, that the right has independent significance and contributes to their distinctness as Aboriginal peoples. Whether someone can call themselves a Mi'kmaq person and pass that identity on to future generations is an essential part of their identity as individuals, communities, and nations. On a practical level, this might also include membership in local bands, unless and until there are other arrangements, such as self-government agreements or modern treaties, or a recognition of traditional Mi'kmaq government.

There is overwhelming historical evidence, reviewed in the RCAP and other studies, that shows that the right to determine citizenship was of central significance to Indigenous nations, and that those rules are what preserved Indigenous cultures and made them distinctly Mohawk, Mi'kmaq, Cree, Maliseet, and so on. The right to determine their own identity is so integral to the existence of Indigenous peoples that it cannot properly be compared to other Aboriginal rights litigated to date, with the exception of the inherent right to self-government, which has not been fully litigated. Indigenous identity and culture are what make each nation distinctive.

A related factor from the *Van der Peet* test is whether the traditional practice or right claimed has continuity with modern day practices. The current practice of bands determining their own membership and other Aboriginal groups determining their own citizenship in self-government agreements, modern treaties, or traditionally within local communities, has continuity with practices relating to pre-contact practices of determining citizenship. The court in *Van der Peet* explained:

I would note that the concept of continuity does not require aboriginal groups to provide evidence of an unbroken chain of continuity between their current practices, traditions and customs, and those which existed prior to contact. It may be that for a period of time an aboriginal group, for some reason, ceased to engage in a practice, tradition or custom which existed prior to contact, but then resumed the practice, tradition or custom at a later date. Such an interruption will not preclude the establishment of an aboriginal right.[184]

The fact that this right has been regulated in part by Canada does not affect the definition of the right or its continuity with past practices. Additionally, the fact that some nations may have stopped determining their own citizenship because of Canada's regulations is no different than Indigenous peoples being prevented from engaging in a commercial fishery because of restrictive fisheries regulations. Even if Canada tried to argue that regulation amounted to a break in continuity, I would argue that the significant history of Indigenous nations determining their own citizenship versus the limited time in which Canada has regulated that right would not result in a loss of continuity given the relatively short time that the right may have been regulated. The fact that the *Indian Act* allows for bands to determine their own membership regardless of who Canada states is an Indian, is further evidence that this right has continuity with past practices and has not been extinguished. What makes the *Indian Act* different from other types of regulation is that, while the *Act* may have interfered with Indigenous identity, it also acknowledged their identities as distinct from all other Canadians.

When considering other *Van der Peet* factors, such as whether the right made the Aboriginal group distinctive, the Supreme Court in *Sappier and Gray* reminded courts that Aboriginal rights are able to evolve into modern forms and should not be frozen in time. With regard to the right to determine citizenship, an evolution of the practice might include the right to decide who has status and band membership and who has citizenship rights within the larger nation. As these communities have evolved over time due to intermarriage, their ability to include the children of mixed relationships should also be recognized as part of that right. By way of analogy, the Supreme Court in *Sappier and Gray* rejected the Crown's argument that the building of wooden homes in modern times by Aboriginal people was not a logical evolution of building wigwams in pre-contact times.

The identities and cultures of Indigenous peoples can no more be frozen in time than can their exercise of their rights. That is to say, if the right to hunt can evolve such that guns can be used instead of bows and arrows, and wood can be used to build houses and not just wigwams, then the Aboriginal right to determine citizenship would protect not only citizens who practice their traditions and live an "Indian mode of life" but also those who have adapted and work as lawyers and politicians advancing their communities interests. In *Sappier and Gray*, the Supreme Court held:

What is meant by "culture" is really an inquiry into the pre-contact way of life of a particular aboriginal community, including their means of survival, their socialization methods, their legal systems, and, potentially, their trading habits. The use of the word "distinctive" as a qualifier is meant to incorporate an element of aboriginal specificity. However, "distinctive" does not mean "distinct," and the notion of aboriginality must not be reduced to "racialized stereotypes of Aboriginal peoples."[185]

Thus, the Aboriginal right to determine citizenship should be recognized because it affirms and protects Aboriginality, as much if not more so than other Aboriginal practices. Just as Aboriginal rights cannot be reduced to "racialized stereotypes of Aboriginal peoples," so, too, is the exercise of the right limited not to citizenship codes, customs, and practices that racialize Aboriginal peoples, like blood quantum codes or the *Indian Act's* descent-based status formulas. Also related is whether citizenship codes that allow for mixed marriages and adoptions would be considered integral only because of European influence.

The Supreme Court in *Van der Peet* held that the influence of European culture is only relevant if the Aboriginal custom is integral because of that influence. However, the court was forced to amend this statement in order to accommodate the Métis in *Powley*. Obviously, the Métis only exist because of the intimate influence of the Europeans. In *Powley*, the court explained that it was necessary to amend the *Van der Peet* test to accommodate the post-contact nature of Métis and their rights: "We uphold the basic elements of the *Van der Peet* test . . . and apply these to the respondents' claim. However, we modify certain elements of the pre-contact test to reflect the distinctive history and post-contact ethnogenesis of the Métis, and the resulting differences between Indian claims and Métis claims."[186] Specifically, the court explained that the only way that Métis peoples could survive is through constitutional protection:

> The constitutionally significant feature of the Métis is their special status as peoples that emerged between first contact and the effective imposition of European control. The inclusion of the Métis in s. 35 represents Canada's commitment to recognize and value the distinctive Métis cultures, which grew up in areas not yet open to colonization, and which the framers of the *Constitution Act, 1982* recognized can only survive if the Métis are protected along with other aboriginal communities.[187]

It would not be an equitable interpretation of section 35 to recognize the post-contact development of the Métis but not allow for the same cultural evolution of Indigenous nations. Similarly, if the test for Aboriginal rights can be amended to address the unique situation of Métis people, the same should be done for the unique right of Indigenous nations to determine their own citizenship. The issue may seem straightforward in *Van der Peet* where the court had to assess a specific practice (fishing), but when the right is more generic (citizenship), the *Van der Peet* test is not as easily applicable. The Aboriginal right to determine citizenship is of such a unique nature that the *Van der Peet* test ought to be amended to allow the finding to be a generic one that would apply to all Indigenous nations. This right could also be categorized as a generic right held by all Indigenous nations as part of the protections afforded to them by section 35 of the *Constitution Act, 1982* to ensure "their survival as distinctive communities."[188] Formulating the right as a generic right, if successful, would allow the numerous Indigenous nations to rely on one court ruling or one agreement with Canada, versus hundreds of individual cases. This right is not like an Aboriginal right to fish, where some Indigenous nations may have once relied on hunting buffalo instead of fishing salmon. All Indigenous nations depended on key areas of governance for their survival and citizenship is one of those core areas. Even federal policies which have interfered with this right in various ways applied to all Indigenous nations equally. Yet despite the generality of the right, the right itself, more than any other Aboriginal right, is what makes each Indigenous nation distinctly Mi'kmaq, Mohawk, or Cree.

Despite the Supreme Court's indication that Aboriginal peoples' relationship to the land is important in Aboriginal rights claims, they suggested that land tenure should not be the sole focus of inquiry:

> In considering whether a claim to an aboriginal right has been made out, courts must look at both the relationship of an aboriginal claimant to the land and at the practices, customs and traditions arising from the claimant's distinctive culture and society. Courts must not focus so entirely on the relationship of aboriginal peoples with the land that they lose sight of the other factors relevant to the identification and definition of aboriginal rights.[189]

This relationship would include Indigenous laws about how it is to be used and by whom. Therefore, by not focusing solely on land, citizenship rules can be protected for those communities that do not have reserves, that have been removed from their traditional territories, or that are now spread over several different territories. Land usage may not even be a factor for certain rights, such as the right to determine citizenship, which is more about the preservation of identity and culture. This allows those living on and off reserve and those on or off territory to partake in their identities, cultures, and communal governments without having to check their rights at artificial borders. Unlike rights such as hunting and fishing that require a land base to exercise, citizenship requires only the Indigenous collectivity and individuals who wish to belong together. Furthermore, Indigenous citizens were always citizens of their particular nations, regardless if they ventured from their traditional territories to hunt, fish, gather, make war, or trade. The fact is, when they returned to their homes, they were still Mi'kmaq, Maliseet, and Mohawk. Therefore, whether a First Nation has reserve lands should not affect their ability to assert an Aboriginal right to determine citizenship.

Having substantiated the right and considered the issue of extinguishment, it is important to remember that Aboriginal rights are not absolute. While Aboriginal rights can and do evolve, the exercise of the right cannot be done in a way that is inconsistent with the original Aboriginal right to determine citizenship. The Court in *Delgamuukw* held that "lands subject to aboriginal title cannot be put to such uses as may be irreconcilable with the nature of the occupation of that land and the relationship that the particular group has had with the land which together give rise to aboriginal title in the first place."[190]

Indigenous nations could not exercise their right to determine citizenship in ways that are incompatible with the exercise of that right by future generations. If a nation enacts laws that ensure their future extinction, it would be inconsistent with the nature of the right itself. It would also be inconsistent with the purpose of the right being constitutionally protected.

While the court in *Delgamuukw* clarified that the limitation on an Aboriginal right was not one that "restricts that use of the land to those activities that have traditionally been carried out on it,"[191] it does mean that modern exercises cannot be inconsistent with the right. Therefore, the right to determine citizenship could evolve to modern circumstances, to include the children of out-marriages/relationships and children adopted from other Indigenous nations. The key to the section 35 analysis of Aboriginal rights is ensuring the survival of Indigenous nations. While the foundational right may be the same for all Indigenous nations, the specific citizenship rules or processes may be completely different. In some instances, bands may reconstitute their membership in an inclusive manner to ensure all of their rightful members are included as an interim measure until larger issues of citizenship are determined. Other bands may decide to work together under the larger nation, while still others may join with currently unrecognized bands and off-reserve groups to work as nations on citizenship issues. This citizenship process may cross provincial boundaries and will ultimately end up including those currently labelled as non-status Indians, off-reserve, Bill C-31 reinstatees, and perhaps some who had previously called themselves Métis. Regardless of the process, there will always be limits on the powers of Indigenous nations, as there are on all governments and nations.

Powerful Rights and Limits on Power

Aboriginal rights in Canada are part of an evolving and complex area of the law. The Supreme Court has provided a basic test for the determination of Aboriginal rights and has incorporated amendments to the test when faced with unique situations, such as Métis rights, commercial rights, or land rights. Although Aboriginal rights are protected in the *Constitution Act, 1982*, the Supreme Court has held that Aboriginal rights are not absolute.[192] Further, those rights must be interpreted in reference to both Canadian common law and Aboriginal laws and perspectives.[193] Another restriction on Aboriginal rights which stems from Supreme Court jurisprudence is the inability of Aboriginal peoples to exercise Aboriginal rights in ways that may harm the public or themselves.[194]

Just as Aboriginal peoples may be subject to various limits on their rights, so, too, is Canada. Canada has the power under section 91(24) of the *Constitution Act, 1867* to legislate with regard to Indians, but this does not give Canada a right to make rules for Indigenous peoples which are harmful to them or that are inconsistent with Canada's fiduciary duty toward them. The protections contained in section 35 of the *Constitution Act, 1982* equally act as a limit on federal and provincial governments with regard to Aboriginal and treaty rights. The court in *Sparrow* explained that section 35 acts as a specific restraint on Canada's power to legislate:

> Federal legislative powers continue, including, of course, the right to legis-late with respect to Indians pursuant to s. 91(24) of the Constitution Act, 1867. These powers must, however, now be read together with s. 35(1). In other words, federal power must be reconciled with federal duty and the best way to achieve that reconciliation is to demand the justification of any government regulation that infringes upon or denies aboriginal rights. Such scrutiny is in keeping with the liberal interpretive principle . . . and the concept of holding the Crown to a high standard of honourable dealing with respect to the aboriginal peoples of Canada. . . .[195]

When the Aboriginal right to determine citizenship is considered in this light, it is obvious that restrictions on powers apply to all parties.

Therefore, Canada lacks the power to legislate the extinction of Indigenous peoples through the status and membership provisions of the *Indian Act*. Given the serious harms inflicted on Indigenous peoples and their nations by virtue of the *Indian Act*'s status and membership provisions, I would argue that Canada does not even have the right to legislate identity or membership. This has not been lost in the debates over Bill C-3 — the bill which amended the *Indian Act* to address some of the gender discrimination raised in the *McIvor* case. Numerous witnesses who appeared before the House of Commons to give evidence in relation to Bill C-3 spoke not only of the harms that the *Indian Act* has caused Indigenous peoples and their nations, but also highlighted Canada's lack of jurisdiction in this regard.[196] Canada has assumed that its power to legislate with regard to Indians knows no bounds, but the Supreme Court's jurisprudence indicates otherwise.[197]

Indigenous laws exist within a complex mix of traditional, domestic, and international laws, all of which are limited in some form or another. Indigenous governments must be subject to limits on power in the interests of both their citizens and the citizens of other nations. This does not mean that, where laws conflict with Canadian or other laws, Indigenous laws must give way. It does mean, however, that the relationship between these laws and others must be the subject of an ongoing and evolving relationship of give and take between Indigenous nations and their citizens, Indigenous nations and Canada, and even Indigenous nations and the international community.

The process of reconciliation between Canada and Indigenous peoples goes both ways. Just as it would no longer be appropriate for one Indigenous group to make war with another over territory, for example, it is no longer appropriate for Canada to try to assimilate Indians. Just as Indigenous nations do not condone Canada using outdated, racist, and assimilatory laws and policies toward Indigenous peoples, Indigenous citizens should not be exposed to similar laws from their own nations. In other words, Indigenous nations are prevented from providing for the extinction of their citizens through restrictive citizenship criteria. The *Canadian Charter of Rights and Freedoms* contains many rights and freedoms, none of which are absolute.[198] An ongoing balancing of rights is required between individuals and legitimate government objectives.

Does the Charter Apply?

Reliance on section 35 constitutional rights by Indigenous nations necessarily incorporates limits on those rights, including not being able to exercise those rights in ways which are inconsistent with the right itself, would harm their citizens, create significant danger to others, or violate international human rights laws. One of the issues facing Indigenous governments today is Canada's demand that the *Charter* apply to First Nations and all agreements between themselves and Canada. The issue of whether the *Charter* applies to Indigenous peoples and governments, and whether it limits the exercise of Aboriginal rights, has supporters on both sides. One limit on the application of the *Charter* is that the rights contained therein apply as between individuals and governments, and do not apply between private parties, unless those actions were carried out at the direction of, or on behalf of, the government.[199] This means that, even if your neighbour yells out something discriminatory, you can't bring a *Charter* claim. Section 32 provides that the *Charter* applies to the federal, provincial, and territorial governments and legislatures,[200] yet the *Charter* is silent on whether it applies to Indigenous governments and, if so, which forms: bands, organizations, self-governing, or Treaty nations. Some have criticized the *Charter* because it was drafted without consultation with Indigenous peoples. In the end, however, it was the collective opposition of Indigenous peoples to the *Charter*'s constitutional entrenchment that led to the inclusion of section 25, which some Indigenous people argue protect their rights from the *Charter*'s application.[201]

Section 25 provides that the rights contained in the *Charter* will not "abrogate or derogate" from Aboriginal rights, treaty rights, or other rights.[202] Although the Supreme Court has not yet determined the full scope of section 25's protection, its inclusion in the *Charter* is seen by many as a positive protection for Indigenous nations. The *Charter* also provides many other rights of both general and limited application. For example, section 7 provides everyone with the right to life, liberty, and security of person. On the other hand, the section which provides everyone in the New Brunswick legislature with the right to work in both French and English is of limited application. One of the more controversial rights of general application has been section 15, the equality right. Some Indigenous peoples feared that non-Indigenous people would use section 15's anti-discrimination provision to argue that there should not be any "Aboriginal" governments.[203] Since its entrenchment, the *Charter* has continued to create controversy as to its applicability to Indigenous peoples and their governments.

The *Report of the Royal Commission on Aboriginal Peoples* (RCAP) reviewed the matter of the *Charter*'s applicability to Aboriginal peoples and concluded that, since Aboriginal peoples enjoy *Charter* protections in their relations with federal, provincial, and territorial governments, they also must have the same protections with their own Aboriginal governments. Despite the fact that section 32(1) of the *Charter* does not specifically mention the applicability of the *Charter* to Aboriginal governments, the RCAP nonetheless concluded that

> it would be highly anomalous if Canadian citizens enjoyed the protection of the Charter in their relations with every government in Canada except for Aboriginal governments. The general provisions of the Charter are designed to provide a uniform level of protection for individuals in exercising their basic rights and freedoms within Canada.[204]

This reasoning is not unlike that used to repeal section 67 of the *Canadian Human Rights Act* (CHRA).[205] Prior to June 2008, section 67 of the *CHRA* provided Canada and First Nations bands with immunity from discrimination claims resulting from decisions or actions taken pursuant to the *Indian Act, 1985*. International human rights groups as well as Indigenous women's and off-reserve Indigenous groups had long advocated for the repeal of section 67 of the *CHRA*. The original intent of that section was to be a temporary measure until Canada and First Nations came to an agreement about how they would amend the *Indian Act*. As that never happened, the immunity stayed in place for decades. An interpretive provision and notwithstanding clause was added to the *Act* so that "due regard" will be given to Aboriginal laws and customs, and nothing in the *CHRA* will "abrogate or derogate" from Aboriginal and treaty rights protected in section 35 of the *Constitution Act, 1982*. However, the principle of gender equity is paramount. Canada heralded the repeal of s. 67 of the *CHRA* as a viable resolution mechanism for Indigenous peoples who felt unfairly excluded from registration as Indians after Bill C-3 passed, or if they felt they were unfairly excluded from membership during its testimony to the House of Commons regarding Bill C-3.[206] Unfortunately, we also learned from the Canadian Human Rights Commission (CHRC) at the same hearings that Canada's position at the Canadian Human Rights Tribunal (CHRT) has been to deny all claims related to status or membership and to challenge the CHRT's jurisdiction even to hear the cases.[207] Therefore, the viability of using the *CHRA* process as a means of addressing discrimination in the *Indian Act* is far from certain.

The *CHRA* cannot necessarily be seen as a viable option to *Charter* claims — at least not yet. The *Charter* contains some provisions similar to that of the *CHRA*. The RCAP reviewed the similar non-derogation clause in the *Charter* and concluded that, while section 25 does offer certain protections to Aboriginal peoples with regard to their Aboriginal and treaty rights, it does not exclude the application of the *Charter* to Aboriginal peoples and their governments.[208] The commissioners felt that Aboriginal peoples are entitled to enjoy the protections of the *Charter* no matter where they live and that Aboriginal governments occupy the same position relative to the *Charter* as do the federal and provincial governments.[209] In other words, if Indigenous governments are to be considered a third order of government, then similar limits will apply to their powers as are applied to the federal and provincial levels of government. The RCAP further argued that, while Aboriginal governments would have the use of the *Charter's* notwithstanding clause, only Aboriginal nations, not local Aboriginal communities, could use it.[210] Similar to the interpretive provisions in the *CHRA*, the RCAP argued that "the Charter must be given a flexible interpretation that takes account of the distinctive philosophies, traditions and cultural practices of Aboriginal peoples."[211] Thus, according to the RCAP, the *Charter* applies to Indigenous peoples and their governments.

The controversy over the *Charter's* applicability was fuelled again in the same year by a new government policy involving Aboriginal peoples. In 1996, Indian and Northern Affairs Canada (INAC) announced the federal government's new policy on Aboriginal self-government: the "Inherent Right Policy."[212] Canada publicly recognized that the inherent right of Aboriginal peoples to self-government was a protected Aboriginal right under section 35(1) of the *Constitution Act, 1982*. The federal government's position with regard to self-government arrangements clearly stated that the *Charter* would apply:

> The Government is committed to the principle that the *Canadian Charter of Rights and Freedoms* should bind all governments in Canada, so that Aboriginal peoples and non-Aboriginal Canadians alike may continue to enjoy equally the rights and freedoms guaranteed by the Charter. Self-government agreements, including treaties, will, therefore, have to provide that the *Canadian Charter of Rights and Freedoms* applies to Aboriginal governments and institutions in relation to all matters within their respective jurisdictions and authorities.[213]

With regard to the interpretation of section 25, the government explained that the *Charter* is about balancing rights:

> The Charter itself already contains a provision (section 25) directing that it must be interpreted in a manner that respects Aboriginal and treaty rights, which would include, under the federal approach, the inherent right. The Charter is thus designed to ensure a sensitive balance between individual rights and freedoms, and the unique values and traditions of Aboriginal peoples in Canada.[214]

While Indigenous peoples had long called for the federal government to officially recognize the inherent right of Indigenous peoples to self-government, the details of the policy were not well received — this notwithstanding that the *Charlottetown Accord* (which was agreed to by all parties, including the Indigenous representatives) would have expressly applied the *Charter* to self-government agreements.[215] Despite the section 25 protection, many First Nations are still opposed to the application of the *Charter* to their governments.[216]

In a recent policy document, *Framework for the Recognition and Implementation of First Nation Governments*, the Assembly of First Nations (AFN) stated that the "current Federal Inherent Right Policy is obstructive of recognition" of the inherent right to self-government, and argued that the "policy must be repealed and replaced."[217] Many First Nations were opposed to constitutionally entrenching the *Charter* back in the 1980s because they feared that the *Charter*'s orientation toward individual rights would threaten Indigenous culture and treaty rights, which were more communal in nature.[218] The AFN's lack of faith in the guarantees in the *Charter* spilled over into the equality guarantee that is now found in section 35(4) of the *Constitution Act, 1982*. During the 1983 constitutional conference, the AFN was the only national Aboriginal organization not in agreement with the adoption of the equality guarantee as part of constitutionally protected Aboriginal rights. While the AFN eventually reversed its position, they did so on the basis that Canada would not interfere with their right to determine citizenship:

> We would like to make it clear that we agree with the women who spoke so forcefully this morning that they have been treated unjustly. The discrimination they suffered was forced upon us through a system imposed upon us by white colonial government through the Indian Act. It was not the result of our traditional laws, and in fact it would not have occurred under our traditional laws. We must make it perfectly clear why we feel so strongly that we must control our own citizenship. The AFN maintains that "equality" does already exist with the traditional "citizenship code" of all First Nations people.[219]

While the AFN may have given in to accepting section 35(4) of the *Constitution Act, 1982*, they continued to resist application of the *Charter* to self-government arrangements. In the end, it would appear that First Nations are still not in control of their citizenship issues, nor have many been able to prevent or resolve discrimination and inequality issues with regard to status and membership in their communities. This may be part of the reason why other political groups representing specific groups of Aboriginal peoples who feel discriminated against by their government may be in favour of both the *Charter's* applicability and the repeal of s. 67 of the *CHRA*.

The Native Women's Association of Canada (NWAC) and many Indigenous women in Canada have taken a position opposite to that of the AFN. They feel that the *Charter* should apply not only to self-government arrangements but also to First Nation band councils.[220] In the 1990s, the NWAC released a document entitled the "Canada Package," explaining their position regarding the federal government's position on self-government. In its review and analysis of the various options being proposed, the NWAC stated that it wanted protections for Indigenous women and that the *Charter* should apply.[221] Should recognition of the inherent right of self-government fall outside the *Charter* and section 35 of the *Constitution Act*, they specifically wanted the *Charter* guarantees (including section 15 equality rights) to apply to all Indigenous peoples.[222] The NWAC had long called for the repeal of section 67 of the *CHRA* as well, but sided with the AFN against the bill as Canada did not include any resources for First Nations to prepare for future claims and to review and amend their laws, codes, and by-laws.

The off-reserve Indigenous peoples of Canada have been represented by separate organizations for quite some time. While they are often made up of large percentages of Indigenous women, their organizations have nonetheless remained a separate political voice. The Congress of Aboriginal Peoples (CAP) has always supported the applicability of the *Charter* to Indigenous peoples, and even supported the NWAC during the constitutional talks when the NWAC was excluded from participation.[223] While the NWAC pursued litigation against the federal government for excluding it from the constitutional talks, the CAP (then the Native Council of Canada) tried unsuccessfully to bring about an agreement among the parties and to acquire a seat at the constitutional table for the NWAC.[224] The CAP's current constituents include status Indians who live off-reserve, many of whom are excluded from band membership or participation in band elections; Métis who are excluded from the Métis National Council and their provincial affiliates; and non-status Indians. The unique make-up of the CAP's constituents is likely the reason why it and its provincial affiliates support the application of the *Charter* to Indigenous governments and agreements. As with the NWAC, the CAP's political positions have waivered in recent years. While its written submission to Canada regarding the Bill C-3 *Indian Act* amendments to address the *McIvor* case were adamant that any amendments must address all gender discrimination, at subsequent presentations they did an about-face and supported the bill. Their position with regard to the applicability of the *Charter* to Indigenous peoples, however, has not changed.

As Aboriginal political organizations differ in their views on the *Charter*'s application, so, too, have the views of Indigenous and non-Indigenous academics. A brief survey of the literature on the issue revealed that, of eighteen articles and books reviewed, thirteen authors argued that the *Charter* does or should apply to Indigenous peoples and their governments, whereas five thought the *Charter* does not or should not apply. The academic debate on this point raises important moral, legal, and political considerations.

Kent McNeil argues that the *Charter* should not apply to Aboriginal governments in Canada.[225] He states that he is not putting forward a legal argument — i.e., as to whether the *Charter* applies to Aboriginal governments as a matter of Canadian constitutional law — and he limits his definition of Aboriginal governments to traditional governments: Indian, Inuit, and Métis peoples with inherent rights.[226] His argument, therefore, is a normative one. He does not agree with those who feel that the *Charter* would protect Indigenous culture and tradition, and thinks there is a danger in applying the *Charter* without first analyzing how it might affect the culture and identities of Indigenous peoples.[227] Boldt and Long agree with McNeil: "Our thesis is that western-liberal tradition embodied in the Canadian Charter of Rights and Freedoms, which conceives of human rights in terms of the individual, poses yet another serious threat to the cultural identity of native Indians in Canada."[228]

The lack of Indigenous courts to help interpret Indigenous culture only exacerbates this problem.[229] Finally, McNeil asserts that Indigenous women in Canada have less to be concerned about, as compared with their counterparts in the United States, since the Aboriginal right to self-government which is protected in section 35(1) of the *Constitution Act, 1982* is limited by section 35(4).[230] To date, there has been no Supreme Court jurisprudence interpreting section 35(4) directly.

Boldt and Long agree and explain that, in the western liberal tradition, the individual is considered "morally prior," whereas in tribal life the individual's self-interest is intertwined with tribal survival. They also explain that Indigenous and western societies have different worldviews:

> We want to stress here that in our discussion of traditional customs relating to group rights we do not propose that Indians are currently uniformly and consistently practising these traditions. However, contemporary Indians have embraced these traditions as their charter myth and as fundamental to their version of the "good society," much as western democratic societies have adopted equality and individual rights as their charter myth and version of the "good society."[231]

Rejection of the *Charter* is more than mere theoretical disagreement for Boldt and Long; it is based on a history of attempted assimilation of Indigenous peoples. It is with this history in mind that Boldt and Long argue, with regard to the *Charter*'s imposition on Indigenous peoples, that Indigenous peoples have good reason to distrust the government and its laws.[232] While the Canadian government argues that the *Charter* would improve the quality of life of Indigenous peoples, it has used the same justification to legislate racist acts and policies in the past.[233] While they do not dispute that Indigenous peoples want protections from the larger society, they argue that they want protections as collectives, not as individuals.[234] Furthermore, since the Canadian government did not create the *Charter* by consent of Indigenous people, the *Charter* should not apply.[235]

Mary-Ellen Turpel (now Turpel-Lafond) questions the "cultural authority" of the *Charter*, though she recognizes that no society is purely individualistic or collectivist.[236] Turpel questions the extent to which the majority in Canada has taken into account the differences between themselves and the Indigenous peoples when creating laws. In her view, "The denial of difference is a political tool of cultural hegemony."[237] She feels that there would be no real change for Indigenous peoples in Canada if the *Charter* and the *Constitution Act, 1982* were to replace the *Indian Act* as the "supervisors" of Indigenous peoples.[238]

Long and Chiste agree that Indigenous communities should be "exempt" from the *Charter* as political and cultural transformation has been limited in

Indigenous communities. They further explain that, while both Indigenous peoples and western traditions support the equality of individuals, the strength of the concept being proposed depends a great deal on its origin — i.e., whether Canada is imposing laws on Indigenous peoples, or whether it originates from a particular Indigenous community's own culture and traditions.[239] These academics feel strongly that the *Charter* should not be applied to Indigenous peoples and .their governments because the *Charter* is not based on Indigenous consent and does not reflect Indigenous culture and traditions.

Assuming that these authors are right and the *Charter* doesn't apply, is there a void in terms of equality for Indigenous peoples? Turpel suggests that the solution is in the development of "community codes" that would deal with the most pressing problems in Indigenous communities.[240] She feels these codes would avert the further "imposition of the human rights paradigm on Aboriginal communities."[241] McNeil, on the other hand, suggests that the solution lies in Indigenous justice systems.[242] He feels that separate Indigenous justice systems should be implemented so that Aboriginal people would not have to rely on Canadian courts to interpret Indigenous culture.[243] Boldt and Long suggest leaving Indigenous cultures as they are and promoting systems that protect human dignity — i.e., respecting collectivities — versus systems that focus on individual rights.[244] Long and Chiste combine these concepts, arguing that "the welfare of Indian peoples will be better served if First Nations have the option of re-establishing traditional social systems and political structures or reforming present ones to reflect their own culturally relevant standards."[245] Their solution represents a combination of Canadian ideas with Indigenous culture: "On balance, Indian nations will best be served by allowing them the option of creating special Indian charters as an alternative to the Canadian charter."[246] While the issue of the *Charter* is an important one to Indigenous peoples, Long and Chiste argue that, "In fact, the reconstruction of 'community' seems to us the most urgent task facing contemporary Indian leaders."[247] Alternatives to the application of the Canadian *Charter* therefore include leaving the issue of rights up to Indigenous groups to manage themselves, setting up Indigenous courts to handle these issues, or drafting Indigenous charters instead.

Turpel argued that the *Charter* should not apply to Indigenous peoples because it lacked cultural authority. However, in an article co-authored with Hogg several years later, she argues that courts would likely interpret the *Charter* to apply to Aboriginal governments.[248] Additionally, Hogg and Turpel both argue that Aboriginal charters are the solution.[249] They think that section 25 of the *Charter* does not provide blanket immunity for Aboriginal governments against the *Charter*'s application, but is meant as a direction for courts to defer to some Aboriginal activities.[250] It is not intended that these Aboriginal charters would displace the Canadian *Charter* (at least not without constitutional amendment), but would exist alongside it.[251]

The RCAP also considered the issue of Aboriginal charters and concluded that, "Where an Aboriginal nation enacts its own charter of rights and responsibilities, private individuals will benefit from its provisions in addition to those of the Canadian *Charter*. An Aboriginal charter will supplement the Canadian *Charter* but not displace it."[252]According to the RCAP, the *Charter* applies with or without supplemental Aboriginal charters, and it offers uniform protections for Aboriginal peoples and non-Aboriginal peoples, regardless of where they live or with whose government they associate, and this can only be to their benefit.[253]

Is the Tension More Apparent than Real?

In the debate about *Charter* applicability, the academics point out an apparent tension between individual and communal rights. Sometimes this is characterized as a tension between Indigenous women's rights and communal First Nation (band) rights. Although the authors reviewed in the previous section argued persuasively that there are often hidden dangers in applying Canadian laws and policies to Indigenous peoples, the fact that they also argue that equality rights are part of Indigenous traditions makes me wonder if this tension is more apparent than real. Patrick Macklem, in his book *Indigenous Difference*, agrees that the *Charter* does pose a risk to the "vitality of indigenous difference."[254] He feels that Indigenous communities have cultures and traditions that are different from western traditions and should not be dismantled through *Charter* litigation simply because Indigenous practices appear different from Western norms of individualism. However, Macklem also argues that the *Charter* should apply, as Indigenous peoples need its protections:

> A blanket exemption from the Charter would enable Aboriginal governments to ride roughshod over interests associated with Charter rights without necessarily furthering interests associated with indigenous difference. In contrast to a blanket exemption, applying the Charter enables the judiciary to develop a much more calibrated approach.[255]

Although the *Charter*'s application to Indigenous peoples could interfere with indigenous difference, Macklem's view is that this risk could be minimized by directing judges to give deference to Indigenous cultures and traditions. This stands in contrast to McNeil's vision of Indigenous courts doing the interpretation. John Borrows, on the other hand, believes that the debate over the *Charter*'s applicability actually hurts the pursuit of self-government for Indigenous peoples and their nations.[256]

Borrows argues that more attention needs to be given to reconciling these differences of viewpoints regarding the *Charter*'s applicability: "By creating a conversation between rights and tradition, the *Charter* presents First Nations with an opportunity to recapture the strength of principles which were often eroded through government interference."[257] Borrows's message is one of practicality; he believes Indigenous peoples cannot ignore the world they live in and must use Canadian tools to advance Indigenous interests: "We require a measure of our oppressors' cooperation to disentangle ourselves from the web of enslavement."[258] He suggests that, while some Indigenous people may find it offensive to use the words, concepts, and institutions of the non-Indigenous majority, it may be necessary in order to carve out a place for Indigenous peoples within Canada where they can enjoy their traditions, customs, and practices.[259] Therefore, why not selectively use these tools when it is to an Indigenous group's benefit? At the same time, he points out, Indigenous traditions are dynamic and change over time, incorporating both "past and present understandings and events."[260] As a result, some Indigenous cultures have adapted to embrace non-Indigenous concepts that are similar to their own. Equality as a concept may have a non-Indigenous name, but it is similar in concept to any number of Indigenous traditions.

One important aspect of this debate is the acceptance of responsibility by Indigenous men for how they treat Indigenous women.[261] Borrows argues that self-government is such an important goal that Indigenous people should refocus their attention on the similarities found between the *Charter* and their traditional values.[262] In this way, non-Indigenous people could not hold up examples of gender discrimination in Indigenous communities as a reason for not supporting Indigenous self-government:

> While colonialism is at the root of our learned actions today, First Nations men must take some measure of responsibility for their conduct and attitudes. It is no longer enough to say "the Indian Act made us do it." Positive acceptance of responsibility is an important step in healing the divisions that have occurred.[263]

Many Indigenous women would agree with Borrows' position, and feel that the *Charter* was not only a victory for Indigenous women when it was enacted, but also provides necessary equality protections for Indigenous women today.[264] The NWAC has advocated for the application of the *Charter* to Indigenous communities, and its real value has been lost in the artificial debate regarding the apparent tension between individual and communal rights.

Each of the authors reviewed above focussed on one specific Indigenous group. That being the case, it is important to point out the limits in the current debate. None of these authors seemed to take issue with the fact that the *Charter* applies to individual Indigenous peoples in their dealings with federal, provincial, and territorial governments; in fact, some of them confirmed its application to

Indigenous peoples. Logically, as Canadian citizens, Indigenous peoples would enjoy the rights, benefits, and protections that other Canadians enjoy, in addition to the rights and protections they might also enjoy as Indigenous peoples. Being Canadian citizens, individual Indigenous peoples could avail themselves of the *Charter* in their dealings with Canadian governments — and have, in fact, done so successfully. Most of the academics reviewed above feel that the *Charter* did apply to individual Indigenous peoples in their dealings with governments. If that is the case, then, practically speaking, to whom does the *Charter* not apply?

The terms "Aboriginal people" and "Aboriginal government" can be defined very differently depending on one's perspective. When academics argue that the *Charter* does not apply, therefore, it helps to know to whom they are referring. They all appear to agree that the *Charter* applies to individual Indigenous people in their dealings with governments, but who are these governments? With regard to First Nations (bands), it is fairly clear that the *Charter* applies to them in their administration of the *Indian Act* and in their dealings with the Indigenous people who live under their jurisdictions. In *Scrimbitt,* the band attempted to use custom law to deny voting rights to its band members who had been reinstated under the Bill C-31 amendments to the *Indian Act.*[265] The band's defence included the fact that other bands in Saskatchewan had similar voting regulations and that it was their traditional custom to exclude Bill C-31 people. The court rejected these arguments and held that the "[b]ill was intended to remedy longstanding discriminatory treatment of Aboriginal women who married non-status Indians. Sakimay's Bill C-31 policy reinstates that treatment and thwarts Parliament's effort to remedy it."[266] The court further held that the refusal by the band to allow Scrimbitt to vote was discrimination on the basis of sex and marital status, and thus violated section 15 of the *Charter.*[267] Though the band tried to argue that economic hardship would follow, the court did not consider the *Charter* breach to be justifiable under section 1.[268]

Similarly, there was no question that the *Charter* applied to the Six Nations Band in *Henderson.* In this case, the only issue after proving discrimination was whether the band's actions were justifiable.[269] The band had enacted a by-law prohibiting non-band member spouses from residing on the reserve. Henderson felt she had a right to live on the reserve with her husband, who was a band member. The court reviewed the decision of the trial court, which dismissed the band's by-law prosecution against the non-band member. Although they found that excluding non-band member spouses of band members was discriminatory, they agreed with the band that the influx of people on the reserve would cause financial hardship to the band.[270] Since the *Indian Act* provides that only Indians can enjoy the use of reserve lands, the court found that the by-law excluding non-band members was saved under section 1.[271] In this case, the *Charter* unquestionably applied to the Six Nations Band, and individual band members and non-band members could both avail themselves of the *Charter*'s protections when dealing with the band. The only question was whether the by-law could be saved under section 1 of the *Charter*, and it was.

Henderson dealt with an *Indian Act* band. There are now self-governing communities that may not be under the *Indian Act*. It would appear that the *Charter* applies to these communities as well. The federal government's *Inherent Right* policy provides that the *Charter* will apply to all of these types of agreements. This, of course, is federal policy and subject to negotiation, but the federal government appears to be fairly firm. Canada's position is that the *Charter* applies to all residents of Aboriginal lands:

> In all instances, in matters related to peace, order and good government and the *Canadian Charter of Rights and Freedoms*, federal laws would prevail over any Aboriginal law passed pursuant to a self-government agreement. Federal and provincial laws of general application and federal laws related to Canadian sovereignty, defence, and external relations will continue to apply to all persons residing on Aboriginal lands.[272]

By way of example, the *Yukon First Nations Self-Government Act* provides that the self-government agreement is made in accordance with the constitution.[273] Section 2.12.1 of the *Nunavut Settlement Agreement* provides that all federal laws will apply, and that the agreement is to be considered a land claims agreement within s. 35 of the *Constitution Act, 1982*.[274] Section 2.15.1 of the *Tlicho Agreement* specifically provides that the *Charter* applies to the Tlicho government in all matters within its authority.[275] Similarly, section 2.18.1 of the *Labrador Inuit Agreement* provides that federal laws apply, and specifically that the *Charter* applies.[276] Although there has not been any significant court decision on the issue, it is unlikely that Indigenous governments can contract out of the constitution. Even if that were possible (given the federal negotiating position) or desirable (given the constitutional protections for Indigenous peoples contained in the constitution), practically speaking, it is unlikely that the courts would interpret First Nation reserves and traditional territories as *Charter*-free zones. Therefore, if the *Charter* applies to everyone and even the *CHRA* has been amended to allow Indigenous people to benefit from basic human rights protections, why the controversy? If the *Charter* applies to individual Indigenous people no matter where they live, applies to non-Indigenous people whether they live on or off reserve, applies to First Nations governments (bands), and even applies to self-governing Indigenous nations, then to whom does the *Charter* not apply? Maybe the problem is that we have been asking the wrong questions.

Are We Asking the Wrong Questions?

Thus far, the questions related to the *Charter* have centred on whether it applies to First Nations (bands), self-governing or self-determining Indigenous nations, and Indigenous individuals, and if so, to what extent? Some authors have looked at the legal question of whether it applies as a matter of constitutional law, while others have looked at whether the *Charter* should apply as a matter of principle. Perhaps the debate continues because the focus has not been in the right place. The tension between an individual Indigenous person's right to belong to his or her Indigenous nation or local community and the nation's right to determine its own citizenship laws is often played out with reference to *Charter* rights. Some of the authors reviewed above spoke about the incompatibility between the individual rights focus of the *Charter* and the communal rights focus of Indigenous traditions. Others spoke of the significant difference between Indigenous traditional values and the European values found in the *Charter*. Still others argued that the *Charter* is imposed on Indigenous peoples and therefore lacks the cultural relevance necessary to legitimize it. Given the education, expertise, and reputation behind these learned opinions, it would appear that the debate is doomed to continue until a decision by Supreme Court of Canada on the matter.

But what if the focus were to shift from the history of how and why the *Charter* was created and how it affects current power structures to one that emphasized its compatibility with Indigenous traditions, the positive protections it offers Indigenous peoples and their governments, and how reconciliation requires some give and take on both sides? If we started looking at the issue differently, other important questions might come to the forefront — such as how can we empower vulnerable groups within Indigenous society to have a voice in this ongoing debate. What if the debate focused on questions like, what harms would befall Indigenous individuals if they were denied *Charter* rights, or whether Indigenous governments would be effective in nation-building if their citizens did not enjoy minimum human rights and freedoms, or whether it makes sense to make the *Charter* inapplicable to Indigenous nations whose own traditions uphold these same values, even if in different ways? We have to remember that the *Charter* represents basic human rights which are accepted internationally and included in the *United Nations Declaration on the Rights of Indigenous Peoples*.[277]

Some of the most vulnerable groups in Indigenous societies have been excluded from status, reserve residency, band membership, voting or running for office in First Nation elections, and participating in cultural and traditional activities. They have been denied equal access to programs and services such as housing, health care and education, citizenship in self-government agreements, and equal shares in land claims and treaty benefits. These vulnerable groups are often denied the right to their Indigenous identities and cultures through communal exclusion, and, ultimately, denied a voice. Meanwhile, mostly male political leaders claim to speak on their behalf, as academics argue the theoretical underpinnings of why the *Charter* does or does not apply, and some traditionalists rationalize including or excluding seven more generations of their own people under the guise of their own personal interpretations of Indigenous traditions. We already know that, despite the repeal of section 67 of the *CHRA*, Canada is vigorously defending all claims of discrimination and trying to deny the CHTR jurisdiction to even hear the cases. It is more important than ever for vulnerable Indigenous people to have minimal protections. Most would agree that the *Indian Act* is an outdated, even racist piece of legislation that cries out to be amended in the interim and replaced in the long term. Recently, National Chief Shawn Atleo of the AFN called for the replacement of the *Indian Act* within five years.[278] In the meantime, many bands continue to use it to disproportionately exclude Indigenous women and children from membership in their communities for a host of reasons, from claims of economic hardship to inter-familial disputes.

The current situation in Kahnawake is a prime example of why minimal protections are needed.[279] The Mohawk Council of Kahnawake passed a law that prevented band members from marrying non-Indigenous persons. Even if the *Charter* came about in a manner that was not inclusive of Indigenous peoples, or contains rights and protections that Indigenous nations did not design in negotiation with Canada, one could argue that the *Indian Act* is a much more offensive piece of legislation. The *Charter* is at least designed to offer protections to all peoples in Canada, Indigenous and non-Indigenous alike. Further, it offers specific consideration for Aboriginal, treaty, and other rights. It could be used to offer protections that would be useful for both communities and individuals. This does not, in any way, prevent Indigenous communities from drafting their own systems and codes to offer higher or traditionally specific protections for their communities and individuals. It does mean, however, that the minimal human rights protections offered in the *Charter* would be available to all Indigenous peoples. The situation in Kahnawake is an extreme example of what happens without basic human rights and freedoms, and helps answer what happens if Indigenous peoples do not have the benefit of the *Charter*.

Perhaps Indigenous communities may enact their own traditional codes which offer better protections for Mohawks, Mi'kmaq, or Cree, for use in their bands, self-government agreements, or other treaty or land claim arrangements. However it is done, the point is that there cannot be a void in the law where Indigenous peoples go unprotected. As Aboriginal and treaty rights evolve and are now protected in the constitution, so, too, must the basic human rights of Indigenous peoples evolve to include modern day circumstances, such as out-marriage, and be protected in various instruments like the *CHRA* and the *Charter*. Why, then, is the issue of *Charter* protection for Indigenous peoples so controversial?

Must we limit the discussion to the default discourse of men versus women or individual versus community? Can we really limit our consideration to individualism when Indigenous women and children seek their rightful place in their communities? By excluding them, Indigenous communities will bring about their own extinction — through legislation, membership codes, or even self-government codes. The future of many Indigenous nations depends far more on the inclusion of their unregistered women and children than it does on preserving male-dominated power structures.

Indigenous women and children and other vulnerable groups must face a two-pronged war to maintain their identities and sense of belonging within their nations: they must first fight with Canada to obtain legal recognition as Indians, then they must fight with their home communities to be accepted as band members. How, after decades of gender and racial discrimination, can Indigenous women and children fight this battle to protect their cultures for future generations if they are not afforded the minimum protections to which every other Canadian is entitled?

The *Charter* offers protections to vulnerable Indigenous peoples from the legacy of assimilation policies and the current financial interests that may lead to their exclusion. If it is possible to use one document — the *Indian Act* — to bring about divisions within communities, why is it so hard to imagine using a less objectionable document — the *Charter* — to create positive outcomes? Protecting current and future generations under the *Charter* affords Indigenous peoples laws that reflect both Indigenous legal traditions and Canadian ones. Indigenous traditions, customs, laws, and codes are carried forward by successive generations to maintain the integrity of each Indigenous nation and ensure its existence into the future. In this way, Canada's constitutional promise to Indigenous peoples that their distinct cultures and identities be protected for future generations becomes the focus.

If the *Charter* has the effect of eliminating discrimination under the *Indian Act,* reinstating those vulnerable groups currently excluded, ridding the *Act* of the discriminatory section 6(2) cut-off and, thereby, saving Indigenous nations and cultures from extinction, then I would argue that this focus on its overarching constitutional promise overcomes the theoretical dilemmas engaged by focusing on its creation or how it affects current power structures. It is also then more in line with the treaty relationship between the Crown and Indigenous nations which govern treaty relations "as long as the sun sets" for our "heirs and heirs forever." From this end of the spectrum, the debate then shifts to one of an overall constitutional promise that is in line with our treaty relationship, and guarantees that everyone benefits from those protections. We must take that bold step forward, out of the status quo and into a new relationship that looks back to move forward — one that is based on a resurrection of our traditions, customs, laws, and values, but which incorporates modern realities, rights, protections, and benefits.

Viewed in this light, *Charter* debates that focus on individual versus community, traditional values versus European values, women versus men, or pure bloods versus half bloods, start to sound outdated and irrelevant. It is doubtful that Indigenous identity and culture could be adequately protected without the *Charter*. It is a vital component of keeping Canada's constitutional promise to protect the identity and culture of Indigenous peoples into the future.

CHAPTER THREE

The Right to Belong:
Charter Equality for Indigenous Peoples

As DISCUSSED IN PREVIOUS CHAPTERS, part of the constitutional promise made to Indigenous peoples by Canada was the protection of their distinctive cultures and identities for future generations. The current Indian registration and band membership provisions of the *Indian Act, 1985* stand in stark contrast to this promise. The *Act* has imposed a scheme of registration on individuals which gives them different types of status with differing rights. It divides families, communities, and nations, and has divided Indigenous nations into smaller local communities whose members are often at the lowest ends of the socio-economic indicators in Canada. Local bands have been further divided into those who live on and off reserve, and those who may or may not have band membership. The divisions within Indigenous communities now find form in the political representation of Indigenous peoples as well. The federal, provincial, and even local band governments attach different legal, social, economic, political, and cultural rights to the various classes and sub-classes of Indigenous peoples.

In the meantime, non-status Indians — women in particular — have taken the lead in asserting their rights for the benefit of status and non-status Indians alike. Jeanette Vivian Corbiere Lavell was one of the first non-status Indian women to challenge legislated divisions in the pre-*Charter* era.[1] Although she was ultimately unsuccessful at the Supreme Court of Canada, she helped lead the way for other non-status Indian women to take the issue further. Sandra Lovelace went straight to the international forum to have her grievance heard, successfully challenging the provisions of the previous *Indian Act*, which led to the Bill C-31 amendments.[2] Section 12(1)(b) of the *Indian Act, 1951* used to result in loss of status for Indian women who married non-Indian men and their descendants.[3] While marrying out no longer results in the loss of status to Indian women, it does have more severe consequences for the descendants of Indian women who married out than it does for the descendants of Indian men who married out.

Reinstated women and their descendants do not have the same type or quality of status as do Indian men who married out, i.e., "double mother clause" Indian men.[4] The double mother clause was supposed to take status away from Indian men whose mother and paternal grandmother were Indians by marrying in, but the vast majority of those who should have lost status did not. This ongoing discrimination has led to numerous legal challenges by non-status Indigenous women. Sharon McIvor, who was a non-status Indian for much of her life, commenced a discrimination case against Canada over twenty years ago.[5] Other non-status Indian women have also brought their claims before the courts, including Lynn Gehl, Connie Perron, and Brenda Sanderson.[6] Claims from non-status Indians have also been brought in other forums, such as the Canadian Human Rights Commission (CHRC).

While some of the politics have changed and support for non-status Indian women has increased since Bill C-31 in the early 1980s, many First Nations and other Aboriginal groups still have a long way to go in showing support for these women — and, ultimately, their own future generations. The 2003 Annual Report of the Assembly of Manitoba Chiefs highlights the ongoing discrimination, stating that "more and more of our women are unable to pass on their status to their children. It is feared that within generations to come there will be no 'Status Indians' in Canada."[7]

Despite the fact that this residual discrimination has been publicly recognized by Canada in various forums, and that Aboriginal organizations have consistently called for the elimination of gender discrimination in the *Indian Act*, the *Act* has not been amended since 1985. As a result of the *McIvor* case, Canada had no choice but to amend the registration provisions via Bill C-3; however, it did so without consulting with First Nations and affected Indigenous peoples. An encouraging sign is the number of First Nations and First Nation organizations that gave evidence before the Standing Committee on Aboriginal Affairs and Northern Development (AAON) in support not only of Sharon McIvor, but of expanding the amendments to remedy gender discrimination in full.[8]

Indian Act Inequality

First Nations individuals, bands, and organizations as well as others had identified gender discrimination in the registration provisions of the *Indian Act, 1951* even before Sandra Lovelace won her international human rights case. While the International Human Rights Committee did not deal with gender discrimination in *Lovelace*, it did find Canada to be in violation of article 27 of the *International Covenant on Civil and Political Rights*, as section 12(1)(b) of the *Indian Act, 1951* prevented Sandra Lovelace from enjoying her culture with other members of her community.[9] Section 12(1)(b) was the section that caused the loss of status to Indian women who married non-Indians.[10] The *Lovelace* case, coupled with the enactment of the *Charter,* meant that, practically speaking, Canada had no choice but to amend the *Indian Act.*[11] The Government of Canada had several objectives in mind when it proposed Bill C-31 in the early 1980s: (1) the removal of sex discrimination from the *Indian Act*; (2) the restoration of Indian status and band membership to those who had lost it due to the former *Act*'s discriminatory provisions; (3) the removal of any provisions that conferred or removed status by marriage; (4) the preservation of acquired rights; and (5) to give bands the option to determine their own membership.[12] Canada had recognized the gender discrimination experienced by Indian women under the *Indian Act* as an "historic wrong."[13] Although the removal of sexual discrimination from the *Indian Act* was one of Canada's main objectives in advancing Bill C-31, the *McIvor* case illustrates that it was unsuccessful. Indeed, gender discrimination is only one of several types of discrimination currently found in the *Indian Act*'s registration and band membership provisions.

Residual Discrimination

While there are no doubt many more claims of discrimination under the *Indian Act* that could be addressed, several of the major claims include: (1) cousins discrimination, (2) the second generation cut-off rule, (3) unstated paternity, (4) siblings discrimination, and potentially (5) Métis scrip. These claims are complex, as they reflect the unequal outcomes of various registration provisions of the *Indian Acts* over time. As different entitlement or registration sections were amended, past inequities were not always resolved; this served either to compound the inequities or perpetuate them in future generations. The situation is made even more complex by the fact that, after 1985, status and band membership no longer went hand in hand. Today there are a wide variety of band membership codes as well as many bands whose membership is still controlled by Canada. This makes remedying these inequalities difficult, to say the least, but the courts have indicated that Canada cannot let difficulty stand in the way of remedying obvious discrimination and inequality.[14] In addition to our *Charter* requiring that we take positive steps to remedy such inequalities, Canada's constitutional promise to Indigenous peoples to protect their identity and cultures for future generations mandates immediate action.

What follows is a brief review of some of the discrimination claims and how these forms of discrimination in the *Indian Act, 1985* contribute to the high number of non-status Indians in Canada, and, subsequently, to their exclusion from the majority of bands in Canada. The first type of discrimination claim is referred to as cousins discrimination because it refers to the inequity of Indian status between cousins within the same family, based on whether they are descendants of reinstated Indian women or Indian men. Manitoba's *Aboriginal Justice Inquiry* was a formal report which recognized this gender discrimination experienced by Indian women and their descendants under the *Indian Act*.[15] The inquiry was in response to the murder of Helen Betty Osborne, which resulted in a conviction of only one of the men present at her murder, and the death of J. J. Harper, former executive director of the Island Lake Tribal Council, after an encounter with Winnipeg police. While the inquiry looked at justice issues for Aboriginal peoples generally, it specifically addressed the historical roots of some of the inequities. The report explained that it was not just the justice system that has failed Aboriginal peoples, but

> justice also has been denied to them. For more than a century the rights of Aboriginal people have been ignored and eroded. The result of this denial has been injustice of the most profound kind. Poverty and powerlessness have been the Canadian legacy to a people who once governed their own affairs in full self-sufficiency.[16]

With regard to discrimination against Indian women under the *Indian Act*, the inquiry found "an extremely convoluted registration scheme in which the discrimination is not readily apparent on the surface. It requires an examination of how the Act treats people to detect the fundamental unfairness."[17]

While Canada argues that the current *Indian Act* treats everyone equally on a go-forward basis, the present determination of entitlement to status is based on previous versions of the *Indian Act* which were discriminatory and therefore bring these provisions into the current *Act*. For new applicants, the discrimination found in the *Indian Act, 1951*, is as applicable today as it was in 1951. The *Aboriginal Justice Inquiry* explained how cousins discrimination occurs:

> Joan and John, a brother and sister, were both registered Indians. Joan married a Métis man before 1985 so she lost her Indian status under section 12(1)(b) of the former Act. John married a white woman before 1985 and she automatically became a status Indian. Both John and Joan have had children over the years. Joan is now eligible to regain her status under section 6(1)(c) and her children will qualify under section 6(2). They are treated as having only one eligible parent, their mother, although both parents are Aboriginal. John's children gained status at birth as both parents were Indians legally, even though only one was an Aboriginal person.
>
> Joan's children can pass on status to their offspring only if they also marry registered Indians. If they marry unregistered Aboriginal people or non-Aboriginal people, then no status will pass to their children. All John's grandchildren will be status Indians, regardless of who his children marry.

Thus, entitlement to registration for the second generation has nothing to do with racial or cultural characteristics. The Act has eliminated the discrimination faced by those who lost status, but has passed it on to the next generation. Similar results flow from distinctions regarding how illegitimate children are treated under the amendments.[18]

The *Aboriginal Justice Inquiry* considered this form of discrimination to be "improper and probably illegal forms of sexual discrimination," and recommended that it be eliminated.[19]

Another discrimination claim is known as the second generation cut-off rule. It was created with the 1985 amendments and means that after two generations of marrying out, the descendants are not entitled to be registered as Indians.[20] With Bill C-31, individuals came to be known as section 6(1) or 6(2) Indians — i.e., full or half Indians. Section 6(1) Indians can transmit their status to their descendants regardless of the status of the other parent, whereas section 6(2) Indians must parent with another status Indian in order to transmit their status to their descendants.[21] The descendants of Indian women who married out are disproportionately represented in both the section 6(2) and non-status Indian categories. This is caused, in part, by the fact that the second generation cut-off rule is applied a generation earlier to the descendants of Indian women who married out than those of Indian men who married out.[22] Some have questioned whether there is any practical difference between 6(1) and 6(2) Indians, seeing they are both registered. Furi and Wherrett provide an answer: "People registered under section 6(2) have fewer rights than those registered under section 6(1), because they cannot pass on status to their child unless the child's other parent is also a registered Indian."[23] Indian women are the primary caretakers of children, so a lack of status for the woman or her children results in lack of access to critical social programs and services to which Indian men and their descendants have ready access.

The second generation cut-off rule is also responsible for the continued decline in the registration of 6(1) Indians. Pam Paul (now Paul-Montour) sounded a warning about this issue years ago. In her report for the Atlantic Policy Congress of First Nation Chiefs (APCFNC), she highlighted the social effects of the second generation cut-off rule on status and band membership in First Nation communities.[24] The second generation cut-off rule will mean fewer and fewer Indians are registered over time, leading to the eventual legislative extinction of Indians and their communities. This type of discrimination is described by the *Aboriginal Justice Inquiry* as a "de facto 'one-quarter blood' rule."[25] Some refer to the status provisions as akin to imposing a blood quantum requirement on applicants that measure their degree of descent from a section 6(1) status Indian (i.e., full blood).[26] Section 6(2) Indians are therefore analogous to half-bloods, and a blood quantum or degree of descent of one quarter or less results in non-status.

These discriminatory status provisions do not just violate equality rights; they also offend traditional laws and customs related to identity and belonging. According to Fiske and George, "The patrilineal provisions and the privileging of individuals with two registered parents stand in direct contradiction to the matrilineal principles of identity and membership."[27]

Even section 6(1) Indian women can be negatively affected by the second generation cut-off rule, regardless of the fact that the father of their children may also be status Indians. It occurs when the woman cannot or will not provide the name of the father of her children to the Registrar at Indian and Northern Affairs Canada (INAC), and is known as unknown, unstated, or unacknowledged paternity. Unstated paternity discrimination is not obvious from the registration provisions of the *Indian Act*, but is affected more by how the Registrar at INAC chooses to process applications for registration. The issue is described by the Native Women's' Association of Canada (NWAC):

> In order for a child to be registered as a Status Indian, the birth certificate must be signed by the mother and the father; that is, the eligibility of both parents to Indian Status must be demonstrated by providing their names. If the mother does not provide the name of the father for the birth certificate, then the assumption made by the government is that the father is not entitled to be registered. This obviously has a great impact on the potential eligibility for registration of the child, because the child will not have Indian Status if the child's mother is registered under 6 (2). Non-reporting of paternity or non-acknowledgement of paternity by Indian and Northern Affairs Canada (INAC) of a registered Indian father will result in the loss of benefits and entitlements to either the child or the child's subsequent children.[28]

The reasons an Indian woman might choose not to disclose the identity of the father of her children often relate to the safety of herself and her children, but the issue is far more complex than simply one of disclosure:

> Issues associated with a lack of privacy in small communities may provide another reason for a woman to prefer not to state the paternity of the child. Other mothers may wish to avoid custody or access claims on the part of the father: leaving the paternity unstated forms a partial protection against such actions by a biological father who may be unstable, abusive or engaged in unhealthy behaviours. Finally, many Aboriginal people argue that decisions related to the registration of the child for Indian Status properly belong to the mother and should not be influenced or driven by external legislative processes.[29]

On the other hand, there are Indian women who do name the father, but, owing to the Registrar's administrative requirements, the child is still not registered. As Mann explains, "Unacknowledged paternity can be said to arise where the mother names the father but not in accordance with the requirements of provincial vital statistics or INAC policy, thereby causing paternity to be considered unstated."[30] It is estimated that approximately 50 per cent of unstated paternity cases result from such administrative issues.[31] It appears, then, that the Registrar's default position is to reject applications for status.

Unstated paternity discrimination results in Indian women being unable to register their children with the same status they themselves have, or not at all in some cases. Once again, this negatively affects the number of Aboriginal people who can be registered as Indians, and often who can be considered band members. This means that hundreds of children descended from Indian mothers will either become lesser status Indians under section 6(2), or will go unregistered and join the ever-increasing group of non-status Indians. These numbers are high; as many as 37,300 children born to section 6(1) registered mothers between 1985 and 1999 were recorded as having unstated fathers.[32] It is also estimated that as many as 13,000 babies with unstated fathers were born to section 6(2) mothers.[33] The burden in differential treatment is born largely on the shoulders of Indian women, who comprise the larger number of single parent households. Mann explains:

> Indian women are more adversely affected by non-registration and non-membership than men because they are usually the primary caregivers of children. Without proper registration status and membership for themselves and/or their children, they cannot access schools, post-secondary education, other benefits for the children, adequate housing to accommodate the family, nor can they inherit band property.[34]

The requirements as to who can be registered as an Indian are specifically delineated in section 6 of the *Indian Act, 1985*: the "evidentiary and administrative requirements for proof of paternity are established entirely as a matter of INAC policy."[35] Thus, not only must non-status and status Indian women fight discriminatory laws, they must also combat INAC's application policies which disproportionately affect them and their descendants.

Siblings discrimination is similar to cousins discrimination in that it involves unequal treatment between Indian men and women and their descendants as well as between those who are unmarried and those who are married. As Furi and Wherrett explain,

> Children of unmarried non-Indian women and Indian men are also treated differently according to gender. Male lineage criteria in the legislation prior

to 1985 permitted the registration of all such male children born before 1985. After the passage of Bill C-31, however, female children born to Indian men and non-Indian women between 4 September 1951 and 17 April 1985 became eligible for registration only as the children of one Indian parent.

The application of the amendments has also led to a situation in which members of the same family may be registered in different categories. One example could occur in a family that enfranchised, and in which the mother is a non-Indian. Under Bill C-31, a child born prior to the family's enfranchisement is eligible for registration under section 6(1), while a child born after enfranchisement is eligible only under section 6(2), since one parent is not an Indian. This affects the ability to pass on status, because the latter child will be able to pass on status to his or her children only if their other parent is a status Indian.[36]

Not only are the descendants of males and females treated differently, but the status assigned to a brother and sister is different. For both sexes, the fact of their unmarried status is also affecting their children's entitlement to registration; it is different from those who were married. This differential treatment in registration status filters into one's entitlement to band membership as well. The Native Women's Association of Canada explained how the law may have changed but it has left behind the same discriminatory effects:

> In 1983, the Supreme Court of Canada ruled in the case of *MARTIN* vs. *CHAPMAN,* that the "illegitimate" *male* child of a status male parent and a non-status female parent would have status and membership, under old section 11(1)(c). However, the "illegitimate" *female* child was not entitled to be registered.
>
> This sub-section has been repealed under Bill C-31, but its legal effects still persist. The separation of status and band membership in the new Act means that the female child is still treated differently.
>
> If a male child had status under old section 11, he will be registered under new section 6(1) and therefore has an automatic entitlement to band membership. His sister, however, will now gain status, but under new section 6(2). She will therefore have only a "conditional" entitlement to band membership.[37]

Although discrimination involving gender, marital status, and blood quantum are the major forms of both residual and new discrimination in the *Indian Act,* other issues can be equally exclusionary. The claim involving Métis scrip takers, for example, is based not on sex, *per se,* but on the legal determination of individual identities as Métis versus Indian, based on the financial choices made by their ancestors. Unlike Indian women who had their status taken from them, descendants of scrip takers have not been reinstated:

> Persons who received or were allotted "half-breed lands or money script," were excluded from status under old section 12(1)(a), as were their descendants. While C-31 has repealed this section, it did not specifically reinstate these persons. To gain status, they must qualify under one of the categories of new section 6.[38]

Canada uses that choice — the one that Indigenous peoples made between treaty monies or scrip monies — as a legal determination of their descendants' identities as either Métis or Indian. There is little justification for such a decision, which was taken without consultation with the affected individuals. Some people who had taken scrip never identified as Métis, and they and their families continued to live as treaty Indians, often on reserve. Many Indian women who married Métis persons, non-status Indians, or non-Aboriginal persons would not have known that they would, at some time in the future, be deemed to have lost their status as Indians, thereby preventing their descendants from registering. Assuming that an Indian woman knew she would lose her status or entitlements if she married a non-Indian, she may have felt that the apparent choice between treaty monies and scrip monies was not really a choice at all, as she was losing her status and had no choice but to take the Métis scrip monies.

If this were the case and a Cree woman took scrip monies as a result, does this make her and her descendants all Métis, even if she and her family still identified with and lived as Cree Indians? Further, does this mean that her descendants must be forever labelled Métis and excluded from registration under the *Indian Act*, regardless of their actual cultural identities, simply because one of their parents chose the only available pot of money to support their families? I doubt that Canada held information sessions to inform individual Indian women about the legal implications of taking scrip money over treaty money in relation to their and their descendants' identities.

The situation works in reverse as well, as Teillet explains:

> Historically, Métis individuals could choose to take treaty and under the 1886 *Indian Act* they would have been considered "non-treaty Indians" which the Act defined as a person of Indian blood who either belonged to an irregular band or followed the Indian mode of life, even if only temporarily resident in Canada. If a Métis individual chose to take scrip he or she was not considered legally to be an Indian. If a Métis individual chose to take treaty, he or she would be entered on the band pay list and, on the creation of the *Indian Act* Registry after

1951, all such individuals were henceforth considered in law to be "status Indians."[39]

The claims of discrimination by these scrip takers are based on the fact that some of them were always, and continue to be, members of their communities and citizens in their larger Indigenous nations, but have been refused legal identity as Indians and are denied the same benefits, rights, and responsibilities as their family and community members. As early as 1988, the Standing Committee on Aboriginal Affairs and Northern Development's *C-31 Fifth Report* also noted the discrimination claims of Métis scrip takers.[40] The issue has still not been addressed.

Other Inequities

Although there are formal claims of discrimination advancing through the courts, the discrimination experienced by Indigenous women and their descendants continues in other, less obvious ways. Many Indigenous women who lost status under the previous *Indian Act* and regained it through Bill C-31 are considered outsiders because they are reinstatees, and are sometimes negatively referred to as "Bill C-31ers."[41] One of the concerns raised by some First Nations during the Bill C-31 consultations was that they feared that allowing these women and their descendants back into the communities would somehow threaten their cultures: "The legislation resulted in a significant increase in the number of people entitled to Indian status in Canada. There were widespread concerns that the influx might overwhelm resources available to bands, and that it might serve to dilute the cultural integrity of existing First Nations groups."[42] Yet most of these Indian women grew up in their communities, and were only excluded later in life because of discriminatory legislation. Marrying a non-registered man did not change who these Indigenous women were as people; it did not alter their culture, or their common history with their communities.

There are many more ways in which Indigenous peoples and communities have been denied legal recognition. As Magnet explains,

> In some cases, Aboriginal peoples or their communities were simply left off band lists, when the band lists were created or substantially revised in the 1940's (band lists largely determine Indian status). In other cases, people lost their Indian status when government "enfranchised" them by force under a policy intended to assimilate Canada's Aboriginal people.[43]

Through no fault of their own, many Indigenous peoples have been excluded from their communities. Unlike Bill C-31 reinstatees, many of them never had their names entered on band lists. Alternatively, they may have once had their names on a band list, but since these lists have been updated, revised, and purged so many times over the years, the result is that hundreds of names were left off the band lists in an effort to reduce the number of status Indians.[44] There is currently no process to review these claims and adjust the status Indian register, nor are there any programs to assist bands in correcting their membership lists.

Charter Equality

The issue of gender equality in Indian registration has often been portrayed as a struggle between First Nations and Indigenous women, or status Indians versus non-status Indians. Yet the preservation of Indigenous identity and cultures has both individual and communal aspects, and certainly should not exclude women and children, regardless of who they married, where they live, how much Indian blood they have, or whether they were born out of wedlock. The assertion that Indigenous nations have a section 35 right to determine their own citizenship is limited by the corresponding right of Indigenous peoples to belong to their communities and partake in the benefits and responsibilities of their cultures. It is also limited by the section 35(4) constitutional right of Indigenous women to enjoy those rights equally with Indigenous men, as well as the section 15 *Charter* equality right. In the section that follows, I review the *Indian Act*, the *Charter*, relevant and analogous case law, academic literature, and government material in support of my argument that the second generation cut-off rule in the *Indian Act* is racial discrimination based on blood quantum/descent and violates the *Charter*'s section 15 equality rights for non-status Indians. This rule is arbitrary and does not relate to the actual cultures and identities of Indigenous peoples. Canada asserts that it has the jurisdiction to determine Indian status, and therefore the power to determine the criteria for registration. Even if Canada's constitutional jurisdiction did extend that far, its powers are not unlimited. Canada's powers are as limited by the *Charter* and *Constitution Act, 1982* as are those of Indigenous governments.

Canada's primary motivation behind amending the registration provisions of the *Indian Acts* over the years was to reduce the number of people for which it was legally and financially responsible. One of the interveners in the *McIvor* appeal, the Abenaki, exposed certain Cabinet documents which acknowledged that the real issue around the second generation cut-off rule was "how some form of reinstatement could be implemented at a reduced cost," and, further, that the ultimate decision rested with Cabinet (not Parliament), whose "final policy decision on reinstatement will be shaped by financial more than any other considerations."[45] While Canada has publicly distanced itself from the assimilatory policies of the past, the fact remains that it has not amended the discriminatory registration provisions in the *Indian Act* whose design was based on those racist policies and views.

It is unbelievable that Canada continues to hold jurisdiction over registration, and that it continues to defend assimilatory registration and band membership provisions. The second generation cut-off rule in particular is incompatible with modern-day concepts of Indigenous identity and citizenship. Criteria based on blood quantum or degree of descent freeze Indian identity in the past when concepts of an "Indian mode of life" included looking like an Indian, wearing moccasins, living on a reserve, or living in a tent.[46] Legislation based on racist ideologies should no longer be a part of our relationship with Indigenous peoples. Canada has to move from apology to action. Addressing the various forms of discrimination contained in the registration provisions of the *Indian Act, 1985* is a necessary interim measure to ensure equality in longer-term solutions.

The Legal Test for Discrimination

I have argued that Indigenous nations have the right to determine their own citizenship. It is possible that this right may also translate into the right of local bands to determine their own membership. As with all rights, this one is tempered by the right of individual Indigenous people to belong to their communities and have equal access to their cultures, which includes the rights, benefits, and responsibilities that go along with that. In this section, I will assess a hypothetical claim of racial discrimination based on what I call blood quantum/descent, but it is first necessary to review the law which has been evolving from section 15 of the *Charter*, which states:

> (1) Every individual is equal before and under the law and has the right to the equal protection and equal benefit of the law without discrimination and, in particular, without discrimination based on race, national or ethnic origin, colour, religion, sex, age or mental or physical disability.

> (2) Subsection (1) does not preclude any law, program or activity that has as its object the amelioration of conditions of disadvantaged individuals or groups including those that are disadvantaged because of race, national or ethnic origin, colour, religion, sex, age or mental or physical disability.[47]

For some time, the legal test outlined in the *Andrews* case was considered the definitive test for assessing section 15 equality claims.[48] The subsequent clarifications that were made to this test in *Law* seemed to have created more confusion than clarity.[49] However, the Supreme Court of Canada in *Kapp* clarified that the legal test for section 15 equality is essentially the test as was originally provided in *Andrews*.[50] Without rejecting *Law* outright, the court did distance itself somewhat from the human dignity aspect of the test.[51] More recently, in *Ermineskin*, the court specifically relied on the equality test as set out in *Andrews* "as restated in *Kapp*" to determine whether discrimination had occurred.[52] Therefore, the test as provided in *Andrews*, restated in *Kapp,* and further clarified in *Ermineskin* will guide my analysis of racial discrimination in the *Indian Act, 1985* based on blood quantum.

The issue in *Andrews* was that the BC *Barristers and Solicitors Act* differentiated between citizens of Canada and non-citizens with regard to admission to the practice of law in the province of British Columbia.[53] Some of the key principles to come out of *Andrews* were:

- equality is a comparative concept;[54]
- the purpose of section 15 was not to eliminate all distinctions from society or religion, and Aboriginal rights would not be included in the *Charter*;[55]
- principles that are regularly applied under human rights legislation are equally applicable to *Charter* discrimination analysis;[56]
- grounds enumerated in section 15 were not intended to be exhaustive, and future cases may expand this list;[57]
- public policy is the jurisdiction of legislatures, and courts are to ensure that public policy is *Charter* compliant;[58]

Based on these principles, the Court in *Andrews* provided a definition of discrimination as:

a distinction, whether intentional or not but based on grounds relating to personal characteristics of the individual or group not imposed upon others, or withholds or limits access to opportunities, benefits, and advantages available to other members of society. Distinctions based on personal characteristics attributed to an individual solely on the basis of association with a group will rarely escape the charge of discrimination, while those based on an individual's merits and capacities will rarely be so classed.[59]

That definition provided for the following test: (1) whether the law imposes a differential treatment between the claimant and others; (2) whether an enumerated or analogous ground was the basis for the differential treatment; and (3) whether the law has a discriminatory purpose or effect.[60]

In any discrimination claim, the initial burden lies with the claimant to demonstrate that an infringement has occurred. The burden of proof will then shift to the Crown to justify the infringement. The court in *Andrews* cited *Oakes* as the test for justifying infringements, but added that the object of the assessment was for the court to balance many factors and avoid rigid or inflexible standards of assessment.[61] The standard of proof for this test is the civil standard — i.e., proof on a balance of probabilities.[62] Thus, the first question in the justification stage is whether the limitation is a legitimate exercise of legislative power to achieve desirable social objectives — i.e., whether it is based on a "pressing and substantial" objective.[63] The second stage involves a proportionality test where the court looks at the nature of the right, the extent of the infringement, the relation between the limit and the legislation's objective, the importance of the right to the individual or group, and the broader social impact of the law and its alternatives.[64] This part of the test requires that (1) the limitation must be rationally connected to the objective; (2) the limitation must impair the right as minimally as possible; and (3) the effects of the limitation must not encroach on individual or group rights so severely that the legislative objective is outweighed by the "abridgement of rights."[65] The more "deleterious" the effects of the legislation, the more important the legislative objective will have to be in order to survive this part of the test.[66] However, given that section 15 was designed to protect groups who suffer from "social, political and legal disadvantage," the government's burden of justifying discrimination is an onerous one.[67]

The subsequent *Law* case commented that, since the decision in *Andrews* had been delivered, there had been some differences of opinion among the members of the Supreme Court of Canada as to the interpretation of section 15, and therefore revised the test.[68] However, the subsequent *Kapp* decision from the Supreme Court clearly indicated that the original *Andrews* decision contained the "template" regarding substantive equality:[69]

> The central purpose of combating discrimination, as discussed, underlies both section 15(1) and section 15(2). Under section 15(1), the focus is on preventing governments from making distinctions based on the enumerated or analogous grounds that: have the effect of perpetuating group disadvantage and prejudice; or impose disadvantage on the basis of stereotyping. Under section 15(2), the focus is on enabling governments to pro-actively combat existing discrimination through affirmative measures.[70]

The Court in *Kapp* further suggested that, "if the government can demonstrate that an impugned program meets the criteria of section 15(2), it may be unnecessary to conduct a section 15(1) analysis at all."[71] They went on to clarify that section 15(2) "supports a full expression of equality, rather than derogating from it."[72] Subsequent to *Kapp*, the Supreme Court in *Ermineskin* explained that the equality test for section 15 had already been laid out in *Andrews* and restated in *Kapp,* and this was the test to use for discrimination claims. My analysis of the second generation cut-off rule will follow the *Andrews* test.

I am a first generation non-status Indian whose parents are a non-Indian (my mother, Erma Creighton), and a section 6(2) status Indian (my father, Frank Palmater). My father was only a section 6(2) Indian because my grandmother (Margaret Jerome) was deemed to be a section 6(1)(c) Indian — i.e., a woman who was an Indian but lost her status upon marriage to a non-Indian (my grandfather, William Jerome), and who was subsequently reinstated after the Bill C-31 amendments to the *Indian Act*. My two children, Mitchell and Jeremy Palmater, would then be second generation non-status Indians. As in the *McIvor* case, had my Indian grandparent been a male, my father and I would have been section 6(1) Indians, making my children section 6(2) Indians. But for the racial discrimination in section 6 in the form of a one-quarter blood quantum rule, my children and I would also have Indian status. In other words, even if Canada were to fix all the sex discrimination in the *Act*, including that identified in *McIvor*, my children and I would still be negatively affected by the second generation cut-off rule, because a "gender-neutral" second generation cut-off rule is still racial discrimination on the basis of blood quantum.

In *Andrews*, the Supreme Court emphasized that equality under section 15 of the *Charter* is a comparative concept, and therefore requires a comparator group with which to conduct the equality assessment. For the purposes of this book, my claimant group represents first and second generation non-status Indians who would be registered as Indians but for the one-quarter blood quantum/descent rule. The Supreme Court of Canada in *Hodge* explained how to choose a comparator group:

> The appropriate comparator group is the one which mirrors the characteristics of the claimant (or claimant group) relevant to the benefit or advantage sought except that the statutory definition includes a personal characteristic that is offensive to the *Charter* or omits a personal characteristic in a way that is offensive to the *Charter*.[73]

In my case, as first and second generation non-status Indians, our most appropriate comparator group are section 6(1) status Indians, who are deemed to be full-blood Indians who have both status and the ability to transmit that status to their children in their own right, without having to parent with another registered Indian. While there will be exceptions, both the comparator group and my group identify as Indigenous, as citizens of our respective Indigenous nations, have common familial connections with our home communities, common histories, laws, traditions, treaties, and territories. In fact, many members of both groups belong to the same families.

Regarding the first step of the section 15(1) analysis, one must first determine whether section 6 of the *Indian Act, 1985* imposes a differential treatment between my claimant group and the comparator group. As between status and non-status Indians, the tangible and intangible benefits allocated to the two groups are strikingly different. Those benefits may vary, depending on the members of each group or the Indigenous nations and local communities with which they are associated, but they are, generally speaking, the same for status Indians. The trial judge in *McIvor* noted the following as some of the tangible benefits tied to status: for the majority of bands, status equates with band membership; entitlement to live on reserve; access to federal programs and services targeted for status Indians; expenditures of Indian monies; use and benefit of reserve lands, such as in specific allotments and the ability to inherit and bequeath lands in a reserve; exemption from taxation for lands and property on the reserve; and specific entitlements to uninsured health benefits and post-secondary education funding.[74]

The court also highlighted some of the intangible benefits attached to status: being accepted by one's Aboriginal community as a "real" Indian; the ability to participate in traditional ceremonies and gatherings; the ability to participate in traditional hunting, fishing, and harvesting practices; a sense of cultural identity and self-worth; and access to and participation in community in order to learn traditional languages and heritage.[75]

As the court in *Corbiere* explained, "The first step is to determine whether the impugned law makes a distinction that denies equal benefit or imposes an unequal burden. The *Indian Act*'s exclusion of off-reserve band members from voting privileges on band governance satisfies this requirement."[76] If voting privileges were enough to satisfy the first part of the section 15(1) analysis in *Corbiere*, then surely the long list of tangible and intangible benefits which are denied to non-status Indians would more than satisfy that requirement. Clearly, there is a distinction in entitlements based on whether one has status or not. The inequality caused by the status distinctions in the *Indian Act* has long been recognized by researchers and academics, as well as human rights and Aboriginal organizations.[77] Canada's own expert witness, Clatworthy, explains that the current set of *Indian Act* rules relating to status and band membership provisions entrenches inequality by creating distinctions between citizens.[78] The RCAP was also highly critical of the distinction made between status and non-status Indians, and the arbitrary means in which they are divided.

Though the *Lovelace* case was problematic in other areas, Justice Iacobucci of the Supreme Court of Canada found the submissions of the non-status Indian claimants relating to their unique set of disadvantages caused by the arbitrary distinctions between status and non-status Indians to be "clearly supported in the findings of the Royal Commission on Aboriginal Peoples" which he cited with approval.[79]

The next step in the section 15(1) analysis is to determine whether an enumerated or analogous ground is the basis of differential treatment. The ground of discrimination that I am using could be categorized in two different ways: (1) racial discrimination or (2) a new analogous ground of blood quantum/descent — which could be an "embedded" type of claim under the main ground of race.[80] The Supreme Court in *Corbiere* provided a useful guide for determining how to establish an analogous ground:

> What then are the criteria by which we identify a ground of distinction as analogous? The obvious answer is that we look for grounds of distinction that are analogous or like the grounds enumerated in s. 15 — race, national or ethnic origin, colour, religion, sex, age, or mental or physical disability. It seems to us that what these grounds have in common is the fact that they often serve as the basis for stereotypical decisions made not on the basis of merit but on the basis of a personal characteristic that is immutable or changeable only at unacceptable cost to personal identity. This suggests that the thrust of identification of analogous grounds at the second stage of the Law analysis is to reveal grounds based on characteristics that we cannot change or that the government has no legitimate interest in expecting us to change to receive equal treatment under the law. To put it another way, s. 15 targets the denial of equal treatment on grounds that are actually immutable, like race, or constructively immutable, like religion. Other factors identified in the cases as associated with the enumerated and analogous grounds, like the fact that the decision adversely impacts on a discrete and insular minority or a group that has been historically discriminated against, may be seen to flow from the central concept of immutable or constructively immutable personal characteristics, which too often have served as illegitimate and demeaning proxies for merit-based decision making.[81]

Despite these guidelines, the Supreme Court has yet to wrap its mind around the underlying racist concepts influencing the determination of Aboriginality. Therefore, the proposal of this new analogous ground is not based on legal precedent, *per se*. While some might argue that such a ground might not be universally applicable to others in society and should therefore not be recognized as an analogous ground, the court has clarified that what might not be a ground for one group in society may still be found to be a ground for Aboriginal peoples:

> First, reserve status should not be confused with residence. The ordinary "residence" decisions faced by the average Canadians should not be confused with the profound decisions Aboriginal band members make to live on or off their reserves, assuming choice is possible. The reality of their

situation is unique and complex. Thus no new water is charted, in the sense of finding residence, in the generalized abstract, to be an analogous ground. Second, we note that the analogous ground of off-reserve status or Aboriginality-residence is limited to a subset of the Canadian population, while s. 15 is directed to everyone. In our view, this is no impediment to its inclusion as an analogous ground under s. 15. Its demographic limitation is no different, for example, from pregnancy, which is a distinct, but fundamentally interrelated form of discrimination from gender. "Embedded" analogous grounds may be necessary to permit meaningful consideration of intra-group discrimination.[82]

I therefore argue that the use of one-quarter blood quantum or degree of descent from a status Indian as a means of excluding Indigenous peoples from registration as Indians is either racial discrimination or an analogous ground of blood quantum/descent because it perpetuates racist stereotypes about Indigenous people based on a physical characteristic over which the affected individual has no control. Further, the government has no business in determining what is an appropriate biological connection to equate with an Indigenous identity through status.

Certainly, if the registration criteria related to other biological measurements such as skin colour or cheek bone dimensions, then section 6 would have been repealed long ago. Or would it? Even today, in sophisticated organizations like the RCMP, an Indigenous person's access to a job posting or promotion could be limited if they do not have "distinctly native features."[83] Blood quantum is no less objectionable a criterion, and no racist criteria should be acceptable for any law, program, or service. There is no blood quantum measurement for Caucasian citizens, nor would I expect the government of Canada to have any role in setting blood quantum levels to determine "whiteness." MacIntosh exposes this ongoing practice in our common law and judicial reason and asks that we finally "liberate our jurisprudence — and Aboriginal peoples — from the harms of social evolutionary thinking."[84] By not addressing discrimination directly in all aspects of our common law and policy, we risk the continued promotion of assimilation to the ongoing detriment of Indigenous peoples.

The fact that blood quantum or descent may only affect a sub-set of Indigenous peoples would not act as an impediment to its recognition as an analogous ground should race alone not capture the nature of the discrimination sufficiently. A future finding that the analogous ground of Indian blood quantum is a species of the enumerated ground of race would not lessen its recognition as an analogous ground. So then, what of the ground of blood quantum as an analogous ground? We know that past *Indian Act* identification or entitlement provisions were based on descent from male blood lines. While the word "blood" was later removed from the *Indian Act,* genealogical descent that preferred the male blood line continued to be the basis of both the registration of Indians and their ability to transmit status to their children. Despite the fact that the word "blood" no longer appears in the *Act* as criteria for identifying Indians, government documents continued to describe the second generation cut-off rule as being a one-quarter blood descent formula.[85] With Bill C-31, Cabinet specifically decided not to extend status to those with "one-quarter blood."[86] This has been referred to as "bleeding off" individuals from their communities, and disproportionately affects Indian women and their children.[87] If we are ever to convince the courts to address this fundamental problem in federal policy, and within their own jurisprudential logic and reasoning, we must call it what it is: the current second generation cut-off rule in section 6(2) of the *Indian Act,1985* is a measurement of blood quantum or degree of descent. The fact that Canada has chosen to use terms such as "genealogical proximity," "degree of Indian parentage," "genealogical connection," or "genealogical standard" does not alter the fact that it is an exercise in racism and forced assimilation.[88] Canada has created, justified, and vigorously defended an identification system for Indigenous peoples based solely on blood quantum, which is clearly an act of racism. It is requiring that all status Indians be "real" Indians as viewed from Eurocentric ideologies around blood purity and race. Aside from being legally unjustifiable, it is morally repugnant.

Having identified the ground of discrimination upon which a section 15(1) analysis would proceed, the next step is to determine whether section 6(2) of the *Indian Act, 1985* has a discriminatory purpose or effect. The preceding has detailed the discriminatory effects, but what of the purpose of section 6(2)? Canada suggested that its purpose in enacting the second generation cut-off rule in section 6(2) of the *Indian Act, 1985* was "[t]o ensure that those registered are sufficiently connected to the historical population that the federal government treated with or for whom reserves were set aside" through descent provisions it refers to as "second generation cut-off."[89] Canada argued that this was one of the objectives of Bill C-31, but neither the trial nor appeal courts in *McIvor* accepted that as one of the actual purposes of the bill.[90] It was a recent add-on by Canada in an effort to limit the potential numbers of Indians that would be registered in the event that McIvor was successful in court.

The Government of Canada claims that Canada's special relationship with Indigenous peoples today must be linked to the historical groups of Indigenous peoples, and has determined that this link cannot carry on past a fictional allocation of one-quarter blood quantum or degree of descent. Cases like *Sappier and Gray* have stated that Aboriginal practices should not be reduced to "anthropological curiosities" or "racialized aboriginal stereotypes," but the identities of Aboriginal peoples are still limited to stereotypical views about what makes an Aboriginal person Aboriginal.[91]

In *Corbiere,* the court found discrimination on the basis that section 77(1) of the *Act* treated off-reserve band members in a stereotypical way — i.e., that off-reserve band members have less interest in their community simply because of where they live:

> Taking all this into account, it is clear that the s. 77(1) disenfranchise-ment is discriminatory. It denies off-reserve band members the right to participate fully in band governance on the arbitrary basis of a personal characteristic. It reaches the cultural identity of off-reserve Aboriginals in a stereotypical way. It presumes that Aboriginals living off-reserve are not interested in maintaining meaningful participation in the band or in pre-serving their cultural identity, and are therefore less deserving members of the band. The effect is clear, as is the message: off-reserve band members are not as deserving as those band members who live on reserves. This engages the dignity aspect of the s. 15 analysis and results in the denial of substan-tive equality.[92]

This is no less true for non-status Indians, whom the second generation cut-off rule excludes on the basis of a personal characteristic — one-quarter blood quan-tum. It presumes that "real" Indigenous people are those with a deemed blood allotment of 50 per cent or more, and any with less blood quantum are somehow less Indigenous and therefore less capable of passing on their identity and culture to their children. This results in the denial of substantive equality for non-status Indians. As the majority of non-status Indians are forced to live off reserve, this makes them dually disadvantaged.

The Supreme Court in *Corbiere* explained that the denial of voting rights to off-reserve band members by virtue of section 77(1) of the *Indian Act* also served to perpetuate the historical disadvantage of off-reserve band members who have im-portant interests in band governance.[93] The fact of their residency off reserve was not enough to totally exclude them from the governance of their communities:

> They are co-owners of the band's assets. The reserve, whether they live on or off it, is their and their children's land. The band council represents them as band members to the community at large, in negotiations with the government, and within Aboriginal organizations. Although there are some matters of purely local interest, which do not as directly affect the interests of off-reserve band members, the complete denial to off-reserve members of the right to vote and participate in band governance treats them as less worthy and entitled, not on the merits of their situation, but simply be-cause they live off-reserve.[94]

Non-status Indians are equally concerned about governance activities in their communities, as they affect their parents, grandparents, and extended families, as well as future generations. The *RCAP Report* also noted that Aboriginal people who live off reserve still want to maintain their identities:

> Throughout the Commission's hearings, Aboriginal people stressed the fundamental importance of retaining and enhancing their cultural identity while living in urban areas. Aboriginal identity lies at the heart of Aboriginal peoples' existence; maintaining that identity is an essential and self-validating pursuit for Aboriginal peoples in cities.[95]

This identity is tied in part to the individual's connection to their traditional territories, which is a large part of their identities:

> Cultural identity for urban Aboriginal people is also tied to a land base or ancestral territory. For many, the two concepts are inseparable. . . . Identification with an ancestral place is important to urban people because of the associated ritual, ceremony and traditions, as well as the people who remain there, the sense of belonging, the bond to an ancestral community, and the accessibility of family, community and elders.[96]

Maintaining an Indigenous identity is no less an "essential and self-validating pursuit" for non-status Indians as it is for status off-reserve Indigenous peoples. In fact, it may be more of a concern for non-status Indians who must face additional hurdles to maintaining their identities.

Canada has created this situation, but it has not taken responsibility for it. It took a class action suit against Canada to arrive at a settlement and an apology for residential school survivors. With regard to the numerous inequities and harms that have resulted from the discriminatory registration scheme, Canada continues to defend it. Mann cited with approval the 1988 Standing Committee on Aboriginal Affairs and Northern Development's report on C-31, which noted the "new and continued inequities flowing from federal control of the definition of 'Indian' and the more limited but still continuing control of the federal government over band membership."[97] Cannon argues that Canada has taken no responsibility for the inequality between status and non-status Indians created by the *Indian Act*:

> The *Indian Act* requires that some Indians — notably the descendants of Indian women who lost (and later acquired) status — be concerned about the "race" of those that they marry. It has created inequality for these individuals, and it exonerates the state from taking responsibility for status Indians.[98]

The negative and hurtful stereotypes described above are all based on empirical realities. The trial court in *McIvor* addressed the issue directly:

> But even if there had been evidence that the new population was more cul-
> turally removed from the original Indian population, their cultural removal
> would be entirely the result of historic sex discrimination. In other words in
> advancing this new purpose, the government is attempting to rely upon an
> invidious effect of its previous discrimination. Consequently, even if there
> were any evidentiary basis for the claim, and there is none, the purpose is in
> fact a discriminatory purpose and therefore could not justify perpetuating
> discrimination under section 1.[99]

The court further explained: "None of the distinctions is designed to take into account actual differences in culture, ability, or merit."[100] Moreover, this type of discrimination on the basis of blood quantum is not justifiable under section 1 of the *Charter*.

Assuming that our claimant group would have been able to satisfy the burden of demonstrating an infringement of section 15(1), the burden would then shift to the Crown to justify the infringement under section 1 of the *Charter* as per the *Oakes* test. Section 1 of the *Charter* provides that "The *Canadian Charter of Rights and Freedoms* guarantees the rights and freedoms set out in it subject only to such reasonable limits prescribed by law as can be demonstrably justified in a free and democratic society." The first step of the justification test asks whether the limitation is a legitimate exercise of legislative power to achieve desirable social objectives. We now have the benefit of the *McIvor* decision to address the historical objectives of Bill C-31. Both the detailed submissions of the parties in *McIvor* and the decisions of the trial and appeal courts bring to light the relevant historical and legal background to the Bill C-31 amendment. The appeal court in *McIvor* listed Canada's legislative objectives for Bill C-31 as follows: (1) the removal of sex discrimination from the *Act*; (2) the restoration of status to those who had lost it as a result of the sex discrimination; (3) the removal of provisions which conferred or removed status by marriage; (4) the preservation of acquired rights; and (5) the ability for bands to assume jurisdiction over their membership codes.[101] Assuming that these are valid legislative objectives, there is no corresponding requirement that, in order to achieve those objectives, the federal government had also to include a one-quarter blood quantum rule. Canada, however, argued that there was an additional objective in *McIvor*: "retain registration as a means of continuing the federal government's relationship with individuals with sufficient genealogical proximity to the historical population with whom the Crown treated or for whom reserves were set aside."[102]

Neither the trial nor the appeal courts accepted "genealogical proximity" as a valid legislative objective of Bill C-31, and explained that a lack of historical connection was never raised by the Minister as one of the objectives of Bill C-31.[103] The requirement of genealogical proximity is therefore not a pressing and substantial objective.

As the courts in *McIvor* have already decided this point, I will only briefly touch on the justification stage of the section 15(1) analysis. As reviewed earlier, the proportionality test involves a complex examination of the nature of the right, the extent of infringement, legislative objectives, the importance of the right, and the social impact of the law and alternatives. This is done by asking questions such as whether the limitation is rationally connected to the objective, and impairs the right as minimally as possible; the limitation must not encroach on the right so severely as to outweigh the legislative objective. Quite often, these questions are considered together. It is also important to remember that the government's burden is an onerous one, because section 15 of the *Charter* was designed to protect those who are socially, politically, and legally disadvantaged. The Supreme Court in *Lovelace* found non-status Indians to be socially, politically, and legally disadvantaged. The court in *Corbiere* found that status Indian band members who are forced to live off reserve are also disadvantaged, and determined that Aboriginality-residence was an analogous ground of discrimination. Although such claims do not require groups of Aboriginal people to prove they are more disadvantaged than another — i.e., it is not a "race to the bottom" — it could be argued that non-status Indians are especially disadvantaged.[104] Non-status Indians lack both status and band membership, and most of them are forced to live off reserve. It should come as no surprise, then, that in such a dually disadvantaged group, the descendants of Indian women who married out are also disproportionally represented.[105]

In *Corbiere*, the Supreme Court determined that the restriction on voting was rationally connected to the aim of the legislation, which they determined to be giving "a voice in the affairs of the reserve only to persons most directly affected by the decisions of the band council."[106] However, the restriction on voting, which excluded off-reserve band members, did not pass the second part of the justification test, since it was not shown that section 77 (1) of the *Indian Act, 1985* impaired the section 15 equality rights of the claimants "minimally." Since no evidence, argument, or authority was provided in support of the claim that it would be too difficult and expensive to accommodate off-reserve band members, the court denied the use of administrative difficulty and cost as a justification to deny a constitutional right.[107] With regard to the second generation cut-off rule, there is no rational connection between section 6(2) and the five accepted legislative objectives. If Canada wanted to ensure that those who were registered had sufficient connections to historic Indigenous communities, it could have used any number of methods to accomplish this. It could have implemented a one-parent rule, or allowed First Nations to determine who status Indians and band members are, as they are best placed to do so. There was nothing in the elimination of sex discrimination and protecting vested rights that required imposing a one-quarter blood quantum rule that would not only exclude non-status Indians from their identities and cultures, but also jeopardize the very existence of the historic Indigenous communities. The discriminatory effects of the second generation cut-off rule are so out of proportion to the legislative objectives as to fail the justification test.

Remedying Inequality for Indigenous Peoples

Having demonstrated that the second generation cut-off rule is racial discrimination, the next step is to determine how to remedy the situation. While there may be a difference of views about this, there appears to be a general consensus that the status quo is unacceptable. The only entity that stands to gain from the disappearance of legally recognized Indians is the federal government:

> [T]he Department of Indian [sic] and Northern Development (DIAND) does not claim responsibility for non-status Indians. The *Indian Act* quite simply works to reduce the number of status Indians in Canada, the state's responsibility toward them, and ultimately, the reserve lands belonging to them.[108]

Substantial remedies are required to address the long-standing historical discrimination against non-status Indians. Their exclusion from registration has not only resulted in exclusion from community membership and a wide variety of benefits, but it also ensures that they lack the political power to access the various negotiation tables that affect their rights. Non-status Indians are "chronically ignored" by governments and denied access to community governance structures that would allow them to advocate on their own behalf and change their status in life.[109]

Remedies

There are many possibilities for remedying the current inequality faced by non-status Indians. Should a court find that section 6(2) of the *Indian Act, 1985* violates section 15 of the *Charter* and cannot be saved by section 1,[110] then the court has various options. These remedies were specifically addressed in *Schachter*:

> A court has flexibility in determining what course of action to take following a violation of the Charter which does not survive s. 1 scrutiny. Section

52 of the Constitution Act, 1982 mandates the striking down of any law that is inconsistent with the provisions of the Constitution, but only "to the extent of the inconsistency." Depending upon the circumstances, a court may simply strike down, it may strike down and temporarily suspend the declaration of invalidity, or it may resort to the techniques of reading down or reading in. In addition, s. 24 of the Charter extends to any court of competent jurisdiction the power to grant an "appropriate and just" remedy to "[a]nyone whose [Charter] rights and freedoms . . . have been infringed or denied." In choosing how to apply s. 52 or s. 24 a court will determine its course of action with reference to the nature of the violation and the context of the specific legislation under consideration.[111]

A court, then, may strike down an offending provision, read down or into a provision, or sever it from the rest of the legislation. The court in *Schachter* also explained that these remedies could be used in combination with an order from a court suspending its order for a specific time period to allow the legislature time to amend the offending provision.[112]

The remedies chosen in Aboriginal cases tend to favour suspensions of orders, so as to allow Parliament time to amend legislation or allow the government time to consult with the Aboriginal group(s) affected.[113] This was the remedy chosen by the appeal court in *McIvor*. However, before one can get into what specific remedies would address the second generation cut-off rule claim, it is necessary to address government reasons for delaying or minimizing remedies.

Federal and provincial governments have both created various excuses in order to delay remedying injustices for Aboriginal peoples, and especially those regarding the rights of off-reserve status Indians, non-status Indians, and Métis. In *Powley*, the provincial government argued that it would be too hard to determine who individual Métis people are, and thus denied them their hunting rights.[114] The court rejected this defence, holding that "the difficulty of identifying members of the Métis community must not be exaggerated as a basis for defeating their rights under the Constitution of Canada."[115]

Another defence often put forward has been that of cost. Governments argue that the cost of respecting a constitutional right would be prohibitive or should result in a justification of the breach of those rights. In *Corbiere*, the Supreme Court of Canada was faced with such a defence by the federal government — that the cost would be too high to include off-reserve band members in band elections — and found that there was no authority that supported the breach of the off-reserve band members' *Charter* rights based on cost or administrative difficulty.[116] The same principle holds true for non-status Indians: Canada gained significant experience in reinstating and registering previously excluded Indians during the Bill C-31 amendments, and certainly could not argue administrative difficulty. It has the expertise and the experience, and registration is based on application — i.e., only those who apply must be processed.

Yet cost is the primary consideration behind Canada's efforts to protect its right to determine and limit the number of status Indians in Canada. Magnet argues that cost is the major reason non-status Indians continue to be excluded from registration under the *Indian Act, 1985* — the federal government's fear of the increased costs associated with adding people to the Indian register.[117] Magnet refers to the government's "public face" regarding non-status Indians, and cites Prime Minister Paul Martin's promise in his speech from the throne in October 2004 to "tackle head on the particular problems faced by the increasing number of urban Aboriginal people and by the Metis. We will not allow ourselves to be caught up in jurisdictional wrangling, passing the buck and bypassing their needs."[118] Magnet goes on to point out the government's "private face," which recognizes the problems faced by non-status Indians yet is unwilling to make the expenditures to alleviate their suffering:

> In private, Ottawa recognizes that non-status Aboriginal people face urgent pressing problems that are basically the same as status Aboriginal people. A 1976 Cabinet memo notes that the "special problems and needs of all classes of native people are similar (recognition, cultural security, socio-economic needs, participation, self-determination)" and that "the Indian Act which defines Indian people . . . is in some ways arbitrary, anachronistic and harsh."[119]

He also notes that despite their private acknowledgment of the problems, their public response is often quite different:

> The Cabinet memo concludes that in a period of "expenditure restraint" it would not be "desirable to extend Indian status, or rights of access to Indian programs, to large additional groups of people." In short, in private, government has decided that while the situation of non-status Aboriginal people is urgent and that Ottawa's response is arbitrary, anachronistic and harsh, the Federal Government will not spend to address these inequalities.[120]

Canada continues to argue that cost is not the chief motivation in maintaining the second generation cut-off rule, but internal documents betray that position. A secret memo from Associate Deputy Minister Drummie, addressed to Minister of Indian Affairs Crombie, stated that the cost of reinstatement was "alarming" and expressed the need to find less costly forms of reinstatement: "It seems evident from the comments . . . regarding the financial consequences of the recommended option that Cabinet's final policy decision on reinstatement will be shaped by financial more than any other consideration."[121]

Based on all indications from the Supreme Court, financial considerations would be insufficient to deny non-status Indians constitutional equality if there were to be a challenge to section 6(2). How a program is funded is a secondary consideration to the protection of the *Charter* right itself. Furthermore, it has long been recognized that courts can fashion remedies to address the right at issue even if one of the effects has an impact of government spending. The court in *Schachter* explained that the issue is whether or not the budgetary impact changes the nature of the legislation significantly from what it was:

> Any remedy granted by a court will have some budgetary repercussions whether it be a saving of money or an expenditure of money. Striking down or severance may well lead to an expenditure of money. . . . It has also been pointed out that a wide variety of court orders have had the effect of causing expenditures. . . .
>
> In determining whether reading in is appropriate then, the question is not whether courts can make decisions that impact on budgetary policy; it is to what degree they can appropriately do so. A remedy which entails an intrusion into this sphere so substantial as to change the nature of the legislative scheme in question is clearly inappropriate.[122]

It is doubtful that the registration of non-status Indians would have the effect of changing the *Indian Act* substantially from what it is; it would still be legislation that determines the beneficiaries of federal programs and services dedicated to Indians. The benefits, rights, and obligations that flow from the *Act* would still be reserved for Indians, but Canada would not be able to exclude Indians on discriminatory grounds. Indigenous people will have to watch carefully post-*McIvor* to ensure that Canada does not do indirectly what it cannot do directly — i.e., "equality with a vengeance."[123] For example, now that McIvor has won (at least in part) her gender equality claim, Canada could not now decide that Indian status under the *Act* no longer has any tangible benefits associated with such status, or change the entitlement criteria to band membership, or reserve residency, which would effectively eliminate much of the benefit gained by *McIvor* in being registered. It would be one thing for Canada to reduce some of the benefits within a program to accommodate unexpected increases in usage if it meant that the country would be in a financial crisis; it is quite another to eliminate a necessary program.

With regard to the types of remedies available — those achieved through the courts or by negotiated agreement — there are any number of practical options. The remedy in *Corbiere* was to declare the words "ordinarily resident on reserve" in section 77(1) of the *Indian Act, 1985*, inconsistent with section 15(1) of the *Charter* pursuant to section 52(1) of the *Constitution Act, 1982*.[124] The Supreme Court of Canada suspended its declaration of invalidity for a period of 18 months in order to allow the government time to amend the legislation. During that time, INAC changed its policy to allow off-reserve voting and provided training to its staff and First Nations, and also provided some funding to assist bands in making the required changes to their election procedures. With regard to the second generation cut-off rule, a court could strike out section 6(2) entirely and give the federal government a set period of time — 18 to 24 months, say — to consult with Indigenous peoples on how best to amend the *Act*. The court would also give some guiding principles on how to best amend the *Act*, or it could declare that the government must reinstate or register certain groups of non-status Indians. In the situation of the few unrecognized bands in Canada, such as the Michel band, their entire communities could be registered under the current provisions of the *Indian Act*.[125] Obviously, that would not apply to any group of individuals wanting band status, but could be an option for those legitimate bands currently not recognized. These kinds of remedies are well within the realm of possibility. Canada reinstated thousands of individuals within a relatively short period of time with Bill C-31, and no doubt has the experience and demographic information to register non-status Indians. Canada has solicited numerous studies on the demographic indicators and future trends of status Indians, both in terms of registration under the *Indian Act* and band membership.[126] Its own expert witness has provided detailed demographic data that could be used in planning and implementation. The only indeterminate issue is how many non-status Indians will actually apply to be registered, which could be far fewer than are entitled.

Various remedies have also been suggested by groups outside the litigation context. The Native Women's Association of Canada (NWAC) has been calling for the repeal of section 6(2)'s second generation cut-off for years. NWAC has further recommended that "Amendments should be made to the Indian Act which would remove all discrimination, present and historical, against Aboriginal women and their children." [127] The Assembly of First Nations (AFN) also feels that the current *Act*'s residual discrimination against Indian women and their descendants has caused significant harm in their communities, and that the second generation cut-off rule has only led to increased litigation by Indigenous peoples to address the discrimination.[128] The AFN reported on the conclusions of First Nations focus groups across the country that called for First Nation control over both status and membership, and that any racist criteria, such as blood quantum, be rejected.[129] The *Aboriginal Justice Inquiry* characterized the second generation cut-off rule as a *de facto* one-quarter blood rule that threatens the survival of First Nations, and recommended that the *Indian Act* "be amended to remove the two generation rule," and that "[t]he category of so-called 'non-status Indians' or 'un-registered' Indians should disappear.[130] There are many more reports and studies that make similar recommendations. The point is that the discrimination caused by the second generation cut-off rule is well recognized and there has been a near-unanimous call for its repeal.

It is important to emphasize that registration and band membership is not being promoted here as a substitution for citizenship under future self-government agreements, but, given that many First Nations are decades away from that stage, it is imperative that inequities among current and future members be dealt with now. The registration of non-status Indians would be an interim solution, but a necessary step forward for individuals, communities, and nations toward mending divisions and achieving equality among their citizens. Since some Indigenous groups base their citizenship rolls for self-government agreements on their former band lists, which in many cases are determined by the *Indian Act*, it is necessary to amend the *Act* to avoid further discrimination even within self-government citizenship lists.

This situation with individual Indigenous people also plays out in communities. When considering remedies, therefore, the focus may be on entire communities as opposed to individuals. The Innu communities in Newfoundland and Labrador are examples of communities that were outside the *Indian Act,* owing to past inequities, and how the federal government turned entire communities of non-status Indians into status Indians and bands by the stroke of a pen.[131] This was also done with Miawpukek (formerly Conne River), and will soon be completed with the Federation of Newfoundland Indians (now the Qalipu Mi'kmaq First Nation).[132] Yet other bands, like Michel First Nation, remain on the outside looking in.

The Innu in Newfoundland and Labrador are now registered as two separate bands, and many of their members are registered under the *Indian Act* as Indians. But the Innu of Labrador were not always in favour of registration. The Innu nation is an example of Canada's power to determine the identity of Indigenous peoples and communities. The Innu are an Indigenous group that were not registered under the *Act* as Indians or bands and originally did not want to be.[133] What they wanted was for Canada to negotiate self-government with them, provide them with programs and services, and treat them equivalently to how they treated status Indians.[134] A Canadian Human Rights Commission report found that the Innu were being pressured by Canada to register as Indians instead of negotiating a self-government agreement:

> But this should not involve any requirement that the Innu be formally placed under the Indian Act. To require the Innu to be so registered would be to elevate form over substance. It would be nothing more than a symbol-

ic act of subordination — to legislation that the Canadian Human Rights Commission itself has described as "outdated and paternalistic." There is no reason why the federal government could not act directly without imposing the process of registration under the Indian Act on the Innu.[135]

While many attempts were made by the Innu to negotiate such a self-government agreement, the federal government refused to provide them with programs and services without registering them under the *Indian Act*.[136] One might ask why an Indigenous group untainted by the *Indian Act* might agree to come under its jurisdiction, but there seemed to be no other avenue to the negotiating table. While communities should not have to be registered as Indians before they can negotiate self-government, it appears that that is Canada's criterion for allowing an Indigenous group to access the negotiating table. This highlights the disadvantaged position of non-status Indians in regard to being able to advocate on their own behalf, or even getting a seat at the negotiating table. Despite INAC concerns over setting a precedent, registering the Innu and creating new bands is not a novel idea, as that is clearly what had been done for the Mi'kmaq of Conne River (now Miawpukek).[137]

In 1984, Miawpukek was registered under the *Indian Act*, and a reserve was created for them in 1987.[138] Miawpukek First Nation is located 224 km south of Gander, Newfoundland, at Conne River. They have about 2300 band members, 1500 of whom live off reserve. The band and INAC have been "engaged in an innovative pre-negotiations process designed to facilitate movement toward a self-government regime for the community of Conne River."[139] Similarly, the Federation of Newfoundland Indians (FNI) is in the process of negotiations with INAC to be declared a band under the *Indian Act*, but without a reserve — a "landless band." The goal is to have their members registered under the *Indian Act*, and, through future negotiations, ultimately gain their own lands.[140] The FNI is recognized by the federal government as the representative organization of non-status Indians in Newfoundland, and is provided operational funding on that basis.[141] When the FNI first started out in 1972, it was the Native Association of Newfoundland and Labrador, and also represented the Innu and Inuit groups of Labrador, as well as the Mi'kmaq from Conne River. The Native Association of Newfoundland and Labrador changed its name when the Innu and Inuit separated from the group in 1975. The Mi'kmaq of Conne River did not separate until 1982. As the Mi'kmaq in Conne River became registered as Indians, followed by the Innu, it became increasingly difficult to see why the FNI members would be excluded. The CHRC conducted a detailed review of the matter, and, in the *Innu Report 2002*, compared the situation of the Innu and the Mi'kmaq at Conne River and concluded the same thing:

The saga leading to registration is an unfortunate one that does not reflect well on the Government. The Innu were offered registration. The offer was subsequently withdrawn and then re-offered. The Innu were told they were getting equivalency without registration, but then told equivalency only applied to programs and services and not to taxation. They were then told they could get taxation exemption if they became registered. When a parallel was drawn with Conne River, the Innu were told that they were different from the Aboriginal inhabitants of Conne River, although an internal government memorandum provided to the Innu under an Access to Information Act request appears to indicate that the only real difference between the Innu and the Mik'maqs of Conne River was that whereas the Mik'maqs had sued the Government, the Innu had not.[142]

Despite such obvious similarities between the three groups, the FNI still had to commence litigation against the federal government before Canada agreed to negotiate the registration of the FNI as a band.

There are other unrecognized bands in Canada in similar positions to that of the Innu and Mi'kmaq in Newfoundland that should also be registered as bands. The Michel First Nation in Alberta is a band that was enfranchised by Indian Affairs and no longer has band status under the *Act*. They are currently suing Canada for having enfranchised their community without having followed the minimal steps required — namely, obtaining informed consent through a majority vote. While the specifics of each community may be different, their relationship vis-à-vis the government is the same: Canada decides who's in and who's out of the *Indian Act*. Some bands are forced to register in order to commence self-government negotiations, while others are arbitrarily excluded.

These situations are somewhat unique, however, and would not apply to the vast majority of non-status Indians in Canada. Remedies such as registering entire communities are therefore not likely to apply with regard to my claimant group — first and second generation non-status Indians excluded by the second generation cut-off rule. That being the case, we have to look to more analogous situations for appropriate remedies. While Sharon McIvor did not challenge the second generation cut-off rule when she brought her gender discrimination claim against Canada, the history, law, and legal analysis is closely analogous to that of my claimant group. There are lessons to be learned both from the *McIvor case* itself and the political response that followed.

Lessons from McIvor v. Canada

The *McIvor* case is especially applicable to my claimant group with regard to the kinds of remedies I could expect, should I be successful with such a claim.

McIvor's claim is highly analogous to mine, and in fact there are issues that cross over, as gender and blood quantum restrictions often go hand in hand. A proper comparison requires some background on McIvor and her twenty-year struggle for justice.

Sharon McIvor was a non-status Indian who, as a result of the 1985 amendments to the *Indian Act*, has since been registered as a status Indian and a member of the Lower Nicola Band in British Columbia:

> Sharon McIvor lacked status from birth, because she traced her Indian ancestry through the maternal line, and her father did not have status. Sharon's parents lived in a common law relationship, and were never married. When Sharon applied to become registered in 1985, Sharon was told that she could only be registered under section 6(2) and not section 6(1), unless she could establish Indian paternity, which she was unable to do. The fact that Sharon was able to establish Indian maternity was not considered sufficient to entitle Sharon to section 6(1)(a) status. Sharon's deceased mother was deemed to have been previously excluded from status due to her non-Indian paternity, and, therefore, she was consigned to section 6(1)(c) under the 1985 Act. In turn, Sharon's children were ineligible for registration.[143]

Her family history and current legal status are similar to those of my own family, in that Sharon McIvor is in a similar position to that of my grandmother, her son Jacob is in a similar position to that of my father, and I am in a similar position to that of Jacob's children (Sharon's grandchildren). However, the McIvor case is complex and the sections under which she has been registered have changed over time as her applications, protests, and appeals have taken over twenty years to be resolved.

McIvor is the first case that challenged the section 6 registration provisions of the *Indian Act, 1985*. The legal principles and political history which form the basis of the decisions in *McIvor* may also apply in my hypothetical claimant group. Sharon McIvor is now a section 6(1)(c) Indian — like my grandmother — and her son, Jacob Grismer, is a section 6(2) Indian — like my father. Therefore, Jacob's children and any future grandchildren are or would be first- and second-generation non-status Indians — like myself and my children. At trial, McIvor and her son Jacob challenged the constitutional validity of section 6(1) and 6(2) of the *Indian Act, 1985* arguing that it discriminates on the basis of both marital status and gender.[144] They did not challenge the band membership provisions or the second generation cut-off rule *per se*.[145] The essence of their claim is that, although the Bill C-31 amendments were meant to address gender discrimination against Indian women who married out, the registration provisions still prefer descendants who traced their lineage through the male line over the female line.[146] Canada defended this claim by arguing that it was an impermissible retroactive application of the *Charter*, that the plaintiffs suffer no harm since they are registered as Indians, and that any infringement was justified in light of the "broad objectives of the 1985 amendments to the *Indian Act* which was a policy decision, made after extensive consultation, balancing the interests of all affected and which is entitled to deference."[147] Justice Ross of the British Columbia Supreme Court (BCSC) found that section 6 of the *Indian Act, 1985* discriminated on the basis of both sex and marital status, violated section 15 of the *Charter*, and was not justified pursuant section 1 of the *Charter*.[148] However, before doing the section 15 analysis, Ross provided a great deal of political, legal, social, and cultural context to the issue that would be relevant in varying degrees to such an analysis.

The trial court noted that the issue of gender discrimination in the *Indian Act* was not new, and that Aboriginal people had been objecting to the gender discriminatory provisions in the *Indian Act*s as early as 1870s. A large portion of the decision was dedicated to reviewing the history of the *Indian Act* and its amendments over time, its imposition on First Nations, and the various calls for the discrimination against Indian women and their descendants to end.[149] As a result of the *Lovelace* case, the enactment of the *Charter*, and significant political pressure, Canada enacted Bill C-31, which was to address two historic wrongs in Indian legislation: (1) "discriminatory treatment based on sex"; and (2) "control by Government of membership in Indian communities."[150] The trial court emphasized the importance of status to Indian women and their descendants, and explained that the lack of status was akin to "statutory banishment" from one's Aboriginal community,[151] and, further, that statutory recognition as an Indian has come to exist alongside traditional concepts.[152]

It is with this contextual background that the analysis of McIvor's section 15 claim led to a finding of discrimination.

The first question to ask is whether the law imposes a differential treatment between the claimant and others which includes an identification of both the benefit at law and the comparator group. McIvor asserted that the benefit at law at issue was to both have and transmit status to one's descendants. Canada's submissions in this regard were conflicting, as it argued that status is not a right that resides in a parent that can be transmitted to one's child, while at the same time explaining that status is based on the entitlement of one's parents.[153] With regard to the tangible benefits of status, such as federal programs and services, Justice Ross explained, "Since parents are responsible for the support of their children, such programs can, it seems to me, be benefits for both parent and child," and was highly critical of Canada's position that status was only a statutory entitlement to programs:

It is my view that the defendants' submission is a strained and unnatural construct that ignores the significance of the concept of Indian as an aspect of cultural identity. The defendants' approach would treat status as an Indian as if it were simply a statutory definition pertaining to eligibility in some program or benefit. However, having created and then imposed this identity upon First Nations peoples, with the result that it has become a central aspect of identity, the government cannot now treat it in that way, ignoring the true essence or significance of the concept.[154]

With regard to intangible benefits like cultural identity, "it is one of our most basic expectations that we will acquire the cultural identity of our parents; and that as parents, we will transmit our cultural identity to our children."[155] Ross further explained:

Although the concept of "Indian" is a creation of government, it has developed into a powerful source of cultural identity for the individual and Aboriginal community. Like citizenship, both parents and children have an interest in this tangible aspect of Indian status. In particular, parents have an interest in the transmission of this cultural identity to their children.[156]

On that basis, the court found status to be akin to nationality and citizenship, and that the benefit of law was registration as an Indian — i.e., status — and the ability to transmit that status to one's descendants.[157] Justice Groberman, writing for the British Columbia Court of Appeal (BCCA), agreed with the trial judge that both tangible and intangible benefits flow from Indian status.[158] While the BCCA did not have to decide whether the transmission of status to one's grandchildren would also be a benefit, the court was inclined to view that it was.[159] The question then moved to the appropriate comparator group.

The BCSC cited the Supreme Court of Canada in *Hodge*, which held that the comparator group is one that mirrors the claimant group relevant to the benefit sought but for the prohibited ground, which in this case is gender.[160] McIvor argued at trial that the comparator group should be male Indians, including male Indians who married out and their descendants — i.e., section 6(1)(a) Indians. Canada argued that the comparator group should be those like McIvor who were reinstated, and therefore limited to those registered in section 6(1)(c),(d), and (e).[161] Justice Ross agreed with McIvor that to treat her the same as all other reinstatees would be to reduce section 15 to a "shell game."[162] In rejecting Canada's argument, the court cited the Supreme Court in *Andrews*, which overturned *Bliss*, which had denied the claim of gender discrimination by pregnant women who were denied benefits on the basis that all pregnant women were treated alike in not receiving benefits.[163] Therefore, the appropriate comparator group for McIvor were male Indians born pre-1985, who had status, married out, and had children, it was the descendants of that group who were the comparator group for McIvor's son, Jacob Grismer.[164] The BCCA focused on the claim of Grismer, as it was the most straightforward, acknowledging, however, that McIvor and Grismer's claims stand or fall together.[165] The court noted that Grismer wanted to compare his group (people born pre-1985 to Indian women who married out) to people born pre-1985 to Indian men who married out.[166] The BCCA found the trial judge to be correct in having accepted the comparator group chosen by Grismer, as it was the most logical group, and the one which was the same in all aspects to Grismer's group but gender.[167]

Both levels of court found the question of whether there was differential treatment between the two groups to be relatively straightforward. The descendants of Indian women who married out could not transmit their status to their own children, whereas the descendants of Indian men who married out could, and this resulted in differential access to both tangible and intangible benefits. On the question of whether the differential treatment was based on an enumerated or analogous ground, Justice Ross agreed with McIvor that "the basis for the difference in treatment is the continuing preference for descendants who trace their lineage along the male line."[168] Another key difference in how the *Act* perpetuates gender discrimination in the present, is that a section 6(1)(c) applicant born pre-1985 cannot look beyond his or her parents for a disentitlement for which to be reinstated. However, applicants under section 6(1)(a) can look as far back in their male ancestral line as necessary to establish entitlement to registration.[169] This inequality is further demonstrated in the fact that there is no second generation cut-off for those born pre-1985 for those registered under section 6(1)(a), whereas there is for those in the section 6(1)(c) category. While the trial court found there to be differential treatment based on marital status and sex/gender, the appeal court held that there was not enough evidence to support a claim based on marital status, and limited the claim to one based on sex. The BCSC found a claim based on sex to be straightforward — had Grismer's Indian parent been his father, his children would be entitled to Indian status.[170] Both Grismer, having been born of an Indian woman who married out, and McIvor, being an Indian woman, could show disadvantageous treatment based on McIvor's gender.[171]

The next question was whether the law had a discriminatory purpose or effect, which the trial court concluded it did. Citing the former Minister of INAC, Justice Ross held:

Minister Crombie quite properly described the discriminatory treatment based on sex in the prior versions of the *Indian Act* as a "historic wrong" and as a "particularly blatant form of discrimination." In my view, the distinctions at issue continue to perpetuate the historic disadvantage experienced by Aboriginal women and those who trace their status through the maternal line. I agree with the submission of the plaintiffs that in so doing the 1985 Act reflects and reinforces the pre-existing disadvantage of a vulnerable group.[172]

Such a distinction based on gender also did not relate to the actual needs or capacities of the claimants.[173] Justice Groberman of the BCCA agreed that these distinctions did not take into account actual differences in culture, ability, or merit, and explained further:

> The impugned legislation in this case is, in my opinion, discriminatory as that concept is used in section 15 of the *Charter*. The historical reliance on patrilineal descent to determine Indian status was based on stereotypical views of the role of a woman within a family. It had (in the words of *Law*) "the effect of perpetuating or promoting the view that [women were] . . . less . . . worthy of recognition or value as a human being[s] or as a member[s] of Canadian society, equally deserving of concern, respect, and consideration." The impugned legislation in this case is the echo of historic discrimination. As such, it serves to perpetuate, at least in a small way, the discriminatory attitudes of the past.[174]

Although the trial decision came out before *Kapp* — regarding section 15(2) — Justice Ross still considered the issue of whether the *Indian Act* was ameliorative legislation and whether it had an impact on McIvor and Grismer's claim. Both McIvor and Canada agreed that Bill C-31 had been ameliorative legislation.[175] The plaintiffs also submitted that they were the targets of such ameliorative legislation. Citing other Supreme Court cases — namely, *Law* and *Vriend* — Ross held that the fact that Bill C-31 had an ameliorative purpose did not save it from a determination of discrimination because it was under-inclusive legislation that specifically excluded members of an historically disadvantaged group.[176] The BCCA agreed with the trial judge on this point. With regard to the justification stage of the test, both levels of court also agreed that the five objectives of Bill C-31 were pressing and substantial objectives.[177]

The trial court addressed a sixth objective alleged by Canada to be one of the objectives of Bill C-31 — namely, genealogical proximity — but held it was not an objective of the bill and was not even mentioned by Minister Crombie at the time.[178] It also held that, even if genealogical proximity had been an objective, Canada could not now rely on the invidious effects of its previous discriminatory legislation to exclude those who allegedly lack a cultural connection to their communities precisely because of that legislation.[179] The appeal court did not overturn the trial judge on this point, and, when listing the objectives of the bill that were specifically supported by the evidence and historical record, Justice Groberman did not include Canada's sixth objective of genealogical proximity.[180] However, Groberman does appear to incorporate that reasoning later on in the decision when he held that Canada's choice to require more than one Indian grandparent was in keeping with the views of some Aboriginal groups and the past legislative regime.[181] It is at this point that logic and legal reasoning start to diverge. In finding that Canada failed to pass the first part of the justification test, Justice Ross agreed "with the submission of the plaintiffs that while the stated objectives of the legislation as a whole are pressing and substantial, the defendants have failed to advance any pressing or substantial purpose for the discriminatory registration scheme that was adopted."[182] The BCCA, on the other hand, held that the objectives were pressing and substantial and did meet the first part of the justification test.[183]

No rational connection was found at trial between the stated objectives and the measures adopted to achieve those objectives: "It cannot be said that the preservation of discrimination removes discrimination in the system of registration."[184] Without any analysis, the BCCA found that there was a rational connection.[185] However, the two courts were of similar minds with regard to minimal impairment, both finding that Canada failed this aspect of the test, albeit for different reasons. At trial, the court found that there were no competing interests, no group would have been disadvantaged by the removal of sex discrimination from section 6, nor would any group have a legitimate interest in perpetuating such discrimination.[186] Finally, while there may be costs associated with remedying discrimination, even Minister Crombie expected that they were unavoidable. In the end, the right at issue is to have status and be able to transmit that status, and what government programs are associated with status are secondary and in the control of Canada.[187] While the BCCA agreed that Canada failed the minimal impairment test, it did so on the limited basis that, as between section 12(1)(b) reinstatees — Indian women — and those affected by the section 12(1)(a)(iv) double mother clause — Indian men — double mother clause reinstatees were give an additional advantage in 1985. As this advantage created in 1985 widens the inequality between Grismer and the comparator group, the legislation fails the minimal impairment test.[188] Their final pronouncements reflect the fundamental basis of their theoretical differences. Justice Ross found that "the damaging effects of the continuing discrimination against Aboriginal women and their descendants are significant," and thus not proportional to the *Bill*'s objectives,[189] whereas Justice Groberman found that "[t]he denial of Indian status to Mr. Grismer's children . . . is not an extraordinary prejudice," and thus the objectives were proportional.[190]

In a subsequent order, Justice Ross ordered, in part, that: (1) section 6 of the *Indian Act, 1985* violates sections 15 and 28 of the *Charter*; (2) section 6 is of no force and effect in so far as it provides preferential treatment for Indian men and their descendants and Indian women and their descendants born pre-1985; (3) nothing affects band membership; and (4) both McIvor and Grismer be registered under section 6(1)(a) of the *Indian Act*.[191] While the order relating to band membership posed some technical difficulties with regard to application, and the order itself was broad, it looks as though the intention was to address gender discrimination on a holistic basis so that numerous other claimants did not have to come to court with nearly identical facts and make the same arguments. However, the BCCA felt that the trial judge erred in trying to remedy all gender discrimination that occurred pre-1985. Justice Groberman found that section 6 violated the *Charter* by providing Indian status to children: (1) who have only one parent who is Indian (other than by reason of having married an Indian); (2) where that parent was born prior to April 17, 1985; and (3) where that parent in turn only had one parent who was Indian (other than by reason of having married an Indian).[192] As a result, the BCCA declared that sections 6(1)(a) and (c) of the *Indian Act, 1985* were of no force and effect and that the declaration would be suspended for a period of one year.[193] McIvor applied for leave to appeal to the Supreme Court of Canada, which was denied on November 5, 2009.[194] Although McIvor has since served notice that she will file a complaint against Canada at the United Nations,[195] the decision of the BCCA will be the one we must deal with regarding any potential amendments to the *Act*.

Canada's response to the decision did not include consulting with Indigenous peoples on how best to implement amendments to the *Act*, or on how they might address larger problems with Indian registration at the same time. Instead, Canada drafted a discussion paper and presented Indigenous peoples with two closely related options for legislative amendments. Canada released this information to Aboriginal organizations in late August 2009 and gave Aboriginal people until November 2009 to offer their views and comments.[196] With few exceptions, the general feeling of Aboriginal groups who spoke out on the issue was that the legislative options did not go far enough to address gender discrimination in the *Indian Act*, nor did they fully address the *McIvor* decision. Despite concerns raised by First Nations and others that full consultation was required, on March 11, 2010, Canada introduced Bill C-3: *Gender Equity in Indian Registration Act*.[197] The bill was introduced by Minister Strahl as a targeted and limited response to the decision of the BCCA. Strahl announced at the same time that there would be funding for the establishment of a national joint committee to look at the larger issues of status and band membership when and if Bill C-3 passed. The essence of the bill was to provide a gender remedy to those in the same scenario as McIvor and Grismer. Entitlement to registration was described as follows:

1. Did your grandmother lose her Indian status as a result of marrying a non-Indian?

2. Is one of your parents registered, or entitled to be registered, under subsection 6(2) of the *Indian Act*?

3. Were you born on or after September 4, 1951?

Those who can answer yes to **all** of the above questions are encouraged to submit an application for registration as an Indian.

If you are the registered Indian parent of·a minor child that fits the above scenario, you may apply on their behalf. Your entitlement to Indian registration will be automatically amended from 6(2) to 6(1) to allow for the registration of your child. No application for this amendment is required as it will be done at the time of your child's registration.[198]

Taking my family situation as an example, under Bill C-3 my deceased grandmother would be deemed a section 6(1)(c) Indian, my deceased father would be deemed as going from section 6(2) status to section 6(1)(c.1) status, and I would go from a non-status Indian to section 6(2) status, still leaving my children as non-status Indians. This obviously does not provide a complete gender remedy; had my grandmother been a grandfather, both he and my father and siblings would have been registered under section 6(1)(a), making our children section 6(2) Indians, as is the case for those who trace their ancestry through the male line.

The bill was debated and passed second reading before being studied at the Standing Committee on Aboriginal Peoples and Northern Development (AAON). During the study phase, the AAON heard from numerous Indigenous individuals, groups, and communities, as well as other parties, such as the Canadian Bar Association, on the bill and potential amendments. The overwhelming majority of witnesses who appeared, including myself, called not only for proper consultations but for the bill to be amended to more properly address the full extent of gender discrimination in the *Act*.[199] Another point that was stressed repeatedly before the AAON was the fact that First Nations challenge Canada's right to determine status and assert their own jurisdiction in this regard.[200] The majority of the AAON agreed with the witnesses and suggested amendments that would better address the full extent of gender discrimination in the *Act*, but these amendments were ruled out of order once it was sent back to the House. Although numerous problems were noted with the bill itself (as opposed to the larger political issues such as jurisdiction), the main problem was that Bill C-3 would create a new category of Indian known as a section 6(1)(c.1) Indian that should have been available to anyone who's mother had lost her status due to marrying out, but is instead limited to those whose mothers married out and they themselves parented a child with a non-Indian. Therefore, people who are section 6(2) Indians because of the gender discrimination faced by their mothers will not benefit from being bumped up from section 6(2) to section 6(1)(c.1) if they themselves either have status Indian children or no children at all. In other words, entitlement to status will now be based not only on the ancestry of one's parents, but also on the ancestry of one's children — which will only apply to the descendants of Indian women who married out. Canada has therefore created a discriminatory remedy for those who have already suffered discrimination.[201]

Sharon McIvor and I, in separate submissions to the AAON, suggested that the most appropriate remedy was to delete the references to a new section 6(1)(c.1) and simply add the following words to section 6(1)(a): "or was born prior to April 17, 1985 and was a direct descendant of such a person."[202] The idea would be that Indian men and women who were born prior to the enactment of Bill C-31 (before April 17, 1985) should all be considered equal in terms of status. This would include any of their descendants who were born prior to 1985. Status would be gender neutral and marriage would not prejudice or advantage anyone. This would mean that Sharon's mother, Sharon, and her son Jacob would all be section 6(1)(a) Indians equally with Sharon's brother and his children. Jacob's children would be section 6(2) Indians, having been born after 1985. Similarly, this would mean that my grandmother, father, and I would all be section 6(1)(a) Indians and my children would be section 6(2) Indians. In other words, the second generation cut-off rule (which was not challenged in *McIvor*) would apply to everyone born after 1985 equally, regardless of gender. To do otherwise preserves the privileged position of male Indians on a go-forward basis. For the purposes of the limited legislative amendment Canada was willing to make with regard to the *McIvor* decision, we had to confine our recommendations to those that could be considered by the AAON. Unfortunately, the AAON, on the advice of several witnesses, decided to recommend a much broader amendment that was ruled out of scope by the House, which leaves us with the bill as originally written. In fairness, it is likely that the House would have ruled our suggested amendment out of scope as well.

So, what does all of this mean for my claim regarding the second generation cut-off rule? The trial and appeal court decisions will be highly informative regarding what historical evidence was considered relevant and what kinds of arguments might be successful. As I did in my hypothetical claim, I can rely on certain key facts identified in the *McIvor* decisions, such as the government's five objectives with regard to Bill C-31, Canada's focus on limiting financial responsibility through a one-quarter blood quantum rule, and certain findings regarding Indian women being historically disadvantaged. Perhaps more importantly, my claim might be an opportunity to highlight certain problematic areas in the court's reasoning, or findings that need to be addressed or reconsidered, such as the appeal court's application (or lack thereof) of various aspects of the section 15(1) analysis, its backdoor approval of a one-quarter blood rule, and its contradictory findings of fact versus conclusions. The kinds of remedies that are available will also help steer arguments one way or another. The BCCA preferred to allow Canada to decide how to amend the *Act*, whereas the Supreme Court in *Corbiere* specifically read down a section of the *Act* and declared a specific provision to be of no force and effect. Obviously, the preference would be to make arguments that would support a declaration that section 6(2) was of no force or effect, so as to limit Canada's flexibility when amending the *Act*.

The lack of consultation post-*McIvor* was of great concern to all Indigenous parties. Therefore, it would be necessary that any suspension of the order for 18 months (as in *Corbiere*) would be for the express purpose of consulting with affected Indigenous peoples and their communities before any legislative amendments are proposed. This was a key issue in *McIvor* that was lacking. I would argue that section 6(2) be declared of no force and effect and give Canada 18 months to consult with Indigenous peoples on how best to remedy the discrimination. Which brings us to the most important aspect of any remedy: the specific finding of discrimination. The BCCA was so far off its finding of discrimination from what the parties originally argued at trial that everyone seemed to be somewhat shocked by the finding. Additional submissions had even been required from the parties regarding the double mother clause issue. Therefore, my arguments will have to be tailored specifically to the second generation cut-off rule and limit any openings for a court to essentially select its own comparator group.

Assuming I was successful in obtaining a declaration that section 6(2) of the *Indian Act, 1985* was of no force and effect because it violated section 15(1) of the *Charter* as it was discrimination on the basis of race or an analogous ground of blood quantum/descent and could not be saved under section 1, then what kind of remedy would I want? If the scope of the case was limited, such that I was not also arguing that Canada lacked jurisdiction to determine status or an Aboriginal right to determine status, then I assume a court would give Canada anywhere from 12 to 18 months to consult with First Nations and come up with amendments. The next question is, what kind of amendments would I seek? Obviously, my position is that no determination of status that is based on blood quantum will ever be acceptable. Therefore, a cut-off rule that is delayed until the third or fourth generation is no more acceptable than a second generation cut-off. The adoption of a true one-parent rule is the most reasonable. It would definitely increase registration, but there would be no flood gates opening that tripled or quadrupled current status population numbers — or at least no demographic studies have indicated as much. Even if it did double the number of status Indians, how would that be a negative for First Nations who are already in nation-building activities? Blood clubs will never have the political power or voting numbers to make any difference in their own communities or in Canada at large. Yet, large nations, rebuilt back to their pre-contact sizes, which have welcomed their citizens back and made them feel part of their nations, are far more likely to have the kind of human resources, volunteers, diverse skill sets and experiences, and additional brain power to help address current socio-economic issues, relationship issues with Canada, and, most importantly, help strengthen the culture, identity, and sense of collective nationhood in each First Nation. If nothing else, a one-parent rule in section 6(1) will act as an impetus for First Nations and Canada to renegotiate their relationship and jurisdiction over Indigenous citizenship, so that control is back in the hands of First Nations and there would be no need for status.

In the end, it is often the political response that is most practically relevant for those who seek to enforce a *Charter* remedy, and so public education and First Nation education will be essential to building support and momentum for such a case. Having a general agreement about potential amendments ahead of time will be much more useful than everyone trying to come up with separate positions after the fact. There is usually more than enough time to do this, as these cases can take upwards of 20 years or more to resolve. That being said, what usually happens is that every other issue is addressed during that time and it is only when a decision has been reached that Indigenous groups and Canada scramble to come up with positions. The *McIvor* case has been extremely useful in putting the issue of status back into the forefront, and has made us all think about what it means to be an Indigenous person, an Indian, a Mi'kmaq, or Maliseet. It would be a mistake to let the momentum slide. There are many other issues around status and band membership that have not yet been addressed. The second generation cut-off rule may be challenged sooner rather than later if certain cases move forward.[203] The Canadian Human Rights Commission may also have an impact, if not on the *Indian Act* directly, on the analysis of section 15(1) of the *Charter* in future cases. We have to be the ones to help guide communal, political, and judicial views about what it means to be Indigenous, and who has the right to make such determinations. It is important to address this issue now because band membership lists are used to determine treaty and land claim beneficiary lists as well as self-government enrollee lists. If we do not address discrimination in registration and band membership now, self-government agreements will do little more than perpetuate the status quo. We owe it to future generations to ensure that the decisions we make today respect their right to their culture and identity in the future.

CHAPTER FOUR

Band Membership

vs.

Self-Government Citizenship

IN THE PREVIOUS TWO CHAPTERS, I advanced the argument that, while Indigenous nations have the right to determine their own citizenship, this right must be balanced against the right of individuals to belong to their nations. For bands to arbitrarily exclude non-status Indians from band membership on the basis of blood quantum or status is as discriminatory as Canada's exclusion of non-status Indians from status on the basis of the second generation cut-off rule. The *McIvor* case highlights other areas of discrimination that are currently being litigated, such as the ongoing differential treatment between the descendants of male Indians and those of female Indians. Not only do the various types of discrimination fostered by the registration provisions of the *Indian Act* offend the equality provisions of the *Charter,* they also complicate band membership codes, which more often than not rely on those provisions to determine band membership. Even self-government agreements that have already been signed are affected by status and band membership rules, and arguably continue to incorporate racist conceptions of Indigeneity that, in some respects, make them little better than the *Indian Act.* Until the issue of blood quantum discrimination and the severity of the harms suffered by the excluded are acknowledged and remedied, self-government citizenship codes will be little more than a perpetuation of the status quo.

Canada is only now coming to grips with the severe harm that results from the loss of identity, culture, and language which resulted from residential schools. These same harms, caused by the registration provisions of the *Indian Act* and by many band membership codes, are equal of severity and impact, despite their different origins. Some attention has been given to status under the *Indian Act* in recent years in academic literature, public media, and through ongoing litigation. While these are positive signs that there may be a shift in ideology, the effects of some band membership codes and self-government citizenship codes cannot be overlooked. As new codes are being contemplated, it is important to acknowledge the inherent dangers so as to avoid codes that echo the divisive registration provisions. This chapter reviews a selection of band membership codes and how they affect Aboriginality in terms of communal belonging or exclusion.

Band Membership

Band membership in Canada is a complex legal, political, cultural, and social issue affecting Indigenous peoples from the eastern shores of Atlantic Canada to the northern areas of Quebec and Ontario, and as far west as British Columbia. The issue of whether a person is a member of a band affects mostly "Indians" — i.e., those who are the descendants of First Nations or *Indian Act* bands, status and non-status alike. The most notable exceptions to the application of the current band membership rules under the *Indian Act* are the Métis and the Inuit. The Métis in Canada either belong to various provincial and national Métis organizations or to the Métis Settlements in Alberta. The Inuit in the northern parts of Canada were never placed on reserves, as they were specifically excluded from the application of the *Indian Act* pursuant to section 4(1).[1] Indigenous nations, on the other hand, have not had full control over their citizenship or community membership for some time. Indigenous nations have been divided into bands, and even band membership codes are creatures of the *Indian Act*. This, of course, has had an impact on individual Indigenous identity as well. Colonial governments took Indigenous nations and reorganized them into smaller, localized bands. This meant that one nation could be divided into·many bands. For example, there are 13 Mi'kmaq bands in Nova Scotia, nine in New Brunswick, one in Newfoundland, two in Prince Edward Island, two in Quebec, and one in Maine. Local issues became the focus as far as the administration of the *Indian Act* was concerned, as it was much easier for colonial governments to manage Indian affairs in individual, fragmented communities, than to deal with larger, more powerful nations.

Similarly, on an individual level, identification came to be based on registration and band membership under the *Indian Act*, as opposed to cultural and political affiliations with a particular Indigenous nation. Many Indigenous individuals now speak of themselves as status and non-status Indians as opposed to Mi'kmaq or Maliseet peoples. The band membership codes that are currently in place have caused many divisions and inequities among members and non-members. As discussed in the previous chapter, this federal system of Indian identification based on blood lines and gender was initially designed to assimilate Indian people. Indian status and band membership became tied to reserve residency rights and access to INAC programs and services, which caused inequality and division among families, friends, and community members. Even with the various *Indian Act* amendments that were made over time and the adoption of self-administered band membership codes, which were separate from the individual registration system, many inequalities remain. Indigenous nations, now divided into bands, have no control over any aspect of the federal rights and benefits that accrue to individuals with membership or registration (status). This situation remains today as bands struggle with bleak membership numbers for the future and even scarcer resources. Bands must consider the future implications of limited membership and citizenship criteria in their treaty, land claim, and self-government negotiations. While self-government agreements and treaty negotiations seem to offer some hope for change, the complex issues of identity and membership based on racist assumptions of the past have yet to be resolved.

Nations Divided

Prior to the 1985 amendments, Indian registration and band membership were basically one and the same. In order to become a band member, one had to be registered as an Indian under the *Indian Act*. After the 1985 Bill C-31 amendments, this was no longer necessarily the case.[2] The bands now had the option, pursuant to section 10 of the revised *Indian Act*, to make their own membership codes, which could differ greatly from the requirements necessary for individual Indians to obtain status under the *Act*. While previously registration and membership were one and the same, there is now a more complex registration system that causes numerous divisions within local band communities.[3] While the intention of the Bill C-31 amendment was to alleviate the gender discrimination found in the old *Indian Act, 1951*, it did not remedy all of it. The new *Act*, in fact, created additional distinctions based on an analogous ground I have called blood quantum/descent. The bands, in assuming jurisdiction over their membership codes, had to decide how they wanted to deal with the effects of the second generation cut-off rule found in section 6. A significant problem was created by INAC when it decided to use the registered Indian population for determining the financial allocations to the bands for federal programs and services, as band membership is no longer necessarily tied to registration. Therefore, if the bands were to create codes that allowed non-status Indians or non-Indigenous people to become members, they would not be federally funded for them.

Bands in Canada received legislative authority to assume control over their own membership from section 10 of the *Indian Act*. However, this section does not provide the criteria with which they must formulate their codes. As of 2002, 241 of the 614 First Nations bands in Canada were identified as having approved band membership codes.[4] For those bands that do not have their own membership codes, the *Indian Act* provisions apply. This is the situation for the majority of bands in Canada, and was in large part a reaction to the costs associated with welcoming new members without having first received funding from INAC.[5] Section 8 and 9 of the *Act* provide the basis for departmental power to maintain band membership lists:

8. There shall be maintained in accordance with this Act for each band a Band List in which shall be entered the name of every person who is a member of that band.

9. (1) Until such time as a band assumes control of its Band List, the Band List of that band shall be maintained in the Department by the Registrar.

(2) The names in a Band List of a band immediately prior to April 17, 1985 shall constitute the Band List of that band on April 17, 1985.

(3) The Registrar may at any time add to or delete from a Band List maintained in the Department the name of any person who, in accordance with this Act, is entitled or not entitled, as the case may be, to have his name included in that List.

(4) A Band List maintained in the Department shall indicate the date on which each name was added thereto or deleted there from.

(5) The name of a person who is entitled to have his name entered in a Band List maintained in the Department is not required to be entered therein unless an application for entry therein is made to the Registrar.[6]

Bands who have opted to take control over their own membership codes under section 10 of the *Act* must also maintain their own membership lists which are distinct from the Indian Register maintained by INAC. INAC's departmental Band Lists contain the names of those individuals who meet registration requirements and who are affiliated with a certain band. INAC maintains two separate lists of Indians: (1) status Indians who are affiliated with bands go on the Band List, which is maintained by the bands if they have their own membership codes, and if not, then members will be included on the lists maintained by INAC; and (2) status Indians who are not affiliated with a band are recorded under a list known as the General List.[7] Section 11 of the *Act* prescribes the rules for the membership lists which are maintained by INAC:

11. (1) Commencing on April 17, 1985, a person is entitled to have his name entered in a Band List maintained in the Department for a band if

(a) the name of that person was entered in the Band List for that band, or that person was entitled to have it entered in the Band List for that band, immediately prior to April 17, 1985;

(b) that person is entitled to be registered under paragraph 6(1)(b) as a member of that band;

(c) that person is entitled to be registered under paragraph 6(1)(c) and ceased to be a member of that band by reason of the circumstances set out in that paragraph; or

(d) that person was born on or after April 17, 1985 and is entitled to be registered under paragraph 6(1)(f) and both parents of that person are entitled to have their names entered in the Band List or, if no longer living, were at the time of death entitled to have their names entered in the Band List.[8]

Two years after the Bill C-31 amendments came into effect, section 11(2) regarding additional membership rules for departmental Band Lists also came into effect. This section applied to bands that did not take control over their own membership and allowed INAC to include other registered Indians, not previously included, on the departmental Band Lists as band members.

Essentially, anyone who was registered as an Indian prior to 1985 — those referred to in section 6(1)(a) — and anyone registered as an Indian under sections 6(1)(b)-(f) and section 6(2) could be included on the departmental Band Lists. As indicated earlier, these provisions are in effect for the majority of bands in Canada, and even some of those bands that have decided to adopt their own membership codes have simply adopted the *Indian Act* provisions or enacted *Indian Act* equivalent codes. Clatworthy notes that at least 377 of 609 bands studied (62 per cent) determine their membership according to the *Indian Act* rules — i.e., section 6 registration provisions. Another 58 bands (10 per cent) apply their own codes which are the equivalent of the *Indian Act* rules.[9] Therefore, the current registration provisions under section 6 of the *Act* affect more than just individual identity. For the majority of bands in Canada, section 6 provides the basis of communal membership and inclusion. Clatworthy compiled a list of the sub-groups that have been created by the Bill C-31 amendments which each band could possibly contain, depending on their particular membership code or lack thereof:

section 6(1) registered (status) members;
section 6(1) registered (status) non-members;
section 6(2) registered (status) members;
section 6(2) registered (status) non-members;
non-registered (non-status) members;
non-registered (non-status) non-members.[10]

With each of these categories comes a different set of rights, programs, and services, and differing levels of community acceptance of the individuals so affected. Other categories of band members, such as status versus non-status, or individuals who are excluded from band membership but are arguably rightful members, have similar interests in their home communities. The separation of band membership and Indian status not only fragments the populations of individual bands into further classes of Indians, but it also breaks down who is entitled to what in terms of programs and services, political and cultural rights, and individual identity and well-being.[11] All of this has an impact on the health and well-being of each local community and their larger Indigenous nation.

Despite the fact that Indigenous nations in Canada had always been self-determining, the majority of bands today — roughly 72 per cent — still allow their membership codes to be determined by section 6 of the *Indian Act, 1985*.[12] Even those that assumed control over their band membership codes have not necessarily loosened the membership criteria or addressed the discrimination which is incorporated through reliance on the *Act*. Sixty-four bands have two-parent descent rules; 22 use a type of blood quantum code to restrict their membership.[13] Unlike Indigenous citizenship from pre-colonial days, membership in most bands today is not automatically granted upon birth, but through an application process. Individuals are required to "apply" to become members, just as they do under the *Indian Act*. Considerations such as what process will be used to determine membership is distinct from the actual criteria, but can have an effect on the number of members. It can also affect how membership is viewed — whether it is seen as no different than membership in any organization, or whether it is viewed as citizenship, a right that passes from generation to generation within a people or nation.[14]

Colonial control over local community membership and Indian registration has interfered with the natural evolution of Indigenous identity. This need to control Indian numbers in order to limit legal and financial obligations appears to have been passed down from federal agents and government policy makers to band administrators and Indigenous leaders. While some First Nations do not subscribe to these views, others, like the Sawridge Band, have developed highly exclusionary membership rules.[15] Now the focus of many band leaders is to ensure that there is enough land, housing, and resources to address the needs of their members, overshadowing concerns about whether their national identity is protected or whether their community will survive into the future. In the past, one could assume that the bigger the nation, the stronger the nation. However, the more recent reliance on federal funds for every aspect of community life means that more band members without Indian status reduces the funding available to provide for basic necessities. Indigenous nations did not become great nations because of federal funding, and while the federal government has a great deal of debt repayment to do, the basis of band membership or citizenship in Indigenous nations should not be based on the government's financial priorities.

One might not expect that bands from the same Indigenous nation would have completely different membership codes, given that they share the same history, culture, traditions, and practices. But extended families can have members who are status and non-status Indians, and band members and non-band members, depending on factors like sex and blood quantum. While some bands allow the adoption of non-Indian children as members and allow the registration of non-Indian spouses as band members, there is no consistency among bands in this regard. Few bands actually incorporate non-status Indians as members. The current rates of exogamous parenting — parenting between Indians and non-Indians, also referred to as out-parenting — also have a major effect on band membership and registration numbers. As of 2002, the rates of exogamous parenting among bands in Canada were:

Low: below 20 per cent (25 bands)
Moderately Low: between 20 - 39.9 per cent (111 bands)
Moderate: between 40 - 59.9 per cent (246 bands)
Moderately high: between 60 - 79.9 per cent (162 bands)
High: 80 per cent or more (49 bands)[16]

Based on the above numbers, the majority of bands in Canada (457 bands, or 77 per cent) have moderate to high rates of parenting with non-Indians. Of these bands, approximately 47,700 individuals, or 6.6 per cent of the population, either had no membership, no registration, or neither registration nor membership.[17] This group was also found to be more likely to live off reserve than on, and made up less than two per cent of the overall on-reserve population.[18] This reality, taken together with the fact that a majority of bands also use *Indian Act* rules for their membership codes, means that the second generation cut-off rule either is affecting or will affect the majority of bands in the near future. Loss of communal membership and legally recognized individual identities as Indians is a significant issue facing Indigenous peoples that cannot wait another 20 to 30 years to be addressed.

Within the next 75 years, it is expected that non-members will grow from the 2002 level of 44,000 individuals to 456,000.[19] Clatworthy found in his study that "[t]he high rates of exogamous parenting which characterize off-reserve populations are expected to result in very rapid growth in the population that lacks eligibility for membership."[20] He concluded: "The vast majority of those lacking eligibility for membership are also projected to lack entitlement to Indian registration."[21] The majority of this group are the descendants of women who have suffered discrimination under the *Indian Act*.[22]

Residual discrimination continues to "cut-off" present and future generations, and may well lead to similar patterns in the future. This, coupled with the second generation cut-off rule, means that large numbers of non-Indians are created who have to live off reserve, which may even affect the rates of out-marriage and, thus, the creation of additional people without status or membership. It is easy to see how such a formula, which was originally designed to assimilate Indigenous peoples, will continue to fulfill its purpose.

The current band membership codes contain a mix of criteria based on *Indian Act* registration criteria or out-dated racial criteria based on notions of blood purity. Some band membership codes also contain residency requirements which disentitle anyone who has not or does not live on a reserve. Requirements related to occupation, health, and financial status which are not applied equally to those who are already members may further disadvantage applicants for membership who suffer the same poor socio-economic conditions as those who live on reserve. Even the cultural and language requirements can be largely out the control of the applicants if they have lived away from the reserve and their extended families because of the discriminatory provisions of the *Indian Act* and band membership provisions.[23]

Band Membership Codes

The Band membership codes reviewed in this section are those that were provided by INAC on an Access to Information request. They are the codes that were originally submitted to INAC after the 1985 amendments to the *Indian Act*. Section 10 of the *Act* allowed the bands to assume control of their membership codes, but they were under no requirement to do so. If they did assume control over their membership, they were required to provide proof that their codes were assented to by a majority of the electors of the band, and to submit a copy of their code to INAC. However, there was no requirement that the bands send updated codes or provide copies of amendments. Therefore, the codes that are accessible publicly through INAC may have been rescinded, amended, or may not be used at all. Clatworthy, who attempted an updated study of the codes, found that not all the bands were still using their membership codes, not all the codes had been approved by INAC, and not all the bands had responded to his requests for updated information.[24] He also notes that, while most bands reported that they are still using their membership codes to determine membership in their communities, some are not. Some bands have a moratorium on new members, some do not follow their codes, and some simply let the chief and council decide.[25] Therefore, while this section refers to various band codes and their possible impact on individuals, the actual impacts will depend in large part on whether the codes are updated, whether the codes are actually used, whether the bands adhere to each aspect of the code uniformly, and how each criterion is interpreted. Despite these issues, the membership codes are illustrative of the general priorities with regard to what many bands consider important to include in membership criteria. These criteria can have significant impacts on individuals as well as on the future of the communities. They are also, more often than not, the starting points for the citizenship rolls in self-government agreements.

The band membership codes analyzed in this chapter were reviewed for several key themes. Each was reviewed to see if it was possible for their code to allow non-status Indians or descendants to become members; whether the band considered culture, customs, or traditional criteria to be important; whether applicants were afforded a probationary period to learn the customs; whether blood quantum or degree of blood was a factor; whether residency was required; and whether they allowed non-Indigenous people to become members in any capacity — through adoption or marriage, for example. This chapter does not undertake a review of each possible criterion, but compares the demographics and rates of out-marriage with the code itself to determine whether and how soon a band has determined its own legislative extinction. I have compared selected band codes with the example band codes selected by Clatworthy. The example band codes represent certain key features, like what kind of code they use and their rates of out-marriage. By providing detailed information on several bands, the rest of the band codes in Canada were ranked according to which example band they most closely matched in Clatworthy's study.[26]

Noting that 236 bands had their own particular codes and 360 bands remained under the *Indian Act* provisions, Clatworthy found that there were four general types of band membership codes:

One-parent rules: A one-parent descent rule declares a person to be eligible for membership based on the eligibility or membership of *one* of that person's parents. One-parent descent rules are found in 90 First Nations or 38 percent of the 236 that adopted membership codes.

Two-parent rules: A two-parent descent rule establishes a person's eligibility based on the eligibility or membership of *both* of that person's parents. Rules of this type are found in 67 First Nations, 28 percent of the 236 with codes.

Blood quantum rules: A blood quantum rule establishes eligibility based on the "amount of Indian blood" a person possesses. In effect, a blood quantum measures the number of Indian ancestors a person has and sets a criterion for membership based on an amount of ancestry. Thirty (30) First Nations (13 per cent of the 236) have adopted blood quantum rules.

A typical criterion is 50 percent Indian blood, a standard set by 21 of the 30, though there are examples of codes that set higher and lower criteria. The "arithmetic" of blood quantum codes measures a person's quantum by adding the quantum of each parent and dividing by 2. The child of parents who are 100 percent and 0 percent Indian is 50 percent, as is the child of two parents who are 50 per cent Indian.

Indian Act rules: These rules are embodied in the Act's Sections 6(1) and 6(2). . . . Forty-nine (49) First Nations, or 21 percent of the 236 that have adopted codes, implicitly rely on the Indian Act rules to determine eligibility for membership. Indian Act rules also pertain to the 360 First Nations that have *not* adopted membership codes and whose membership is, therefore, still regulated by the Act.[27]

In every region in Canada, one can find examples of the above types of codes, some of which have additional criteria such as residency requirements or cultural knowledge. So, while one First Nation may have adopted a one-parent code that allows for the possibility of a non-status Indian to become a member in theory, in practice, if they do not have enough traditional knowledge or they do not live on the reserve, they could still be excluded from membership. There is no way of knowing how bands interpret and apply their codes without full disclosure of their membership activities.

The St. Basile Band (formerly known as the Edmunston Band, but now the Madawaska Maliseet First Nation) in northern New Brunswick, is part of the larger Maliseet Nation that occupies parts of New Brunswick. Their membership code allows the descendents of their "original" members to apply to be considered as members.[28] Although their code contains a one-parent descent rule, it does not guarantee that the applicant having only one parent who is a band member will be granted membership status. It appears to mean that, while they are not barred outright from applying, as is the case in the majority of Atlantic bands, they could still be barred due to additional criteria.

The code tends to read the same as Canada's submissions in *McIvor* — i.e., they characterize Indigenous peoples as a historical group, and everyone who came afterward is either a new group (such as restored or reinstated people) or are their descendants.[29] This view sees Indigenous peoples as having only existed at some point arbitrarily frozen in time. Any current Indigenous peoples are only the watered-down descendants of that group and not the actual Indigenous group itself. This restrictive view not only allows Canada to limit how many generations of descendants can be considered Indian, but membership codes that are framed in this way incorporate this type of backdoor assimilatory ideology to their own detriment.

The code provides that individual applicants must submit their applications for membership in the band to the membership committee. This committee is made up of eight people, being two representatives from each of the four "original" families as defined in section 3. (2) of the code.[30] This membership committee reviews the information submitted by each applicant and makes a recommendation to the chief and council on whether to accept or reject the application. A majority of council can accept or reject an application for membership, and any applicants who are denied membership and want a review of that decision must apply to the band tribunal. The band tribunal itself is also made up of a committee comprised of the four "original" families. This focus leads one to wonder what will become of the community when the original families have departed. Will they no longer be a historical Indigenous group?

This code differentiates between different types of members — i.e. "original," "restored," "descendant," and "adopted" members. Each category details how each person came about their membership — for example, whether they always had membership or whether they are a newcomer. The criteria applied to each of the membership categories is quite different. The original and restored members are entitled to have their names entered on the band membership list as of right, whereas the two categories of descendant members, the descendant and adopted members, must not only apply for membership, but must meet additional criteria not required of the original and restored members. For example, the two categories of descendant members must show that they have Indian blood and are descendants of a member of the St. Basile Indian Band. This is not required of the original or restored members, and allows non-Indigenous and non-registered women who married registered Indian men to gain Indian status and band membership regardless of the fact that they were not Indigenous and did not have "Indian blood." According to these rules, these women and their children would be members as of right in the band, but the descendants of Indigenous band members (band members with Indian blood) would have to prove they have Indian blood. The only children who appear to be able to be band members on a go-forward basis are those with Indian blood and not those non-Indigenous children who were legally or traditionally adopted by band members. It is thus apparent that the blood/descent criteria is applied selectively and only to certain types of members — i.e. those outside the historical group.

An additional part of the application process for potential members to Madawaska would be to demonstrate their knowledge and loyalty with regard to the "ways of life of the Band."[31] Nations can be divided into several bands, and it is not clear in some of these codes if they are referring to local practices or those of the larger nation, although in most cases, it is likely a combination of the two. On one hand, this type of criterion could be viewed as a means of protecting and promoting the culture and traditions of their local community. On the other hand, the code does not provide for how the membership committee would determine whether one has met the standard of being familiar enough with the language, customs, and history of the band to merit membership, and whether intervening factors such as residential schools, previous *Indian Act* discrimination, lack of housing on reserve, and assimilationist policies against Indigenous peoples in general would be considered in weighing the factors in an applicant's qualifications. One aspect of this code that could be useful is that it allows for a five-year probation period for applicants to obtain the required knowledge. The only unclear part of this probationary period is whether there is a residency requirement, as one of the criteria speaks to how long the applicant has lived among the band. A question which might be raised by "new" members is whether the original and restored members are also all loyal and know the ways of the band, and whether the additional criteria imposed on "new" members are fair and just in light of the lack of similar requirements for "original" or "restored" members. Do all the original and restored members know the language and the customs of the band? If not, one must consider the issue of the fairness of having different criteria for different member categories.

Another issue that might affect how Madawaska views its membership numbers is the extremely high rate of out-marriage in their community[32] — measured in 1992 as 93.5 per cent, one of the highest out-marriage rates for all the bands in Canada.[33] Their Bill C-31 population at the time (those who were restored under the 1985 amendments and whose children were immediately affected by the second generation cut-off rule) was 42 per cent.[34] This is also high, and can affect the number of people in the future who can have both registration and membership. According to Clatworthy's analysis of bands with similar membership codes, St. Basile (Madawaska) is most like the Sheshaht Band (now known as the Tseshaht First Nation) in terms of population forecasts.[35] While initially their registered Indian population should increase for the first 60 years to about 73 per cent larger than its current level, the same population is expected to gradually decrease to about 50 per cent larger than its current level, based on the Tseshaht comparison.[36] The membership population, on the other hand, will increase at first and then level off.[37] However, these forecasts for Tseshaht are based on their low out-marriage rates and their one-parent descent rule. These projections also do not reflect the further restrictions that might be imposed by the subjective membership criteria. Although the St. Basile Band can be generally compared to the Sheshaht band in terms of population forecasts owing to the type of membership code they have, St. Basile's significantly higher rate of out-marriage and their own additional membership criteria mean that they are likely to have a lower registered Indian population and much lower membership numbers than their comparison band. This is significant both for the future of the community as a whole, which currently has barely more than 230 registered Indians associated with their band, whereas the Sheshaht have over 679 registered Indians.[38]

The Eel River Band (now referred to as Eel River Bar First Nation) in northern New Brunswick has a band membership code that lays out the formula for its own extinction within a few generations. As explained in the Introduction, this is the band from which my family descends, of which my father, Frank Palmater, was a member, and of which I will be a member. This band is also part of the larger Mi'kmaq Nation that occupies New Brunswick, Nova Scotia, Prince Edward, Newfoundland, Quebec, and parts of the United States. Their code is an example of a two-parent membership rule. It does not state who shall make the decisions regarding membership, nor does it provide an appeal or review mechanism for applicants. In order to be a member, one basically had to be a registered Indian and band member prior to the Bill C-31 amendments in 1985, or both one's parents had to be or were entitled to be band members — i.e., the two-parent rule. This band has no other criteria, such as cultural knowledge, residency, or language. Though they do not specifically reference blood quantum, they have incorporated blood quantum/descent through their adoption of the *Indian Act* provisions. In effect, the code would bar all section 6(2) registered Indians from applying for membership, because section 6(2) Indians are registered by the fact that only one of their parents is a section 6(1) Indian and a band member. With only one parent as a band member, they would automatically be excluded as members, even if they lived on the reserve or spoke the language or had substantial familial, social, and historical ties to the community.[39] If this was still Eel River's code, then my father would have been barred from membership as a section 6(2) Indian, but I understand it has been amended. While one incentive for the band to have this kind of criteria is that they would be able to keep membership numbers low and, therefore, have fewer members for which to provide programs and services, the significant downside is that the population projections for this community are grim.

Eel River Bar had an out-marriage rate of 54.7 per cent in 1992, and had a Bill C-31 population of 19.1 per cent.[40] Clatworthy noted that Eel River Bar is most similar in population forecasts to that of the Golden Lake Band.[41] Therefore, as with Golden Lake Band, Eel River Bar can expect only modest growth in its registered Indian population in the first 25 years of the projection period (1991 to 2016), which would be followed by "very rapid declines in the size of the population."[42] By the end of the projection period, the registered Indian population would be reduced to about 40 per cent of its current level.[43] The population entitled to membership is expected to decline for the entire projection period (1991-2091), such that within 50 years the band's population would be reduced to 50 per cent of the current level and, at the end of that period, it would have been reduced to only five per cent of the current level. These grim figures are made worse by the fact that the Golden Lake Band only had an out-marriage rate of 32 per cent for those living on reserve, whereas Eel River Bar's is over 54 per cent.[44] The Golden Lake First Nation (now Algonquins of Pikwakanagan) have an on-reserve registered population of 408 and an off-reserve population of 1574, whereas Eel River Bar's current population is only 319 registered Indians on reserve and 281 off.[45] The base level populations where each band starts from also affects how quickly their populations can diminish by virtue of the *Indian Act* registration provisions or their own band membership codes, as is the case with the restrictive two-parent descent codes. Eel River Bar, already a tiny community, cannot afford to exclude significant numbers of potential members if it wishes to continue as a community into the future. Given that this is my home band, I would hope that bringing knowledge of this urgent situation to the community would encourage them to amend their code for the benefit of our current and future generations.

The Parry Island Band (now known as Wasauksing First Nation) is located on Georgian Bay in Ontario and is comprised of the Ojibway, Odawa, and Pottawatami peoples.[46] Within their band membership code, the Parry Island band assert their inherent right to determine the citizenship of their own First Nation, and explain that the purpose of their code is both to preserve their cultural and political integrity and to ensure that "future generations will continue to enjoy the rights and obligations" of citizenship.[47] At first glance, their code seems to be based on sound considerations. However, on further reading, it uses a blood quantum rule to determine "citizenship."[48] The blood quantum ranges from 50 per cent and 65 per cent to 75 per cent. Their specific type of acceptable "blood" is what they refer to as "First Nation blood." This is what allows them to accept band members from other bands who would not necessarily be of Ojibway or Parry Island community blood. It would appear by this code that Parry Island will allow the blood of other Indigenous nations to be inter-mixed with that of their community, but not the blood of any others. However, given that status under previous *Indian Acts* allowed non-Indigenous women to become members, their blood quantum analysis appears to be largely a work of fiction. This code also establishes a citizenship roll, enrolment officers, and a citizenship committee comprised of elders, council, youth, and regular citizens.[49] The citizenship committee makes the recommendations regarding the acceptance or rejection of each application to the band, which has the final decision.[50] There is no review or appeal mechanism, except that applicants who have had their applications rejected may reapply if they provide new information.[51]

Parry Island Band had an out-marriage rate of 51.6 per cent in 1992, and their Bill C-31 population was 34.4 per cent.[52] Clatworthy noted that their band membership code most closely resembles that of the Gibson Band (now known as the Wahta Mohawk).[53] The Gibson Band's membership code also used a blood quantum rule.[54] Therefore, the registered Indian population in Parry Island (based on the Gibson Band projections) is expected to remain stable for the first 15 years of the projection period (1991-2006), but will rapidly decline throughout the rest of the projection period (to the end of 2091), until it is reduced to about 25 per cent of its current size.[55] Similarly, the membership population will remain stable for the first 15 years of the projection period, and then rapidly decline until the membership population is reduced to only 17 per cent of the current level by the end of 2091.[56] According to Clatworthy, "The last child with eligibility for membership is projected to be born during the 2081-2086 period. After that time, no descendants of the current member population would qualify for membership."[57]

The Gibson band's rate of out-marriage is 66 per cent and their registered Indian population is currently 169 on reserve and 510 off reserve for a total of 679.[58] Parry Island's total registered population is 991.[59] By way of comparison, the Gibson band has a blood quantum requirement of 50 per cent, whereas Parry Island's requirements are 50 per cent blood quantum for people born before 1990, 60 per cent blood for people born between 1990 and 2010, and 75 per cent blood for people born after 2010. This formula mixes both an increasing blood quantum requirement with very high rates of out-marriage (51.6 per cent). As a result, both bands will see their last eligible child entitled to membership born much sooner than other bands.

The last example of a band membership code is one that follows the *Indian Act* rules either by choice (i.e., having assumed control of band membership and enacted their own code which follows the *Indian Act*), or by default (choosing not to assume control over band membership, so that the *Indian Act* rules apply by default). This situation applies to the majority of bands in Canada. The sample band I have chosen is the Millbrook Band in Nova Scotia, which forms part of the larger Mi'kmaq Nation in the Atlantic region. As of 1992, the Millbrook Band's membership was determined solely by the requirements of the *Indian Act*.[60] It was the same case for Six Nations (now referred to as Six Nations of the Grand River).[61] Therefore, the closest comparison for the Millbrook Band in terms of registration and membership population is Six Nations of the Grand River.[62] Since Six Nations did not adopt their own band membership code, its membership is still determined by the *Indian Act*, which means that INAC's Indian Register and membership list for Six Nations would likely contain the same individuals (i.e., if one was registered, one was a member).[63] The population entitled to membership is expected to grow in the first 35 year period (1991-2026) but will then rapidly decline until it is 20 per cent smaller than the present population by the end of the projection period (2091).[64] Clatworthy concludes: "Further declines in the size of the member population would occur beyond the projection time frame."[65] These two bands are very similar in that their out-marriage rates were almost identical at 27.3 per cent and 27.5 per cent, respectively. Similarly, their Bill C-31 populations were 24.4 per cent and 22.6 per cent, respectively.

While there were many similarities between the two bands, there is also one significant difference between the Millbrook Band and Six Nations that could affect their "extinction dates." How fast their registered populations would decline is affected by their current population numbers. In 1991, Millbrook's registered population was 809, whereas Six Nations' registered population was 16,697.[66] This gives Six Nations more time to address their membership issues. In the end, the *Indian Act* rules for determining band membership have similar results to using sections 6(1) and 6(2) to determine the registration status of Indians. The second generation cut-off within section 6 means that band membership is also limited by the second generation cut-off. Coupled with the reality of out-marriage, the *Indian Act* rules for determining both registration (status) and band membership spells the eventual legislated extinction of status Indians and band members for both Six Nations and Millbrook.

While all these band membership codes fall into one or another category, what is not reflected in those categories is the additional criteria that may be used to further restrict membership numbers that make the actual forecasts of future population numbers entitled to membership likely larger than they are in reality. The numbers reviewed above cannot therefore be viewed as worst case scenarios.[67] Whether or not individuals will be approved for membership based on these additional criteria, or even how these criteria are interpreted or applied by various band councils or membership committees is also unknown. For example, the Mowachaht Band only had a 1.4 per cent Bill C-31 population and a 21 per cent out-marriage rate in 1991.[68] Their current registered population is 316 off reserve and 235 on reserve, for a total of 541.[69] They also adopted their band membership code on the basis of their "inherent right to determine who their own people are" and created the rules based on the belief that their "ancestral roots never fade."[70] The basis for their rules appear to be taking into consideration their future generations. But other factors can also lead to a decline in population numbers, depending on their application. According to their rules, the following people are some of those entitled to have their names entered on the band membership list: anyone whose name was or was entitled to be on the Band List prior to the adoption of the code; anyone who has two parents who are band members; anyone who has one parent who is a band member; and anyone under the age of 18 who is of Aboriginal descent and has been adopted by a band member.[71] They are a band whose population forecasts closely resemble that of the Sheshaht Band: membership numbers will rise initially and then level off, whereas registration numbers will eventually decline.[72]

What is different about the Mowachaht Band membership code as compared to the majority of codes is that they also include the following provision which details how band members can lose membership in the band:

6.(1) Notwithstanding any other provision of these Rules, a person who is of the full age of eighteen years and who is entitled to be a member of Mowachaht Band of Indians and who is registered in the Mowachaht Band List and who is a grave threat to the Mowachaht Band or the members of the Mowachaht Band may have his name removed from the Mowachaht Band List and lose entitlement to have his name so registered.

By way of example, grave threat includes continued child sexual abuse, continued selling of liquor or drugs to children or endangering the lives of Mowachaht Band members.[73]

The section goes on to provide that no one will be removed from the band list without a fair hearing, a recommendation by the membership committee that he or she be removed, and a vote by a majority of the adult band members to remove that person's name.[74] The membership committee consists of five people appointed by the band who are band members and live on the reserve.[75] It is not known how many band members have actually lost their membership status from this provision, nor is the scope of this provision known. It also appears from the wording of their code that the off-reserve band members do not have a say in membership applications or decisions about the loss of membership by individuals, because residence on the reserve is one of the criteria for being a membership decision-maker.[76]

Several other bands have similar provisions regarding how band members can lose membership status. The Ehattesaht Band, for example, is a community of Nuu-chah-nulth (formerly known as the Nootkas) located in British Columbia, with a Bill C-31 population of 5.8 per cent and an out-marriage rate of 7 per cent in 1991.[77] Their current registered population is 209 off reserve and 116 on reserve, for a total of 325.[78] Their membership code provides that "Ehattesaht Indian Band Membership Rules shall protect, nurture and pay special attention to Nuu-chah-nulth Culture, Heritage, Traditions and Language, as practiced by our forefathers now and in the future," and "shall especially protect and safeguard the Ehattesaht/Nuu-chah-nulth Identity, of our children now and forever."[79] They go on to explain that their philosophy of government is based on a better life for all their people and that their chief and council speak for their children and elders.[80] They further explain that their membership rules will be used as "the vehicle for the continuing existence of Ehattesahts as Aboriginal People and ensuring the longevity of the Ehattesaht Communities by: Safeguarding all, what we were, what are now and what we hope to be in the future as Ehattesahts."[81]

Like the Mowachaht, the Ehattesaht Band also resembles the Sheshaht in terms of population projections: membership initially increases and then levels off, whereas registration numbers eventually decline.[82] In part, they include as band members those who were previously on the band list, those with two parents who are band members, illegitimate children whose registration was rejected, and native children adopted by Ehattesaht Band members.[83] They also include: "All those persons who can prove their Ehattesaht/Nuu-chah-nulth Ancestry through direct or collateral lineage, whether maternal or paternal."[84] This appears to be an inclusive membership code allowing those with direct familial connections to the band to become members. Their code goes on to specify who is not entitled to apply, which includes those without Aboriginal descent, which is defined in their code as someone "who can not prove a blood relationship to an ancestor."[85] It also includes a section on what applicants need to include with their applications and what rules they need to live by in order to be granted band membership. The most important criterion for membership, as stated by the code, is the respect of Ehattesaht traditions and customs.[86]

Another criterion involves a residency requirement.[87] This could prove to be very exclusive of otherwise eligible band members in the future, and significantly reduce the otherwise level membership population numbers forecast by the Sheshaht model. Given that their current off-reserve population nearly doubles that of their on-reserve population (209 versus 116), a significant number of potential band members could be excluded by this requirement.

Another difference between this code and others is that the Ehattesaht Band includes a provision on how some members can lose their membership — namely, female band members can lose their membership upon marriage to a non-band member. This provision only applies to female band members and is similar to the kind of discrimination challenged by Sandra Lovelace and Jeanette Lavell.[88] While the band may argue that this code is not based on *Indian Act* provisions but merely represents their tradition in this regard, one must remember that any Aboriginal right to determine citizenship based on section 35 of the *Constitution Act, 1982* cannot discriminate between men and women as per section 35(4).[89] Similarly, any claim of protection of their membership traditions through section 25 of the *Charter* would also be limited by section 28, which ensures that all rights are granted equally to men and women.

The above marrying-out provision only speaks to marriages between members of different bands. It does not speak to the possibility of a marriage between a female band member and a non-Indigenous person — although, if one follows the same logic, the band will presumably withdraw her membership. If this is the case, and the rate of out-marriage remains steady or increases, then more and more female band members will be at risk of losing their band membership, affecting their children's rights as well. The band would have re-created the section 12(1)(b) scenario all over again, further reducing band membership numbers under the guise of tradition. Male band members do not have to be concerned with losing their membership by virtue of marriage.

The Matsqui Band is part of the Sto:lo Nation of British Columbia, with a registered population of 135 people off reserve and 99 people on, for a total of 234.[90] In 1991, they had a Bill C-31 population of 30.8 per cent and an out-marriage rate of 63.8 per cent. Based on this information, the Matsqui Band most resembles the Sheshaht Band in terms of population forecasts. Not only did the Matsqui Band enact their membership code in order to "protect the cultural integrity" of their community; they also designed their code with a view to maintaining "social harmony" and "enhancing economic stability" among the members of the band.[91] This is one of several bands that explicitly stated that economic reasons form part of their membership criteria and decisions. Their band membership code allows base enrolees (those previously entitled to have their names on the band list) and the children of base enrolees to be band members.[92] The code also allows "restored members" (those who had lost status under the old *Indian Act* and regained it with the Bill C-31 amendments) to be members, but does not allow the children of restored members to become members until "the Band is granted or acquires additional lands to accommodate them."[93] Despite the population forecasts for band membership rising initially and then levelling off, this additional criterion could drastically reduce their membership numbers if the amount of land they acquire never exceeds the land required for current band members and for special projects such as schools, offices, and economic development projects.

This criterion is obviously beyond the control of potential applicants for membership and is further complicated by residency criteria for those who are already approved band members. There is also an "abandonment of residency" clause which states: "If any member abandons his residence on the Matsqui Reserve for a minimum period of one year, that person may be removed from the Matsqui Band list if his absence causes the Matsqui Band to assume a financial liability on his behalf."[94] It is not clear from the code what form that financial liability would take, but a strict application of this provision could significantly reduce membership numbers, given that the majority of the registered population at Matsqui already live off reserve and many may have to move away for work, school, or personal reasons, given the high rate of out-marriage. This clause appears to discriminate between on- and off-reserve band members based only on residency and finances. The *Corbiere* case held that Aboriginality residence was an analogous ground under section 15 of the *Charter* and that the denial of voting rights to off-reserve band members amounted to discrimination.[95] With regard to the Matsqui, not only do they differentiate between band members on the basis of reserve residency and finances, but they could deny band membership itself on that basis.

The Sucker Creek Band is part of the Cree Nation from Alberta.[96] They had a Bill C-31 population of 36.5 per cent, an out-marriage rate of 64 per cent in 1991, and their current registered population is 1,672 people off reserve and 681 on reserve, for a total of 2,353.[97] Their population forecasts most closely resemble those of the Gibson Band (Wahta Mohawks), especially with regard to their registered populations.[98] This band, too, asserts its "inherent right and traditional authority to control its membership," and bases its membership code both on the "principles of fundamental fairness and the rules of natural justice" as well as the "values, customs, and traditions of the Sucker Creek Band."[99] The band adds an additional interpretive provision which aims to protect the individual Aboriginal and treaty rights of its members against its own membership code:

> This code shall not be applied or interpreted in any manner that abrogates or derogates from or denies any of the existing aboriginal and treaty rights of the members of the Sucker Creek Band or of any of the existing Aboriginal and Treaty rights of any individuals that might apply for membership to the Sucker Creek Indian Band.[100]

This section could invalidate several of its own membership provisions. For example, the Sucker Creek membership code provides that children with parents who are both band members are automatically entitled to become band members upon submission of proof of parentage, whereas children who only have one parent who is a band member must both make application to and seek approval of the band council. [101] These latter applicants are also subjected to further considerations not imposed on the former group:

1) The person's previous conduct and circumstance as is relevant to the person's compatibility with the customs and way of life of the Sucker Creek Band;

2) The person's knowledge of the history, customs, culture and way of life of the Sucker Creek Band; or

3) The person's contribution or potential for contribution to the benefit and well-being of the Sucker Creek Band.[102]

They further add that admission will be contingent on proof that the member will not be "harmful to the interests of the band" and that the band council has the sole discretion to determine whether or not it has "sufficient land, housing and resources to provide services to present and additional members."[103] The Sucker Creek Band also reserves the right to consider any other factor raised by any other band member in relation to an application for membership.[104]

This means that, in addition to having a population significantly affected by high rates of out-marriage and a high Bill C-31 population, they can expect to have a registered Indian population of less than 25 per cent of its current size by

2091.[105] If they apply their membership code strictly to the children who only have one parent as a band member, then it is reasonable to assume that they could expect declines in membership population similar to those who have two-parent band membership codes. Their additional discretionary factors, such as ensuring they have sufficient land, housing, and resources, could affect their future membership populations and even lead to moratoriums on membership.[106] Although the code is based on fairness and justice, it would appear that any irrelevant issue can be taken into consideration. Without knowing how this code is applied in practice, it leaves the door open for inappropriate personal issues to find their way into the decision-making process. Similarly, if members are found to have an Aboriginal right to belong to their nation, and therefore a similar right to belong to their band, it would appear that the band code would be over-ruled by virtue of the Aboriginal rights having paramountcy.

Economic factors influence the determination of membership in Sucker Creek as well as other bands with membership codes. The difference is that not all bands have been so forthright about stating this in their codes. Economic factors are often out of the control of individual applicants and can act as major obstacles to obtaining membership status if that criterion is strictly applied. A few bands have even instituted a fee for specific types of membership applications and appeals that may also be prohibitive to some. Having a specified blood quantum or being directly descended from a blood relative was also common to a good number of band codes. Some bands have even included a provision that, after so many years of their band membership code being in effect, they will perform a review of their list to ensure that every person on it is of Indigenous descent. One matrilineal band adapted their code to adjust to modern realities of out-marriage and incorporated patrilineal descent to determine membership where necessary. The issue of children being adopted into and out of a band was addressed in a significant number of membership codes as well. Many of the bands restricted membership to those adopted children who were of "Indian blood." Some also incorporated some form of residency requirement, either in terms of their initial membership application criteria or incorporated into their rules on how to lose band membership. Knowledge of the band's traditions and customs and ways of life were also common criteria for new applicants, as was a commitment to the common good of the band or having ties to the community. The purpose of the probationary period was to allow new applicants time to meet one of two criteria: to learn the traditions and customs of the band or to take up residence on the reserve.

Other factors that have been taken into account when reviewing applications for band membership in various codes include: being of good character; whether one's behaviour might encourage criminal activity or whether one has a criminal record; the applicant's medical report or records; being financially stable or self-supporting; the contribution of personal and economic resources to the band;

one's skills and employment record; knowing the traditional language; being affiliated with the tribe; a knowledge of band government; the responsibility to foster and respect one's people; respect for the elders; respect or obedience to the chief and council; participation in band affairs; the performance of community service; and compliance with band by-laws and regulations. It is interesting to note that few, if any, bands made any exceptions in their membership codes for applicants who may have trouble meeting any or all of the criteria due to life circumstances caused by previous discriminatory applications of the *Indian Act* within their families. Some bands also had provisions that allow members to submit petitions if they do not wish certain individuals to become members. It was not clear under what circumstances this might be relevant.

Regardless of the additional criteria, as long as the bands fit into the two-parent, blood quantum or *Indian Act* codes, they have doomed themselves to legislated extinction. Their additional criteria, depending on how they are implemented, may help extinguish their communities at a faster rate. The one-parent codes offer the most hope, as long as the additional criteria do not limit membership and end up maintaining the status quo. Some individuals and bands are putting their faith in future self-government agreements and hoping that citizenship codes will offer a new way to rebuild communities and nations. But if self-government agreements base their citizenship codes on the *Indian Act* or band membership codes that incorporate those same criteria, then one must ask whether self-government agreements are really the solution, or do they merely maintain the status quo under a new guise?

Self-Government Citizenship

Self-government agreements are no longer just an idea for the future, something to aspire to, or a distant hope. A number of self-government agreements have already been negotiated, ratified, and implemented. There are also comprehensive land claims agreements, referred to as "modern treaties," that have been negotiated to include many of the same powers and authorities that can be found under a self-government agreement. While the negotiations for both types of agreement are based on their own separate federal policy, they can, in effect, bring about similar results for the bands or nations that partake in them.[107] Among the Indigenous nations or groups that have negotiated self-government agreements are the Carcross/Tagish, Kwanlin Dun, and Westbank First Nations.[108] Among those who have negotiated comprehensive land claim agreements, or modern treaties, are the Council for Yukon Indians, the Sahtu Dene and Métis, and the Nisga'a.[109]

Within these comprehensive claims agreements, some of the groups have also been able to negotiate self-government-type provisions or agreements, so the self-government agreements reviewed in this chapter could be from agreements that have originated from either or both of these processes. It should also be noted that the majority of bands, Indigenous nations, and Indigenous groups in Canada do not have self-government agreements. As federal policy favours negotiation tables where the province is a willing partner, there are many Indigenous groups who are unable to commence tri-lateral negotiations owing to provincial opposition or lack of interest. While bi-lateral negotiations may be possible, Canada's stated preference is to have the province or territory at the table.[110]

The RCAP's Aboriginal "Citizen"

The Royal Commission on Aboriginal Peoples commenced in 1991 and issued its final report in 1996, comprising five volumes and 4,000 pages.[111] It had 440 recommendations, calling for everything from official recognition of the Métis to the dismantling and replacement of the Department of Indian Affairs. The *RCAP Report* was generally well-accepted among Aboriginal people, and created an expectation of positive response from the federal government. The response, entitled "Gathering Strength," outlined a four-pronged approach to address the RCAP's recommendations:

Renewing the Partnership. This commitment included an initial Statement of Reconciliation acknowledging historic injustices to Aboriginal peoples and the establishment of a $350-million "healing fund" to address the legacy of abuse in the residential school system. Other elements related, among other things, to the preservation and promotion of Aboriginal languages; increased public understanding of Aboriginal traditions and issues; the inclusion of Aboriginal partners in program design, development, and delivery; government willingness to explore how existing systems might be improved; and addressing the needs of urban Aboriginal people more effectively.

Strengthening Aboriginal Governance. Initiatives identified under this heading pertained, among other things, to developing the capacity of Aboriginal peoples to negotiate and implement self-government; the establishment of additional treaty commissions, as well as Aboriginal governance centres; the creation of an independent claims body in co-operation with First Nations; a Métis enumeration program; funding Aboriginal women's organizations to enhance women's participation in self-government processes; and the possible development of an Aboriginal government recognition instrument.

Developing a New Fiscal Relationship. The government's goals in this area included working toward greater stability, accountability, and self-reliance; developing new financial standards with public account and audit systems that conform to accepted accounting principles; assisting First Nations governments to achieve greater independence through development of their own revenue sources; and enhanced data collection and information exchange.

Supporting Strong Communities, People, and Economics. This objective entailed devoting resources to improving living standards in Aboriginal communities with respect to housing, water, and sewer systems; welfare reform to reduce dependence and focus on job creation; a five-year Aboriginal human resources development strategy; expansion of the Aboriginal Head Start program; education reform; increased focus on health-related needs and programs; improved access to capital; and the establishment of urban youth centres.[112]

Since that time, the government's approach to the *RCAP Report* has been the subject of numerous criticisms by domestic and international human rights bodies.[113] More recently, the UN Special Rapporteur prepared a report on the situation of human rights and fundamental freedoms of Indigenous peoples and included references to the *RCAP Report* in many of his recommendations, which were released in 2005.[114] He concluded his report on Canada by observing:

> Despite the progress already achieved, Aboriginal people are justifiably concerned about continuing inequalities in the attainment of economic and social rights, as well as the slow pace of effective recognition of their constitutional Aboriginal and treaty rights, and the concomitant redistribution of lands and resources that will be required to bring about sustainable economies and socio-political development.[115]

He also made recommendations related to housing and the increasing of the land and resource base of Aboriginal peoples, which also referred to the recommendations of the *RCAP Report*.[116] Despite the fact that the government has been slow to adopt the recommendations of the *RCAP Report*, the report itself provides a detailed argument for the protection of Indigenous nations that may affect how future self-government agreements are structured.

With regard to the negotiation or renegotiation of treaties, land claims, and self-government agreements, the RCAP started on the premise that the "authentic renewal of treaty relationships will require realignment not only on the part of the Crown but also on the part of Aboriginal and treaty nations."[117] It was also the contention of the authors of the *RCAP Report* that the relationship between Indigenous peoples and the Crown was based on a nation-to-nation relationship, and that evidence of this could even be seen in such historical documents as the *Royal Proclamation of 1763* which referred to "Nations or Tribes of Indians."[118] British and French relations with Indigenous peoples were conducted on the basis "of the assumption that their Aboriginal counterparts possessed the political, territorial and economic characteristics of nationhood."[119] They went on to define an Aboriginal or treaty nation as "an indigenous society, possessing its own political organization, economy, culture, language and territory."[120] The *RCAP Report* also notes that the problem for Aboriginal nations came largely with the *Indian Act* in 1876, which divided Aboriginal nations into bands and imposed a certain uniform administrative and political structure on them. This imposition was a deliberate attempt to break up Aboriginal nations and fulfill their goal of assimilation of Aboriginal individuals into the larger society.[121]

Thus, the RCAP recommended that Canada's future development "must be guided by the fact that there are three orders of government in this country: Aboriginal, provincial and federal," and this involves a vision of self-government that (1) "involves greater authority over a traditional territory and its inhabitants, whether this territory be exclusive to a particular Aboriginal people or shared with others," and (2) "greater control over matters that affect the particular Aboriginal nation in question: its culture, identity and collective well-being."[122] With regard to self-government, the RCAP explains that most self-government agreements would involve both territorial and communal jurisdiction.[123] Territorial jurisdiction would involve authority over a specific territory and its inhabitants, and the jurisdiction over the members and residents would be mandatory.[124] Communal jurisdiction would be exercised over the membership of the Aboriginal group, and would depend on the voluntary association of members with the group and the voluntary submission of these members to the group's jurisdiction.[125] The RCAP also cautioned that with the right to exercise self-government came inherent limitations.

The entities entitled to exercise self-government could take various forms, from single-entity approaches by one Aboriginal nation to multi-layered approaches that might be taken by traditional confederacies such as the Haudenosaunee or Wabanaki.[126] In their view, however, the right of self-government vests in Aboriginal nations and not in "small local communities" — i.e., bands. In this, they refer to the 60-80 traditional Aboriginal nations in Canada, as opposed to the 634 *Indian Act* bands and their local communities.[127] These Aboriginal nations are described as political and cultural groups:

> Aboriginal peoples are not racial groups; they are organic political and cultural entities. Although contemporary Aboriginal peoples stem historically from the original peoples of North America, they often have mixed genetic

heritages and include individuals of varied ancestries. As organic political entities, they have the capacity to evolve over time and change in their internal composition.[128]

While the RCAP agrees that Aboriginal nations have the right to determine who their citizens are, and that this right is protected under section 35 of the *Constitution Act, 1982*, they also believe that this right is subject to two important limitations:

> First, it cannot be exercised in a manner that is discriminatory towards women or men. Second, it cannot specify a minimum "blood quantum" as a general prerequisite for citizenship. Modern Aboriginal nations, like other nations in the world today, represent a mixture of genetic heritages. Their identity lies in their collective life, their history, ancestry, culture, values, traditions, and ties to the land, rather than in their race.[129]

Since the RCAP recommended that self-government be exercised by Aboriginal nations, and that many Aboriginal nations would have to reorganise themselves after many years of being divided into bands and smaller communities, they felt that the reconstitution of Aboriginal nations ought to be done fairly, arguing that inclusive membership codes ought to be a pre-requisite to the exercise of the right of self-government by any Aboriginal nation:

> This process of reconstitution must be an open and inclusive one that does not shut out people by reference to overly restrictive or irrelevant criteria. An Aboriginal group that restricts its membership on an unprincipled or arbitrary basis cannot qualify for the right of self-determination.[130]

Membership disputes are inevitable, given the significant number of non-status Indians who are excluded from their nation by membership rules. Significant fairness issues at the band level could seriously affect the right of Indigenous nations to exercise self-government.[131]

This does not change the fact that, according to the RCAP, one of the core areas of jurisdiction of Aboriginal self-government is anything that can be considered "of vital concern to the life and welfare of a particular Aboriginal people, its culture and identity."[132] This includes the right of each Indigenous nation to determine its own criteria for residency in their territory, elections and referenda, and their own citizenship/membership.[133] The federal Inherent Right Policy also includes membership, elections, and residency rights as items for negotiation in self-government agreements.[134] Citizenship in Indigenous nations is an important aspect of self-government rights under section 35 of the *Constitution Act, 1982*, and the RCAP contends that any rules laid down by Indigenous nations with regard to citizenship "must satisfy certain basic constitutional standards flowing from the terms of section 35 itself":

> The purpose of these standards is to prevent an Aboriginal group from unfairly excluding anyone from participating in the enjoyment of collective Aboriginal and treaty rights guaranteed by section 35(1), including the right of self-government. In other words, the guarantee of Aboriginal and treaty rights in section 35 could be frustrated if a nation were free to deny citizenship to individuals on an arbitrary basis and thus prevent them from sharing in the benefit of the collective rights recognized in section 35.[135]

The first of these limitations is found in section 35(4), which guarantees Aboriginal and treaty rights equally to male and female persons. Citizenship codes could not discriminate on this basis, as it would offend section 35, the very section protecting their collective right of self-government.

The RCAP explained that there is a second limitation to the criteria that can be used to make up citizenship codes in Aboriginal nations: Aboriginal nations cannot be viewed as racial groups, but as political and cultural groups.[136] While the issue of blood quantum was a controversial one in some Aboriginal communities, the RCAP was of the view that a minimum blood quantum had no place in section 35 self-governing Aboriginal nations:

> It prevents an Aboriginal group from specifying that a certain degree of Aboriginal blood (what is often called blood quantum) is a general prerequisite for citizenship. On this point, it is important to distinguish between rules that specify ancestry as one among several ways of establishing eligibility for membership and rules that specify ancestry as a general prerequisite. By general prerequisite, we mean a requirement that applies in all cases or that only allows for very limited exceptions. For example, a citizenship code that requires that a candidate must be at least "half-blood," except in cases of marriage or adoption, would lay down a general pre-requisite and as such, in our view, be unconstitutional. By contrast, it would be acceptable for a code to specify, for example, that someone with at least one parent belonging to the group qualifies for citizenship, so long as this provision represents only one among several general ways for an individual to qualify for membership, including, for example, meeting such criteria as birth in the community, long-time residency, group acceptance and so on.[137]

The RCAP further recommended that the *Charter* and international norms and standards apply to these codes, in addition to the requirement that they be consistent with section 35 of the *Constitution Act, 1982* generally, and specifically with regards to section 35(4).[138] In addition to being citizens of their Aboriginal nations, they would also be Canadian citizens, and for some, they may also be members of sub-groups, such as clans, within their nations.[139] In the end, the RCAP recommended that persons could be considered eligible for citizenship in an Aboriginal nation on the basis of the following: "community acceptance, self-identification, parentage or ancestry, birthplace, adoption, marriage to a citizen, cultural or linguistic affiliation, and residence."[140] But what the RCAP has recommended and what has occurred within self-government agreements can be very different.

Self-Government "Enrollees"

The Council for Yukon Indians (CYI), the Government of Canada, and the Government of the Yukon signed an Umbrella Final Agreement on May 29, 1993.[141] This was a major comprehensive land claim agreement, or modern treaty, which pre-dated both the RCAP and the federal government's Inherent Right Policy on self-government.[142] The *Yukon Agreement* provided lands, financial compensation, training, provisions for sharing management of lands, resources, and royalties, economic development measures, and provisions for self-government for the 14 member First Nations of the Council of the Yukon Indians.[143] The Teslin Tlingit Council, Vuntut Gwitchin, Champagne, and Aishihik First Nations were the four First Nations to sign their self-government agreements pursuant to the *Yukon Agreement*.[144] The CYI also represents the Carcross/Tagish, Ehdiitat Gwich'in, Nacho Nyak Dun, Gwichya Gwich'in, Kluane, Little Salmon Carmacks, Nihtat Gwich'in, Selkirk, Ta'an Kwach'an, Tetlit Gwich'in, Tr'ondek Hwech'in, and White River First Nations.[145] Agreements have now been signed with 11 of the CYI's member First Nations.[146] While some aspects of the agreements can vary slightly to suit community needs, the main components of the *Yukon Agreement* are seen in each of the individual community agreements, especially for matters such as "Eligibility and Enrolment."

Each of the sections related to eligibility read identically in each of the agreements except for minor additional wording specific to each community. For example, Chapter 3 of the *Yukon Agreement* provides the basic "Eligibility and Enrolment" criteria that must be found in the individual First Nation agreements. The *Yukon Agreement* defines an adopted child as including any natural person who has been adopted according to the laws of Canada or Aboriginal custom. It defines a descendant as including anyone who directly descends by a maternal or paternal line, notwithstanding any intervening adoptions. A minimum blood quantum of 25 per cent (described as "Indian ancestry") is the base criteria for enrolment.

Although there are alternative ways of becoming an enrollee, some of those alternatives are also based on blood quantum/descent. For example, one can become an enrollee by being a descendant of someone with minimum blood quantum, or being an adopted child of someone with minimum blood quantum, adoptions not requiring blood descent. The focus appears to remain on the blood quantum of enrollees. The only exception is someone who has a "sufficient affiliation" with the community and can apply to be enrolled. Presumably, this includes non-Indigenous spouses who have lived in the community for a long time. All 11 First Nations that have negotiated final agreements have the same provisions with respect to "Eligibility and Enrolment." Given that most of these codes were enacted after the *RCAP Report* was released, one can presume that they had the benefit of the RCAP's insight into citizenship issues. However, it is easy to see Canada's influence in these codes through the negotiation of a 25 per cent minimum blood quantum. Citizenship codes, such as those adopted by the CYI communities, simply carry on the second generation cut-off rule, as opposed to providing alternatives for their communities. It appears that whether by status, membership, or citizenship, Canada does its best to enforce a blood quantum rule.

The Westbank First Nation is located in the Okanagan Valley of British Columbia, one of seven communities that belong to the Okanagan Nation, who are part of the Salish.[147] The Westbank First Nation has a self-government agreement with the Government of Canada concluded in 1993.[148] This bi-lateral agreement was negotiated under the federal *Inherent Right Policy* and did not include the province of British Columbia as a party.[149] Since then, the Westbank First Nation has embarked on a tri-lateral treaty negotiation with the Government of Canada and the Province of British Columbia and, at the time of writing, was in stage four of a six-stage treaty negotiation process.[150] Section 70 of the *Westbank Agreement* provides that the Nation has jurisdiction in relation to their own membership. Interestingly, the agreement also provides that the Westbank First Nation will not be precluded from "using its best efforts to establish a process whereby all Members who are not registered as Indians shall be entitled to be registered as Indians under the *Indian Act.*"

Section 72 of the agreement refers to the constitution of the Westbank First Nation that would deal with membership rules for their people. The *Westbank First Nation Constitution* was last amended in July 1997, and includes provisions specific to the initial membership list and to how new members would be added to their membership rolls.[151] Section 7.3 provides: "On the date this Constitution comes into force, the names on the band list maintained by INAC for Westbank shall constitute the names on the Membership Roll."[152] Therefore, the charter group for Westbank First Nation are all those who had previously qualified for band membership under the *Indian Act*. Since their band membership list was maintained by INAC, it means that they did not have their own membership code, and relied on the provisions of the *Indian Act* which determine membership through status. Therefore, the Westbank First Nation incorporates the same discrimination into their new code.

The Nisga'a, who are also from British Columbia, adopted a more traditional form of eligibility criteria. The *Nisga'a Final Agreement* was signed on April 27, 1999.[153] Their agreement provides several important clarifications with regard to the status of certain laws: (1) that the *Constitution Act, 1982* is not altered by virtue of their agreement; (2) that they are no longer a band under the *Indian Act*, nor are their lands considered reserves (for the purposes of the *Indian Act* or section 91(24) of the *Constitution Act, 1867*); and (3) that the *Charter* applies to the Nisga'a Lisims Government in all matters over which it has jurisdiction.[154] One of those areas over which it has jurisdiction is the administration of the "Eligibility and Enrolment Criteria" for their agreement. Chapter 20 of the Nisga'a Agreement provides for the Eligibility Criteria:

a) of Nisga'a ancestry and their mother was born into one of the Nisga'a tribes;

b) a descendant of an individual described in subparagraphs 1(a) or 1(c);

c) an adopted child of an individual described in subparagraphs 1(a) or 1(b); or

d) an aboriginal individual who is married to someone described in subparagraphs 1(a), (b), or (c) and has been adopted by one of the four Nisga'a tribes in accordance with Ayuukhl Nisga'a, that is, the individual has been accepted by a Nisga'a tribe, as a member of that tribe, in the presence of witnesses from the other Nisga'a tribes at a settlement or stone moving feast.[155]

There is no reference to the *Indian Act*. Their primary focus seems to be ancestry as traced through the mother's side of the family. The provision that allows the descendants of those who have Nisga'a ancestry and a mother who was born into a Nisga'a tribe may save some applicants, but it is not clear from the whole section whether it includes all descendants from successive generations as eligible enrollees, or whether they are speaking only to the first-generation descendant of the person with Nisga'a ancestry and a mother who belonged to a Nisga'a tribe. Given that the Nisga'a have incorporated the *Charter* into their agreement, it is possible that the distinctions made between members based on sex would not pass a section 15 equality test. Although the Nisga'a might argue that their eligibility criteria are based on tradition, and, as such, are protected under section 25 of the *Charter*, it is more likely that section 28 of the *Charter* would apply to ensure equality between the sexes. Even though their agreement is protected under section 35(3) as a modern treaty or land claim, section 35(4) would also ensure that the rights thereunder are protected for male and female Aboriginal people equally.[156] Given today's rates of out-marriage and the grim population forecasts for most bands, it would seem that an enrolment criterion based on maternal descent would exclude a large number of people based only on the gender of their ancestor. Even if this reflects their traditional practices, and may have worked well for many generations pre-contact, the modern reality of children from mixed marriages means that traditional practices must evolve to fit the modern circumstances of their people. If they do not, then the very existence of their community is at risk.

Other final agreements involving communities from the same province or territory often have eligibility criteria which tend to be similar to one another in terms of format, clauses, and criteria. The Council for Yukon Indians is an example of an umbrella agreement which requires that the individual communities include certain clauses from the umbrella agreement in their individual agreements. The *Gwich'in Comprehensive Land Claim Agreement* and the *Sahtu Dene and Métis Comprehensive Land Claim Agreement* involve communities from the Northwest Territories.[157] Both groups have agreements which provide that a person will be entitled to be enrolled as a participant in the land claim if that person is a Canadian citizen and a Gwich'in (for the former) or a Sahtu Dene or Métis (for the latter).[158] In both cases, if that person is not of the Indigenous origin of that community, they can still be enrolled if they are a Canadian citizen of Aboriginal ancestry resident in the settlement area and are "accepted" by the specific community.[159] "Acceptance" is defined as meaning that the person is "sponsored by a person eligible to be enrolled," and "was approved by a process" to be determined by the relevant community.[160] These agreements do not further specify what counts as Indigenous, or how far back one can go to establish descent from the specified group, or what level of ancestry is acceptable for Indigenous peoples outside the specific group. These provisions are similar in nature to the band membership codes reviewed earlier that allow for non-band descendants to be considered as band members if they are proven to be of First Nation ancestry, or have membership in another band. Communities such as the Sahtu focus on their blood lines to establish citizenship, yet they also allow non-Sahtu Indigenous people to become citizens. So the distinction appears to be between Indigenous and non-Indigenous blood lines, similar to that found in some band membership codes. These communities are willing to accommodate mixed parenting between different Indigenous nations, but not with non-Indigenous people. Those who have been excluded on this basis may feel that they have been discriminated against on the basis of blood quantum or race.

Other agreements have different criteria based on their specific communal needs. Some of the eligibility criteria used in other agreements include the following: a person who was on the voters list to approve the agreement or is of one-quarter Inuvialuit blood; a person who was a member of one of the eight Cree Indian bands of Quebec or is a person of Cree ancestry ordinarily resident in the Territory; a person who was a member of the Naskapi Band or a person of Naskapi ancestry ordinarily resident in the Territory; and a person of Inuit ancestry and is resident in or has a connection to the Settlement Area or is a person with at least one-quarter Inuit ancestry. What is important to note in these agreements is the focus on the charter group being comprised of those people who were originally entitled to be band members under the *Indian Act* prior to obtaining land claim or self-government status. These agreements also give band members a type of preferential eligibility, in that they are automatic members or enrollees, as opposed to those who must go through a community acceptance process. It also means that those who were wrongfully excluded from band membership or status previously are disadvantaged in the self-government and land claim process, as they are unlikely to have been on the voters' list, and, therefore, not in the charter group or in the group of automatic enrollees. Depending on their "blood" levels or status as non-registered Indians, they might not become enrolled at all.

If that is the case, and more flexible provisions are not present, then I have to seriously question whether the majority of the self-government agreements, including modern treaties, offer something better for Indigenous peoples in comparison to Indian status and band membership, or whether self-government agreements serve to maintain and promote the status quo — i.e., status under the *Indian Act* determines individual identity, communal identity, and access to Aboriginal and treaty rights. Serious analysis of this issue has been largely overshadowed by all the publicity related to land claims agreements, self-government, and modern treaty agreements, large natural resources partnerships, and economic development agreements. It cannot be overstated how important these types of agreements are for Indigenous peoples, as they redistribute land, natural resources, and revenues back to the Indigenous communities from which they were originally taken. However, my point is that the intangible benefits of communal identity and culture are equally important to non-status Indians and others who are excluded from the consultation, negotiation, and agreement process of self-government agreements and modern treaties. By relying on the *Indian Act* or blood quantum as a means of determining self-government citizens or enrollees, a vicious cycle is created whereby those who want in are excluded from the decision-making process. Self-government agreements were meant to be more than just a continuation of the status quo; they were meant to honour the inherent right of self-government for all Indigenous citizens and not only those deemed to be Indigenous from Canada's perspective. It looks as if self-government agreements have a long way to go to make good on the claim that they offer the solution to status and membership issues that will continue to affect our future generations.

Rethinking Indigenous Identity and Belonging

Who are the people who identify as Indigenous, and why are there such differences among the people who claim to be Indians, band members, treaty beneficiaries, land claims enrollees, or self-government citizens? It would seem that one's identity as an Indigenous person — such as a Maliseet, Cree, Mohawk, or Mi'kmaq — would also include a corresponding legal identity as an Indian, a communal identity as a band member or citizen of an Indigenous nation who has signed a self-government agreement. The fact that these groups are often not the same are indicative of the two most discriminatory modes of denying Indigenous identity: registration under the *Indian Act* and blood quantum/descent (which are one and the same in many instances). The only way to ensure that Indigenous nations and their cultures thrive into the future is to ensure that the individual and communal identities of Indigenous peoples are protected. This is the very promise that is contained in section 35 of the *Constitution Act, 1982,* and that promise should inform every aspect of relations between Canada and Indigenous peoples. Further, this promise is based on the goal of all peoples to ensure that their identities are passed on to future generations so that they may also have the cultural context from which to live the "good life." If this is to happen, Canada must abandon its biological notions of Indigeneity, take steps to undo the harm that has been caused, and step back from making future determinations of Indigeneity. Indigenous peoples are also responsible for acknowledging the damage that has been done by the incorporation of colonial notions of Indigeneity and taking positive steps to undo the harm by being more inclusive in their nation-building exercises.

Avoiding the Traps of the Past

Indigenous identity and concepts of belonging involve complex legal, social, cultural, and political factors that do not easily lend themselves to one-size-fits-all solutions or quick fixes. Bill C-31 has been described as an attempt by the federal government to eliminate some of the discrimination against Indigenous women under the *Indian Act*, yet it is also an example of how this relatively quick fix not only failed to address all the discrimination against Indigenous women in the *Indian Act*, but created new forms of discrimination. Many Indigenous peoples are refocusing their efforts on healing, rebuilding their communities, learning their languages and traditions, and seeking the teachings of their elders so that they can learn from their collective histories. Also important in this process of healing and rebuilding is the need to acknowledge what has caused them the greatest harm in the past, consult on what they want for their future as communities and nations, and ensure that, as they move forward, they avoid the traps of the past. What can make this process difficult is the fact that colonial-based concepts about Indigenous identity and rights still frame our discussions about how to move forward. The problem with the *Indian Act*, band membership codes, self-government citizenship codes, and even Aboriginal rights jurisprudence, is that they continue to be based on out-dated ideologies that do not reflect modern realities. After reviewing these legal mechanisms for determining identity, I have identified one fundamental concept which is preventing any real progress in reconciling Indigenous identity and rights with Canadian laws and policies: it is that Indigenous cultures are defined as though they were frozen in the pre-contact period. This concept underlies the characterization of Indigenous peoples as "historic communities" which are deemed to have existed only at a period of time in the pre-contact era, and who are now, as time goes by, slowly disappearing through intermarriage and assimilation. It also explains the legislative genesis of requiring one-quarter blood quantum to be a recognized Indian, and how some Indigenous communities have internalized and accepted this criterion of "authenticity." It further explains how courts and governments can require that Indigenous traditions, customs, and practices must be different from those of non-Indigenous peoples to be truly Indigenous, and how some Indigenous communities have come to view anyone who does not follow these traditions as non-Indigenous.

This next section will focus on the two criteria which are inherently tied to both colonial concepts of freezing Indigenous identity in time and those that have also been internalized by our own communities: blood quantum and pre-contact tradition. What can be interpreted as an inherent part of identity (ancestry) can also be interpreted in a way that is racist and destructive (blood quantum). Similarly, few could question tradition as essential to one's culture and identity, but freezing traditions in pre-contact times means the community can't exist in today's world. The days of waiting for Canada to fix the problems it has created are long over. The current bills being considered in Parliament are an indication of a shift back toward paternalistic laws and policies. The core group of bureaucrats, academics, and politicians who advocated for assimilation have come up with less overt ways of accomplishing the same goals, all under the guise of bringing Indigenous people into Canadian society. If we do not address these self-destructive identity concepts now, they may be too difficult to undo in the future.

Connection to one's culture and identity is not only part of the good life, but its denial may also risk the lives of the youth in our communities. Children receive their identity and culture from their parents. When this natural process is blocked, some youth cannot find a proper context for their lives, and suicides can be the devastating result.[161] One need only look to the youth of a nation to see how healthy the nation is as a whole. For example, the Aboriginal population in Canada is a very youthful one, much younger than the non-Aboriginal population.[162] The median age of the Aboriginal population is 27 years, compared to the non-Aboriginal population, which is 40 years; and 48 per cent of the Aboriginal population is under 24, compared to 31 per cent of the non-Aboriginal population.[163] Non-status Indians are the fastest-growing Aboriginal population, and could become the youngest of the Aboriginal populations by 2026.[164] Given that Indigenous communities comprise such high numbers of youth, issues faced by Indigenous youth affect the whole of Indigenous communities, including parents, grandparents, caretakers, educators, and elders. Some of the issues Indigenous youth face today are lower levels of education than other Canadians, and disproportionately higher rates of incarceration and suicide, especially among males. Teen pregnancies among Aboriginal female youth are six times that of other Canadians.[165]

In addition to the regular pressures that every youth in Canada must deal with, Aboriginal youth in particular "also have to deal with stereotypes, low expectations and incidents of outright racism in their encounters with non-Aboriginal society."[166] Many of these youth suffer the same pain that their parents, grandparents, and extended families have suffered with regard to the loss of land and the suppression of languages, cultures, and identities.[167] The majority of Aboriginal youth are not about to disappear or assimilate into Canadian society, but youth between the ages of 15 and 29 are at the highest risk of making ill-fated choices for themselves, especially if they do not have a clear, healthy sense of identity: "They seek a place in society that affirms their value as citizens and as Aboriginal persons."[168] When young Aboriginal people cannot make this crucial link between their identity, acceptance in their community or nation, and their culture, they are at increased risk for poor health and educational achievement, lower workforce participation levels, and suicide.[169] Suicide rates for Aboriginal youth far surpass that of other Canadians, and in fact "have reached . . . calamitous proportions — rates said to be higher than those of any culturally identifiable group in the world."[170] The reasons for this are many and complex, but researchers have emphasized the fact that if one's cultural identity has been marginalized because of colonization, or "the trustworthy ways of one's community are criminalized, legislated out of existence, or otherwise assimilated beyond easy recognition, then the path for those transitioning toward maturity becomes much more difficult."[171] The continual increase of the non-status Indian population and the corresponding increase in Indigenous peoples who are denied band membership represent a significant risk to the health and future of our communities.

Youth represent our link to future generations, and their continued exclusion as non-status Indians or non-band members poses risks to our communities. The potential harms to our youth from disconnection from their cultures are too significant to be ignored. It is important to note that these high rates of suicide are not prevalent in all First Nations communities, and in fact, "nearly 90 percent of suicides occur in less than 10 percent of communities."[172] Chandler and Lalonde studied Aboriginal youth suicide rates from the period 1987 to 1992, and each community from which each youth originated was also noted, together with an assessment of whether indicators of "cultural continuity" were present.[173] Some of these markers of cultural continuity included whether the community had some measure of self-government, had litigated for title to their traditional lands, or whether they had community centres dedicated to preserving their cultures.[174] The study found that: "[b]ands that evidenced all of these cultural continuity factors had no youth suicides during our first study window." The study further found that, "[b]y contrast, bands that evidenced none of these 'protective' factors suffered youth suicide rates many times the national average." The study concluded that both individual and cultural continuity are strongly linked.[175] It would seem prudent, then, to find solutions that ensure that Indigenous youth are included in their communities and nations, and that their identities as Indigenous peoples are recognized, legitimized, and encouraged. Studies have shown that First Nations who like the way they are and feel proud of themselves tend not to engage in higher-risk activities.[176] Those who participate in activities, among other healthy activities, which have a basis in tradition are also more likely to stay in school and perform better.[177] Those who do not have the benefit of this cultural context are at far greater risk of many high risk activities, the most tragic of which is suicide.[178]

Perhaps the feature that is most referred to in discussions about Indigenous identity, culture, and citizenship is ancestry. Indigenous people are often referred to as the "First Peoples" of this country, as their ancestors were here prior to the settlement and assertion of sovereignty by Europeans and the establishment of Canada as a state. It is their ancestors who protected and maintained their rich cultures. The importance of ancestry and the links between current generations with their ancestors cannot be overlooked.[179] At the same time, there are those who confuse the concept of ancestry with racial purity, or blood quantum. While most agree that the concept of blood quantum for determining identity is racist and discriminatory, and serves no useful purpose in maintaining Indigenous difference, the fact remains that this method of determining membership or identity remains firmly rooted in the minds of some Indigenous peoples. It is important to establish that strict reliance on ancestry as determinative of Indigenous identity can result in membership codes that have the same exclusionary effects as blood quantum.

Indigenous ancestry is a source of pride for most Indigenous peoples, be they Mohawk or Mi'kmaq, status or non-status, on or off reserve. In fact, their particular ancestry is part of what sets them apart from immigrant minorities who make their own claims for recognition. The Supreme Court of Canada in *R. v. Van der Peet* cited the fact that Aboriginal people were "here first" as the main reason they are unique as compared to minority, ethnic, or interest groups in Canada:

> In my view, the doctrine of aboriginal rights exists, and is recognized and affirmed by s. 35(1), because of one simple fact: when Europeans arrived in North America, aboriginal peoples were already here, living in communities on the land, and participating in distinctive cultures as they had done for centuries. It is this fact, and this fact above all others, which separates aboriginal peoples from all other minority groups in Canadian society and which mandates their special legal, and now constitutional status.[180]

Thus, the fact that modern Indigenous peoples are descended from the Indigenous peoples who were here at contact is considered important by courts for determining Aboriginal rights. Indigenous peoples are different from ethnic minorities or immigrants because they are indigenous to this continent, have special relationships with the land, have constitutionally protected rights based on their claims to the land and its resources, and are the only cultural or political group in Canada who can treat, or conclude treaties, with Canada.[181] The Supreme Court in *Powley* made a critical clarification about the importance of ancestry in determining identity, and held that such ancestry could be acquired through birth, adoption, or other means.[182] The court specifically refrained from further defining "ancestry," but explicitly rejected the use of blood quantum and offered the following guidance:

> We would not require a minimum "blood quantum," but we would require some proof that the claimant's ancestors belonged to the historic Métis community by birth, adoption, or other means. Like the trial judge, we would abstain from further defining this requirement in the absence of more extensive argument by the parties in a case where this issue is determinative.[183]

As commonly understood, ancestry refers to the fact that one has descended from a particular nation or culture, which signifies a link to common history, ancestors, territory, traditions, customs, beliefs, and culture. It is this ancestral claim, versus the generic claim for minority recognition as an ethnic group, that has been recognized as supporting various legal rights, and separates them from the claims advanced by interest groups and ethnic minorities.

The more difficult issue is how to ensure that the concept of ancestry is not misconstrued so as to reinforce the notion of racial purity through blood quantum. Although ancestry speaks of familial connections to past and future generations, there is no requirement that those family and communal ties must be determined through degree of descent. The ancestral connection between Indigenous peoples spans generations, and connects present individuals with ancestors as well as with future generations. This ancestral connection is not lessened by the fact of intermarriage. Multiple ancestries can be a great source of pride for Indigenous peoples and could encourage feelings of citizenship in common with other Canadians. However, this is not possible if section 35 reconciliation means Indigenous identity must give way to Canadian identity every time there is a union of the two. I am proud to be an Indigenous Canadian, so long as I can be both Indigenous and Canadian without the latter trumping the former.

Tom Flanagan and Alan Cairns are academics whose critiques of Indigenous peoples and policies have received a great deal of attention, and could affect future policy in this area. Flanagan does not approve of Indigenous people receiving benefits on the basis of who their ancestors are, since these benefits are not available to other Canadians.[184] He asserts that "Indians did not do anything to achieve their status except be born, and no one else can do anything to join them in that status because no action can affect one's ancestry."[185] Flanagan's point only has merit if, in fact, Indigenous identity and culture are determined solely on the basis of ancestry, defined as blood quantum. His point is not true if Indigenous citizenship can be acquired through adoption, residency, or marriage. Flanagan does not apply his logic equally to the Canadian situation. Many Canadians have not done anything to become Canadian other than be born, but that does not make them any less Canadian. He does not question the right of Canada to make birth a criterion for citizenship, but does so for Indigenous peoples. Cairns, on the other hand, believes that a democratic liberal society depends on the "fraternity" of its citizens.[186] His goal is to "nourish" the "commonalities" between the two, and to let the differences fall by the wayside — so long as what is nourished is a Canadian identity and what falls by wayside is the Indigenous identity.[187]

What is forgotten here is that ancestry is deeply significant to many Indigenous peoples. Ancestry viewed as the totality of familial, communal, historical, and territorial ties to their peoples is preferred to a concept which focuses solely on direct descent by birth. Forgetting about one's Indigenous ancestry would mean forgetting about one's parents, grandparents, community, territory, and history. The assumption made by those such as Cairns and Flanagan is that, in order to partake of the "modern" labour market, education, and society, one must forfeit one's identity as an Indigenous person.[188] Nothing about living in a house, getting an education, or becoming a lawyer requires that one's identity be forfeited, unless Indigenous identity is defined by racist stereotypes. Macklem argues that indigenous difference is not racial, but is comprised of culture, territory, treaties, and sovereignty.[189] Macklem explains that the ancestral connection between Indigenous peoples and the land also forms a major component of Indigenous identity, and that this, combined with participation in cultural practices, generates a "shared sense of continuity with the past," and a clear link between ancestry and identity.[190] At the same time, Macklem warns against defining Indigenous identity solely in terms of the past; ancestral factors can contribute to Indigenous identity, but they cannot be the entire basis of it, otherwise these identities would be frozen in time.[191]

Like all cultures, Indigenous cultures "undergo dramatic transformations in response to internal and external circumstances and developments."[192] Constitutional protection of Indigenous identity does not mean that Indigenous peoples cannot also have allegiances to their fellow citizens, be Canadians, and, at the same time, remember, assert, and protect their Indigenous ancestry and identity. Macklem argues that they can have many allegiances and still maintain their identity.[193] Were it not for events of the past that did not respect the democratic principles espoused by liberals, Indigenous people would not be forced to choose between their ancestral identities and Canadian ones:

> If Aboriginal nations had been treated as formal equals in the distribution of sovereignty effected by European expansion, their sovereignty would have been respected. It was not and, as a result, allegiances of Aboriginal people became multi-dimensional. The multi-dimensionality of Aboriginal allegiances is in fact partly a function of the denial of formal equality and, as such, should not be used as a weapon to force Aboriginal people to choose between two unpalatable scenarios.[194]

John Borrows also finds it troubling that Indigenous Canadians are denied the benefit of multiple ancestries and allegiances:

> While I think restrictions on Aboriginal citizenship are necessary to maintain the social and political integrity of the group, I must admit that I am troubled by ideas of Aboriginal citizenship that may depend on blood or genealogy to support group membership. Scientifically, there is nothing about blood or descent alone that makes an Aboriginal person substantially different from any other person. While often not intended by those who advocate such criteria, exclusion from citizenship on the basis of blood of ancestry can lead to racism and more subtle forms of discrimination that destroy human dignity.[195]

While Macklem and Borrows both agree that borders are necessary to protect Indigenous cultures, they diverge on how to construct those borders. Macklem was resistant to the idea of Bill C-31 reinstatees being welcomed back to their communities, whereas Borrows felt that Indigenous identity was strong enough even to incorporate non-Indigenous people as citizens.[196] Indigenous peoples existed pre- and post-contact and "have a right and legal obligation as a prior but ongoing citizenship to participate in its changes."[197]

The social realities that Indigenous peoples face today are that they live among other Canadians, frequently intermarry, and have other relationships that often result in children.[198] This has been the case for centuries. Consequently, there are no Indigenous groups in Canada that are completely made up of "pure" Aboriginal peoples — even if there were a test to determine such a status.[199] This fact, however, does not in any way detract from their distinct status as Indigenous peoples.

Often, fears of assimilation are really fears about loss of blood purity, and the reaction of some Indigenous groups has been to reinstate blood quantum as a band membership criterion and to place moratoriums on mixed-marriages in an effort to stave off dilution.[200] Kymlicka does not believe that blood quantum is a legitimate criterion for determining the membership of societal cultures like Indigenous nations.[201] While ancestry may be an important aspect of the distinctness of societal cultures, Kymlicka cautions against this being misunderstood as a requirement for individual members to have to meet blood quantum minimums.[202] He notes that there are high rates of intermarriage between Indigenous groups and North American populations, and, as a result, the number of "Indians who are of solely Indian descent, is also constantly shrinking, and will soon be a minority in each case."[203] He explains that national minorities are more properly understood as "cultural groups," as opposed to racial or descent groups:

> The desire of a national minority to survive as a culturally distinct society is not necessarily a desire for cultural purity, but simply for the right to maintain one's membership in a distinct culture, and to continue developing that culture in the same (impure) way that the members of majority cultures are able to develop theirs. The desire to develop and enrich one's culture is consistent with, and indeed promoted by, interactions with other cultures, so long as this interaction is not conducted in circumstances of serious inequality in power.
>
> So, the unavoidable, and indeed desirable, fact of cultural interchange does not undermine the claim that there are distinct societal cultures.[204]

The fact remains that the concept of blood quantum originated from "nineteenth-century European bio-genetic models" and has nothing to do with traditional concepts of Indigeneity.[205]

Indian agents who enforced blood quantum rules on Indigenous nations were operating under long discredited theories: "most of the tribal rolls used to determine blood quantum were compiled . . . 150 years ago. The Indian agents performing the count operated under the same archaic assumptions about biology and culture that produced now-discredited fields such as eugenics and phrenology."[206] Eugenics was a social philosophy based on the idea that human traits could be improved through various kinds of intervention in order to produce a healthier, more intelligent society. Eugenics led to forced sterilization and selective breeding, and served as one of the justifications for the holocaust. Phrenology, now considered a defunct field of study, involved determining an individual's personality traits by reading the bumps and fissures on their skull. Phrenologists gathered thousands of Aboriginal skulls from men, women, and children in order to study them.[207] As Lawrence explains, "Native American skulls were examined with a view to determining whether degrees of 'racial mixing' could be measured":

> These studies were used until the 1920s by federal officials as a measure of racial purity to determine who was and who was not a full-blood Indian. . . . Tribal enrolment lists from the early twentieth century based on such racist biology continue to be the legal documents used to determine heirs in awarding land claim compensation.[208]

It is from this type of pseudo-scientific background that blood quantum came to be used as the criterion by which to determine the "purity," and thus the identity, of Indigenous peoples: "When racism is understood as rooted in biological difference, the blood quantum is not only racist, but it makes racism possible in the first place. Without the blood quantum as a measure of race, discrimination based on racial identification would not be possible."[209]

If First Nations adhere to this ideology they "will author their own demise,"[210] and the words of the former Deputy Superintendent General of Indian Affairs, Duncan Campbell Scott, will be fulfilled: "Our object is to continue until there is not a single Indian in Canada that has not been absorbed into the body politic and there is no Indian question."[211] The difference between ancestry, broadly defined, and blood quantum is that ancestry can incorporate familial and communal ties as well as a shared history and culture, whereas blood quantum focuses exclusively on racial purity. Fears of assimilation have led some bands to institute blood quantum codes that accelerate the extinction process for their communities. But cultural interchange and mixed marriages can happen within communities without fundamentally changing the identity of Indigenous peoples. Ancestry is about shared families, cultures, histories, and territories, not blood or cranial measurements.

Other seemingly benign criteria can have similar exclusionary effects, depending on how they are defined and applied. In the case of ancestry, it can be a source of pride and inclusion when defined as a connection to common ancestors, histories, territories, and cultures. But if ancestry is defined as blood quantum, then it becomes exclusionary and will result in diminished communities. Criteria based on tradition fall into that same category. Traditions, customs, and practices are important parts of Indigenous cultures, but if they are rigidly defined as pre-contact practices, then their use as criteria for determining identity or citizenship will result in arbitrary exclusions. What is often lost in the debate over the importance of tradition is the diverse connections Indigenous people have to their culture, territories, and communities. Is it more important that individuals hunt with traditional weapons after having completed the traditional ceremonies to be a Mi'kmaq citizen, or can they honour the tradition of hunting a moose for their family but use a modern weapon to do so? Similarly, must one be an elder to advocate on behalf of one's community, or can one respect the traditional principle of contributing to one's community in a modern way, as a lawyer, a doctor, or a teacher? The answers all depend on how traditions are defined or limited.

Tradition can be an important aspect of Indigenous identity as it connects the generations of the present with those of the past, with a view to protecting their culture and identity for future generations. There is no such thing as a culture that has not evolved. Societies are not static. They constantly adapt to changing circumstances, and evolve with each new discovery. Some societies and religions have their fundamentalists who try to preserve customs and practices as they believe they originally were, but for the most part even these tend to evolve with time.[212] Indigenous identity should be flexible enough to adapt to modern circumstances, while maintaining connections to traditions as they have evolved over time. A singular focus on pre-contact tradition mandates that someone be the arbiter of what constitutes valid tradition. Schouls argues that Indigenous identity should not be determined from rigid traditional criteria, as doing so actually jeopardizes it:

> The identification approach suggests that individual Aboriginal identity should not be regarded in a deterministic fashion, originating from traditional cultural or political attributes. Rather, Aboriginal identity is more properly understood as a relational phenomenon; one acquires it by virtue of one's connections to others through ancestry, shared historical memories and territories, and shared commitment to one another in community over time. This approach, in other words, lends flexibility to Aboriginal identity; it can be shaped to meet challenges posed by new circumstances without jeopardizing the integrity of Aboriginal identity itself.[213]

In order for Indigenous communities to exercise their right to be self-defining, they must allow flexibility in their definitions, so as to be inclusive of Indigenous people living in today's world, as opposed to pre-contact times.[214]

It is this struggle between perceptions about Indigenous identity of the past with modern day expressions of Indigenous identity that cause angst in some communities. These differences in perspective have been labelled a debate between individual versus collective rights, essentially pitting modern expressions of individual Indigenous identity against communally held traditions. However, not all academics view the debate in this light. Schouls explains that the issue is really more of a "demand for individual political inclusion at the Aboriginal community level" than an individual versus collective issue.[215] He further explains that "rights to community inclusion are important because healthy individual identity is understood to be the outcome of individuals possessing power to influence the course of relations that they consider integral to their self-image."[216] Multiple expressions of Indigenous identity must be granted equal status and influence in the development of the community's identity.

Canada's laws and policies have interfered with Indigenous conceptions of who they are and even how they view their own traditions. The current Indigenous leadership, aware of the devastating effects of the *Indian Act* and its policies, have an obligation to avoid perpetuating that damage in their own laws:

> While colonialism is at the root of our learned actions today, First Nations men must take some measure of responsibility for their conduct and attitudes. It is no longer enough to say "the Indian Act made us do it." Positive acceptance of responsibility is an important step in healing the divisions that have occurred.[217]

Now that Indigenous nations and local communities are aware of the damage that *Indian Act* divisions have caused, they have to take steps to remedy the damage independent of any additional remedies that are owed to them by Canada. Individuals with the least amount of traditional knowledge could include those who have been denied the opportunity to access their community elders and extended families to learn their traditions and customs. Traditions can be learned and community connections re-forged, but the rebuilding of extinct communities would be much harder to accomplish. Therefore, Schouls argues, "Perhaps more pertinently, for those possessing identity and wishing to re-establish community affiliation, no communal roadblocks should be placed in their way, since these individuals often did not lose those affiliations through any choice of their own."[218]

The result of using these kinds of narrow definitions is what Schouls calls "a descending scale of legal identity security."[219] These definitions may give absolute certainty in the mind of the user as to who is an Indian, for example, but they also lead from full to half to non-Indian status before the first generation has had a chance to even think about the ramifications. What he is most opposed to are "dictatorially imposed" views about what Aboriginal identity should or should not be, whether they are based on tradition or not:

> Aboriginal persons regularly disagree with one another about what makes for an Aboriginal way of life. Cultural and political images of community identity are regularly contested, often in the name of values of equality and freedom from domination that relational pluralism champions. It is unfair, therefore, that certain Aboriginal persons should be allowed to impose their preferred view of an Aboriginal way of life on those who may disagree with it simply in the name of cultural survival based on the purported moral superiority of traditional cultural principles and values.[220]

Traditional practices and modern ways of life can be reconciled. One can be Indigenous and still participate in many other social settings in Canada. Borrows points out that most Indigenous communities had oral traditions, and therefore "time is dynamic and includes both past and present understandings of events."[221] Therefore, reliance on tradition does not preclude its modern day exercise in forms that have adapted and evolved with their cultures. Modern forms of Indigenous identity can and do reflect both past and present influences. "At the same time, it must be recognized that understandings of tradition itself change by enveloping new concepts."[222]

The focus for Indigenous identity and communal belonging should be based on these intergenerational connections and changes as opposed to specific traditional practices frozen at certain points in time. Traditions can be respected in many different ways, and could also be in the form of a commitment to learn and preserve traditional practices versus using them as a screening tool. Asante explains that the self-government goals envisioned by Indigenous peoples should not reconstitute their nations on race or blood: "Their bond would be those of culture and identity, not blood — their unity would come from their shared history and their strong sense of themselves as people."[223]

Asante notes that political organizations representing identity groups often find it easier to focus on one aspect of identity, such as race. The effect of this singular focus is that other social categories of identity are excluded.[224] Minow argues that the real intent of these stringent rules is to end the debate in favour of certainty: "Sometimes legal rules are designed to close off discussion — to cut off some inquiries based on the view that certainty may be more important than truth or even more important than fairness."[225] The benefit of absolute certainty is far outweighed by the harms caused to Indigenous peoples and their communities as a result.

Most Indigenous communities are now bands created under the *Indian Act*. Contemporary Indian governments are no longer traditional in nature but have been forced to conduct their affairs according to the *Indian Act*. This is not to say that tradition is no longer an important part of their communal identity; there has been a resurgence of traditionalism in many Indigenous communities. At the same time, these communities and their traditions and cultures have changed over time. Just as it would not be fair for non-Indigenous governments to use cultural adaptation against Indigenous communities to say that they were no longer Indigenous or deny them their Aboriginal rights, it is equally unfair for Indigenous communities to use loss of language, culture, or tradition against their own members to deny them their rights and identity. It is not the fault of non-status Indians that Canada has created a discriminatory system that divides individuals from their communities. Their right to belong to their communities is no less powerful than it was pre-*Indian Act*.

The government has divided communities and attempted to sever important individual and communal connections to language, culture, tradition, history, territory, treaties, and ancestors. In the words of Prime Minister Harper, the goal was to "kill the Indian in the child."[226] It is important for Indigenous communities to undo the harm that has been done, not through rigid citizenship criteria that perpetuate the harms done by federal assimilation policies, but through rekindling those important connections. Lomayesva explains that the problem with current Indian identity is that it was a term created outside the context of each Indigenous nations' traditions, and he argues that "the term Indian cannot be defined by reference to any set standards based upon blood or cultural belief. It must be understood to describe a type of connection between an individual and tribal community. Thus, to be Indian is to possess a type of connection between oneself and a tribal community."[227] To define Indigenous identity solely in reference to traditionalism "creates a standard of identity centered upon an archetype of what an Indian should be."[228] Linking Indigenous identity strictly to traditionalism has the same effect as blood quantum, and leads to discussions about whether an Indigenous community or individual are "pure," or, conversely, whether they are "contaminated":

> Implicit in this line of thought is that the greater tribal cultures are influenced by contemporary western society the less pure (or more contaminated) they are. It is not difficult to make the next step, and conclude that a contaminated culture is less Indian. It is this lesson which on some level has been accepted by American Indians themselves.[229]

According to Lomayesva, traditional criteria can hurt rather than help protect Indigenous identity: "Terms like traditional do not aid to understand the underlying nature of the Indian. The diverse and changing nature poses substantial problems in identifying a consistent definition of Indian identity."[230] Indigenous communities that base their identity on blood or rigid traditional criteria will remain small and easily fragmented as opposed to those that base their communal identities on the ancestral, historical, familial, and territorial connections that form the basis of their nations. These latter will find a much wider basis of support and will find the effort of nation rebuilding much easier.[231]

Rigid applications of traditional criteria can have the same effects as the status provisions of the *Indian Act*, except that traditional criteria would be more subjectively applied. Multiple expressions of Indigenous identity must be granted equal status within Indigenous communities in order for those communities to be just and have a chance at surviving into the future. There should be no roadblocks placed before individuals who wish to reconnect with their identity and their communities. Traditional practices and beliefs can be reconciled with modern practices and realities; to do otherwise freezes traditions and creates an archetypal "Indian" standard that few could hope to meet. Whereas reliance on strict traditional criteria can fragment a community, reliance on a variety of key connections provides more opportunity for the sharing and reclaiming of identities. Traditional practices can be learned and respected by both current and new citizens so long as they are not dictatorially imposed or used to harm people. Important communal connections can also be made through common history, ancestry, familial ties, territories, and treaties. These connections allow for a wider base of support and make nation rebuilding much easier. More important, the inclusion of Indigenous citizens through varied connections helps ensure the survival of their identities and cultures for future generations.

The responsibility to protect Indigenous identity and culture for present and future generations is a significant task. Excluding someone from his or her family, local community, or nation can have devastating effects on individuals and nations alike, and may lead to outcomes such as suicide or alcoholism.[232] The decades of separated communities and family members have resulted in the serious negative social indicators referred to in the *RCAP Report*. Unfortunately, Indigenous people have been governed by the *Indian Act* and policies imposed by the federal government for so long that many have internalized these divisions. Canada has made many Indigenous individuals and communities so dependent on financial transfers for the basic necessities of life that often the focus has shifted from seeking justice from Canada to protecting today's resources.[233] Indigenous identity is important to Indigenous peoples, and their participation in their culture as a necessary context for their lives is considered one of the "goods" of the liberal good life. Indigenous cultures are entitled to evolve and adapt to changing circumstances, like any other society, and still retain their identity as Indigenous. This includes the intermarriage of Indigenous peoples with non-Indigenous peoples and the mixed-heritage children who come from those relationships. Blood quantums imposed on children of mixed-marriages and relationships evolve not from Indigenous traditions and practices, but from the debunked sciences of eugenics and phrenology that seek to measure the purity of races. Even tradition, if used as the sole criterion for identity, can be exclusionary. How do we overcome this apparent stalemate? We know tradition is important to Indigenous identity and nationhood, but we also know that it can trap our concept of identity in the past. We need to look past the individual criterion itself and look at how cultures are maintained.

The reason traditions are so important to Indigenous cultures is because they are a connection between the present and past generations. Traditions tie us not only to our ancestors, but to friends, families, and communities in the present. This connection, which helps form our sense of identity and belonging, can then be passed on to future generations, thereby completing the circle of relations necessary to maintain a culture. This makes tradition somewhat like ancestry in that the ultimate goal is to maintain and pass on those connections to our cultures and identities. This being the case, then, perhaps if we switched our concept of Indigenous identity and culture from a focus on singular criteria such as status, blood quantum, residency, marriage partner, or tradition, and concentrated on the totality of our connections to our Indigenous nations, we could escape the archetypal identity which freezes us in the past. In so doing, the list of who gets included or excluded will be based more on whether there is a legitimate connection between the individual and the nation than on the privileging of those who meet some arbitrary criterion but may have no real connection to their nation. This could also help alleviate the double standards that exist between those who live on or off reserve or those with or without status. Under a connections-based citizenship system, a person who may be a non-status Indian but who volunteers in the community, has multiple familial ties there, respects the traditions, and has expressed their loyalty to the nation might be a good candidate for citizenship, whereas someone who has status but has never had any contact with their community, has no familial connections, and has no interest in learning the culture might be a less likely candidate.

Connections to the community through common history, familial ties, territory, and culture have more relevance in determining Indigenous identity, rebuilding Indigenous nations, and protecting future generations than any one subjective criterion. Indigenous people have changed and will continue to change as their cultures and identities adapt to modern circumstances. While many changes maintain links to traditions and past customs, some have incorporated the negative effects of colonialism. It is imperative that Indigenous nations and local communities do not cut off their citizens in an effort to keep up with government policies or economic incentives. A membership or citizenship code that requires that new members must reside in the community, speak the language, and have knowledge of the customs and traditions of the community effectively denies membership to the majority of Indigenous peoples in Canada because the majority of Indigenous people in Canada live off reserve,[234] the majority of Indigenous languages are in jeopardy,[235] and the majority of Indigenous people do not live in conditions conducive to maintaining their·culture and traditions.[236] Changes should be incorporated in citizenship codes because they are in keeping with the cultures of nations, not because they blindly follow what has always been done or because there is economic pressure to do so. Otherwise, the excluded will have no choice but to resort to litigation and human rights claims. If Indigenous peoples are not willing to give their own people a second chance, how can we expect anything else from the rest of society?

Completing the Circle

While federal and provincial governments have legitimate policy reasons for wanting to know who Indigenous peoples are, they do not have a right to define Indigenous nations through government-imposed definitions. The right of an Indigenous nation to determine who its citizens are is a legally protected right under section 35 of the *Constitution Act, 1982.* If Indigenous nations are going to preserve their status as self-determining peoples rather than vanishing races, they need to reclaim their jurisdiction over citizenship. There is no need to maintain the archetypal "Indian"; Indigenous peoples in Canada are legitimate peoples and have the right to their lands and resources.[237] A people can grow and expand and incorporate people from other nations and still have a connection to a common history, ancestors, and traditional territories.

The current conflict between on- and off-reserve band members, or status and non-status citizens, is not about individuals versus communities, women versus communities, or real Indians versus wannabes. The conflict originated and has been sustained by Canada's goal of eliminating Indians and freeing up land and resources for the settler population. Canada's public political positions, including the prime minister's apology for the residential schools, stand in conflict with the positions they take in court. The conflict in Indigenous identity is Canada's continued interference with our identities. Saying First Nations can choose their own band members appears to be empowering, but in reality, Canada has confined Indigenous identity to the *Indian Act*, and attempts to use our traditional means of identification will be countered by restrictive government funding policies. We have to help our communities recognize that the conflict between status and non-status was created by Canada, and that this conflict serves only Canada. We need to see the concerns of Indigenous women, non-status, and off-reserve Indians in a new light that shows their passion to be part of their communities. First

Nations seriously interested in nation-building ought to welcome loyal citizens. Social conflict is inevitable, but how it is resolved depends on whether there is external interference or support and whether there is a mutual desire on behalf of both Indigenous individuals and communities to make the necessary changes for the ultimate benefit of future generations.

The question that naturally follows is, what is the best way to start this process? Several academics have considered this complex issue, and have advanced general ideas about how we might address the current conflict within First Nations regarding identity and belonging. Asante argues that the success of Indigenous self-government hinges on the idea of Indigenous nationhood and joining the various ways in which Indigenous peoples have been defined:

> The ideas of nation and social integration need to be joined. This union is important because whereas the idea of "nation" is the "bounded nature of all political communities and the embeddedness of all claims to constitute a distinct and autonomous political community," social integration is that "web of relationships that constitutes a people as a 'social collectivity' existing independently of common subjection to the rule of a particular state."[238]

She essentially argues that Indigenous nations must socially integrate the reality of the varied identities adopted by their members in order to be viable nations. This means that the many ways of being Indigenous should be accepted by Indigenous communities in order to achieve social harmony. Her proposed solution appears to be in line with the demographic realities facing Indigenous nations today. The most recent census notes that the "Descendants of the First Peoples of Canada represented 5.4 per cent of the country's total population."[239] Interestingly, the census also noted that "[p]eople with Aboriginal ancestry are more likely than the total population to report multiple origins. In 2006, 62.4 per cent of people with Aboriginal ancestry also reported other origins, compared with 41.4 per cent of the total population of Canada."[240] That is a reality which many Indigenous communities will have to address if they are to maintain their communities into the future. The outdated concepts of blood purity are not in line with current ethnic realities, which only serve to further the notion of the "vanishing race."

If Indigenous people are to preserve and protect their identity as individuals and communities, Borrows argues, we must also adopt a more fluid way of defining our identity, especially since one in every two Aboriginal people marries a non-Aboriginal person.[241] He views Indigenous identity as incorporating local, national, and international influences. At the same time, he argues that some restrictions are necessary to maintain the social and political integrity of the group, so long as they are not based on racist criteria:[242]

However, while I do not favour limits on citizenship on racialized grounds, it may be appropriate to have rigorous citizenship requirements on other grounds, to protect and nurture these communities. Aboriginal peoples are much more than kin-based groups. They have social, political, legal, economic, and spiritual ideologies and institutions that are transmitted through their cultural systems. These systems do not depend exclusively on ethnicity, and can be learned and adopted by others with some effort. Therefore, Aboriginal peoples could consider implementing laws consistent with these traditions to extend citizenship in Aboriginal communities to non-Aboriginal people. If non-Aboriginal people met certain standards that allowed for the creation and reproduction of these communities' values, then these people should have a way to become Aboriginal citizens. The extension of this responsibility would respect the autonomy of Aboriginal communities, while at the same time recognizing the need to consider our interdependence as human beings.[243]

Borrows's solution opens the door for Indigenous nations to rebuild by including not just Indigenous peoples with mixed ancestries as citizens but leaves the possibility open to incorporate others.

Another perspective is that of Cornet, who suggests that band membership provisions may be the "bridge" to self-government arrangements that include recognition of Aboriginal citizenship.[244] She argues that the federal government could declare the *Indian Act* status provisions inoperative and use band membership codes to determine who Indigenous peoples are until self-government agreements have been negotiated. Her proposed solution may still involve reliance on some degree of descent, but only in the sense that citizenship can be acquired by birth, like Canadian citizenship.

Cornet's solution is somewhat similar to that proposed by Lawrence, who argues that the transformation of how we think about Indigenous identity does not have to wait until every Indigenous nation has signed a self-government agreement with citizenship codes.[245] She explains that interim processes like the amendment of the status provisions under the *Indian Act* and changes to band membership provisions could help extend some benefits to Indigenous people in the present. She also argues that Aboriginal organizations should challenge the section 6(2) cut-off in the *Indian Act*, but her ultimate solution to Indigenous identity and citizenship involves a focus on confederacies rather than *Indian Act* bands:

> The confederacies represent a way out of the deadlock of fragmentation and divisions that Native people have been sealed into by the Indian Act for two reasons — they not only present the possibility of renegotiating

the boundaries that have currently been erected around different categories of Indigeneity, but they envision a potentially sufficient land base to
do so. While Bill C-31 Indians may struggle for the right to be members
in their mothers' communities, the fact remains that the generations of
individuals excluded from Indianness by gender and racial discrimination
within the Indian Act will not all be able to rediscover "home" within the
approximately six hundred existing postage-stamp-sized communities that
are currently called "First Nations." The only really viable way in which
urban Native people would be able to have access to Native land is through
the prospect of being citizens of the original Indigenous territories — the
lands that correspond to those that were held by the different Indigenous
nations at the time of contact. We must be clear, though, that if First Nations genuinely want an end to the divisiveness of the current system, they
cannot create new national entities that simply replicate its logic.[246]

For Lawrence, the focus is not so much on the entity (bands, nations, or confederacies) as on the criteria that determine who is in and who is out. These new
entities would be similar to the historical confederacies, like the Iroquois Confederacy or the Wabanaki Confederacy, for example, but she does argue that both
the registration provisions and band membership codes have to be fixed in the
interim. New entities can easily adopt the discriminatory criteria of the past and
prevent communities and individuals from being able to move forward.

While Garroutte takes her examples from the tribes in the United States,
the principles she extracts are equally applicable to First Nations in Canada.[247]
Garroutte noted that cultural definitions of who is an Indian always seem to be
applied to individuals rather than to tribes as a whole. She argues that cultural
definitions lead to obsession with tribal "authenticity."[248] So many Indians tie
up their identities with the concept of distinctiveness that this easily gets tied
up with the extreme end of "otherness," such that no one can ever meet such a
high standard. There are "good reasons why Indian communities might want to
forgive themselves, and others for the cultural losses they have suffered."[249] After
reviewing the harms suffered by American tribes due to blood quantum codes,
she proposes a definition of tribal identity based on kinship. Her definition of
kinship is based on a relationship to one's ancestors that is not fractioned by
blood quantum, and allows for the incorporation of non-tribal members to be
adopted into the tribe. Her solution envisions a concept of kinship that is not
rooted exclusively on ancestral connections but can also be obtained through
learned behaviours. A flexible definition like this would honour one's ancestors
and at the same time not shame "mixed-bloods," or those who become part of
the community through a means other than birth. Her vision of kinship presup-
poses a commitment to traditional values without seeing the culture as frozen

in a particular time period, making her solution based on reciprocity between individuals and their communities:

> But it does encourage them to see even those who are on the margins of other definitions of identity — the non-enrolled, those of low blood quantum, the culturally dispossessed, and even the "new Indians" — as individuals who carry in their very bodies a powerful and important connection to the ancestors, and thus as potential relatives who possess personal worth and unique talents. And it allows these people to become relatives in the fullest sense, as they are taught to turn their talents to the benefit of Native communities and learn to live in reciprocity.[250]

Both individuals who are included in the community and the community itself will have to give a little, but both will grow from the exchange. Lomayesva, who also uses the U. S. experience, proposes a similar solution:

> I suggest that the term Indian cannot be defined by reference to any set standards based upon blood or cultural belief. It must be understood to describe a type of connection between an individual and tribal community. Thus, to be Indian is to possess a type of connection between oneself and a tribal community.[251]

While he does not expand on this concept or explain how this connection could be made, he emphasizes that focus should be on the relationship between the individual and the community rather than trying to "essentialize" what an Indian is in terms of blood or culture.[252] Schouls makes a similar argument:

> Aboriginal identity is more properly understood as a relational phenomenon; one acquires it by virtue of one's connection to others through ancestry, shared historical memories and territories, and shared commitment to one another in community over time. This approach in other words, lends flexibility to Aboriginal identity; it can be shaped to meet challenges posed by new circumstances without necessarily jeopardizing the integrity of Aboriginal identity itself.[253]

The emphasis should be on the many possible factors that demonstrate a real connection with the Indigenous nation, not on singular criteria. The singular focus on just about any criterion for membership could be used to exclude people. What is required is a demonstration of key connections between the individual and the people through a combination of factors which may be different for one person (e.g., familial connections) than for another (e.g. loyalty to the nation).

The fact that solutions are possible does not mean that change will be easy. Some First Nations are in the process of changing their membership codes, while others have never adopted one. Some have already negotiated self-government agreements which have criteria based on blood quantum/descent that are arguably discriminatory. Some First Nations are presently in the grip of intense membership disputes that are affected by decades of federal interference in determining identity and linking identity to funding. Where the once historic goal was to become large, powerful nations, now some bands are trying to limit numbers owing to limited resources and fears of political takeovers by new members. Communities that are using their traditions to exclude people are not allowing for the many ways in which Indigenous identities have evolved and adapted to the circumstances around them. While political groups advocate for the inclusion of their members in their Indigenous nations and fight against ongoing discrimination within the *Indian Act* and band membership codes, they, too, have fallen victim to the same kinds of criteria that create discrimination. They are trying to assert their Indigenous "authenticity" in the only way that the federal government will allow them: by proving direct blood lines to Indigenous peoples in order to access funding, access seats at negotiating tables, and speak with "authenticity." There is now even a trend to "traditionalize" these organizations out of fear that they will not be seen as "Indian" enough.

This issue cannot be examined from a purely theoretical perspective. The practical, everyday realities of Indigenous peoples and their communities requires closer examination. What follows is a look at two different Indigenous groups: one a First Nation and the other an Aboriginal organization set up to advocate on behalf of the excluded. What is common to both groups is the difficulty they have had with regard to membership issues. Membership disputes can be difficult, as they involve long-held beliefs, traditions, and colonial ideologies which have been internalized. It is no wonder, then, that some communities like Kahnawa'ke are having such serious membership disputes and why some communities may have decided to avoid dealing with the matter altogether. Kahnawa'ke is well known for its membership code, which was adopted outside the *Indian Act* context and has been the subject of much controversy both inside and outside the community.[255]

Kahnawa'ke is a Mohawk community located in Quebec. It has been in the media in recent months defending the eviction notices it sent to the non-Indigenous spouses of Mohawk residents based on their residency by-law, which prohibits non-Mohawk members from residing on the reserve.[256] Their membership code has also received attention for its 50 per cent blood quantum requirement, and a moratorium on mixed marriages.[257] Alfred, who wrote about Kahnawa'ke Mohawk politics in *Heeding the Voices of Our Ancestors*, also examined both the traditional and contemporary methods the community has used to determine membership. He has come to understand the conflict within the community as "the necessary by-product of rejecting the legacy of an unjust history and the struggle to re-integrate traditional values in the community."[258] He describes the struggle in relation to membership:

> As part of the traditionalist movement and the eventual development of a nationalist ideology in Kahnawake, imposed Canadian definitions of Indian status and criteria for eligibility to reside within Mohawk territory were explicitly rejected by the Mohawks. Control over membership and the definition of Mohawk status was recognized as the core power necessary to recreate a community based upon traditional Mohawk values.[259]

Unfortunately, in ridding themselves of the *Indian Act's* direct influence on membership, they ended up incorporating the colonial ideologies about race and blood purity embedded in the *Act*. They abandoned their traditional ideologies for those they thought would protect their community. Alfred highlighted the community's most recent report, which reviewed the membership criteria and procedures, and concluded that they were not as effective as hoped:

> In general, it must be noted that many of the processes and institutions established through the current Membership Law have failed to live up to its preamble. Instead of developing a sense of community, they have led to disharmony and anger. Instead of respecting the principles of dignity and compassion, they have promoted accusations and resentment. Instead of replacing foreign laws such as the Indian Act, they are often still cited in the decision-making process.[260]

Not only does the report recommend that a "total reworking of the law" be considered, but that other laws, like the Election Law, be consistent with the Membership Law.

Their 1981 law placed a moratorium on marriages to non-Indians and the adoption of non-Indians. Anyone who broke this law was deprived of the benefits of Mohawk membership. After 1984, the law read so that new members had to meet a 50 per cent blood quantum requirement. In 2004 when the new law came into force, the Mohawk Registry (which kept the names of all members) divided the members into different categories: those who were of "native lineage" and who had been on the previous registry, and those who became automatic members. Those with "acquired status" became entitled to residency, but not membership. These individuals included women who acquired status by marriage and whose marriages were still intact, or they were widows.[261] One of the main concerns with this law is its lack of enforcement power. They are currently in the process of trying to set up a Court of Kahnawa'ke, as they would like to charge, fine, or imprison residents in Mohawk territory who are non-members.[262] They could also suspend membership privileges for anyone who would "cohabitate with or rent accommodations to non-members."[263] In 2006, the council approved a project called the "Affiliated Individuals Project." This was intended to find out how many people were affiliated with the community, who they were, and where they lived.[264] It was thought that this information might be useful for possible future consultations, and to allow the membership department to forecast impacts on membership statistics. "We have been able to contact at least two thirds of these individuals and have found that for the first thousand people contacted there were a thousand more who were their descendants."[265] The membership department appears to be quite concerned about the *McIvor* case and the extent to which they may be forced to accept new members.[266]

At the same time, they also realize that, in comparison to other Indigenous communities in Canada, they have stricter membership requirements: "When it comes to lineage it appears that we are the most difficult on our own people."[267] They have also noted problems in terms of the actual decision-making process with their Council of Elders. "Numerous complaints have been received" regarding the decisions and conduct of the Council of Elders alleging the "inconsistent treatment of applicants."[268] Their original goal was to have a law that was "malleable" and could adjust to changing needs, and to focus less on blood quantum and more on residency rights and the rebuilding of "ancestry and family ties."[269] However, in practice, this does not seem to be the case. One striking example of the inconsistencies to come out of their Elders Council is when a certain Indigenous lineage quantum is accepted for one sibling and not for another.[270] While not in their mandate, the Council of Elders continues to "feel an obligation to the community not to allow further erosion of our culture and bloodlines."[271] Additional complaints against the Council of Elders by community members include

> assertions of unnecessary prying into personal lives as well as dismissive treatment and harmful statements made during hearings.
>
> In addition, many community members insist that the real reasons for unfavourable decisions are not publicly stated. For example, the published reason may state a reason such as "no connection to the community or culture" while the applicant insists that this is obviously untrue and that the stated reason is "personal history such as troubles in their past."[272]

Other issues include lack of redress for community members for unfavourable decisions; lack of transparency and accountability by the Council of Elders; the insistence of the Council of Elders on interpreting the criteria to include blood quantum (when it does not); the issue of whether to include Mohawk Nation members or only Kahnawa'ke community members; and the issue of citizenship versus membership and the political agreements that may have been made with other Mohawk communities to establish who is a Mohawk. The report's conclusion is telling: "Few of our community would actually fit into the strictest mode of lineage calculation as evidenced by the application of strict blood quantum consideration, clan association and ties to the community," and that "if the community were truly traditional, not many would be refused."[273]

Despite all the work, consultations, and studies done to date in Kahnawa'ke regarding membership, they are still struggling with the issue of Indigenous identity, membership, and citizenship, and how best to bring about positive changes to ensure the survival of their people. This community could achieve many of its goals and include many of the concerns of its community members by reuniting the important relationships between Indigenous identity and belonging through connections. The connections that individuals have to their communities and nations, and vice versa, are inseparable from one another. All individuals have had separate life experiences, all of which have shaped their identities. Similarly, communal identities are not frozen in time, but grow, evolve, and adapt to changing circumstances. An identification system that focuses on the inter-relationships or connections between individuals and communities and allows for alternative ways of identifying those connections will accomplish many of the goals cited by Kahnawa'ke. This will allow individuals the freedom to be part of their community and to form safe attachments by being free to identify as Mohawk. It also fits with Kahnawa'ke jurisdiction over deciding who does and does not belong.

Just as First Nations can struggle with identity and membership issues, so, too, can the very organizations which purport to advocate on behalf of those who are excluded. The New Brunswick Aboriginal Peoples Council (NBAPC) is a provincial affiliate of the Congress of Aboriginal Peoples (CAP), both of whom claim to represent the interests of status and non-status Indians living off reserve.[274] In order to be a member of the NBAPC, one must provide documentary evidence that one is a direct descendant of a person with Aboriginal ancestry.[275] Further, applicants must be able to trace their blood relative back to a "known" ancestor no earlier than July 1, 1867.[276] This means that, if the person one relies on as their Indigenous relative was born in 1725 and died in 1790, their ancestry would be too remote in terms of blood quantum or degree of descent to entitle them to membership in the NBAPC. This result seems somewhat counter to those the NBAPC represents, as it is often blood quantum in the *Indian Act* or band membership codes that make them the excluded group to begin with. What is even more ironic is the choice of date to limit the remoteness of descent from an Indigenous ancestor. Indigenous nations did not begin or end on July 1, 1867, and choosing the date of Confederation seems to be the ultimate example of assimilation at work. What does confederation have to do with Indigenous identity?

Not only must applicants prove their blood link, but the code also specifies that non-Indigenous spouses of approved members cannot become full members. However, even these rules are not applied equally among applicants. While it is not obvious from the *Constitution and By-Laws*, in practice, the Membership Committee makes additional requirements of non-status Indians not made of status Indians. For example, non-status applicants must provide documented proof of their Indigenous ancestry in order to qualify for membership; status Indians, on the other hand, need only submit their status card.[277] This is despite the fact that the NBAPC's *Constitution and By-Laws* specifically states: "The federal Indian Act is irrelevant to issues of membership, community participation or beneficiary entitlement."[278] This rule also has the effect of privileging non-Indigenous women applicants over Indigenous women applicants. A non-status Indigenous applicant would be required to provide proof of Indigenous ancestry, whereas a non-Indigenous woman who gained status through marriage would not have to do so. This has resulted in the further anomaly that the non-Indigenous spouses of status Indian members get to become full members of the NBAPC, whereas the non-Indigenous spouses of non-status Indians members do not.[279] This is an odd result for an organisation that claims to represent the interests of non-status Indians. These situations are bound to result when membership codes try to mix blood quantum criteria with *Indian Act* status. Neither is a true reflection of one's Indigenous identity, but perpetuates the reliance on racist and sexist criteria for determining membership.

Some First Nations discriminate against their members on the basis of residency — i.e., whether they live on the reserve — in terms of whether or not they can be members, whether they can vote in elections or run for office, or whether they can have access to programs and services provided by the band.[280] Until amendments were made to the *NBAPC Constitution* at the 37th Annual General Meeting in 2008, the NBAPC arguably discriminated, in the same way, against their off-reserve members as against anyone who was not resident in the province.[281] Just as off-reserve band members in First Nations could not vote or run for office in band elections, the NBAPC refused to allow their non-provincial members to vote or run for office in their elections.[282] While the NBAPC criticized some bands for failing to provide information or programs and services to off-reserve band members, the NBAPC appeared to be doing the same thing.[283] Given the long history of the NBAPC's advocacy to combat discrimination under the *Indian Act* and band membership codes, it is surprising that their own codes perpetuated this injustice. Perhaps what this shows is that off-reserve Indigenous people have been affected by assimilation as much as on-reserve Indigenous people and will require just as much time to deal with these complex issues of membership.

Earlier in this section, I reviewed the solutions that have been proposed by various authors. Some of these offered alternatives to the current *Indian Act* status provisions and band membership codes. They also highlighted the dangers in using restrictive traditional criteria which have the effect of freezing Indigenous identities in time. A common theme was the importance of Indigenous nations having control over determining their own citizens. There is a general consensus in the literature that Canada has no moral or legal authority to determine either individual or communal identities. Any of the proposed solutions will obviously not come without debate, struggle, and social conflict, as the examples illustrate. However, the benefits that accrue to individuals and communities in revitalizing their cultures and identities far outweigh the challenges they may face in arriving at a consensus. All the ideas reviewed above are reflected in some way in the recommendations I will make in the section that follows. In coming up with over-arching principles that could be used by Indigenous nations to determine citizenship, I am cognizant of the fact that there is no one-size-fits-all solution. Each Indigenous nation must engage in a community process to determine which cultural factors are most important to them, how they will weigh the importance of each factor, and the processes they will use to make such determinations.

The principles I will propose take into account several challenges reviewed in previous chapters: (1) governments, courts, and many Canadians, tend to view Indigenous cultures as frozen in pre-contact times; (2) there has been a long history of government interference in both individual and communal Indigenous identity; (3) Indigenous nations are not races of people that can be determined through biological determinations such as hair colour or blood quantum; (4) Indigenous nations are not currently organized in their traditional forms; and (5) self-determining peoples exercise their powers within a context of domestic and international legal laws which must be reconciled. While the laws of Indigenous nations will be paramount over federal laws in core areas like citizenship, individual Indigenous citizens will have the benefit of both the laws of their nation and the laws of Canada. Thus, communal laws are limited by the laws which benefit individuals, and vice versa. These challenges must be kept in mind when Indigenous nations consult with their local communities and individual citizens. Some Indigenous nations are not as united on a nationhood basis, which means that power is at a local rather than a national level. This fact will be more prominent for some Indigenous nations than others. Even taking into account all these significant challenges, there are still fundamental principles which can guide discussions about citizenship.

The underlying basis of any community's citizenship principles must be the connections individual citizens have to their nation. I see it as a flexible concept which will serve as the foundation of any code and will inform the appropriateness of each citizenship criterion, whether at the band membership level or at the nation level. This flexibility must be built in to accommodate the ongoing struggles faced by Indigenous peoples in maintaining their cultures and traditions in the face of assimilatory laws and policies. My suggestions come from my views about the traditional concept of relationships, which is circular in nature and is common to many Indigenous communities. The relationship between an individual and their nation is experienced differently by each generation and the wealth of these experiences needs to be passed on and shared with families, friends, acquaintances, co-workers, elders, advisors, leaders, children, and other communities. These relationships will evolve over time, just as a community's traditions, customs, and practices do. The circle can only be complete if an individual who identifies as Mi'kmaq is recognized as Mi'kmaq and is welcome into the local Mi'kmaq community as a Mi'kmaq. One cannot be a Mi'kmaq for some purposes and not others and still maintain a secure identity. This identity must be reflected in all forms: social, political, cultural, and legal. Even the relationship between the individual and their nation is circular and reciprocal. Just as individual Mi'kmaq citizens would expect all the rights, benefits, and privileges associated with being Mi'kmaq, so too can the Mi'kmaq Nation expect that their citizens live up to their civic duties and responsibilities and make sacrifices for the benefit of their nation when needed. The Mi'kmaq Nation will only survive into the future and thrive if it finds a way to build a bridge between its traditional structure (seven districts) and its current structure (bands) as well as the chiefs, elders, and political organizations now speaking on behalf of Mi'kmaq people. So long as the Mi'kmaq Nation has individuals who are willing to commit to the continuance of their identity, culture, government, and nation, it will survive the current social conflict that is the result of cultural growth, adaptation, and survival.

Loyalty, commitment, sacrifice, volunteerism, and civic duty will come freely from Indigenous citizens who have their individual and communal identities recognized, supported, and protected. This kind of protection extends to all rightful citizens, regardless of sex, blood quantum, or place of residence. In exchange for communities embracing their members for the harms they have suffered through Canada's assimilatory laws and policies, residential schools, forced relocations, disproportionate incarceration rates, underfunded social programs, and stolen lands and resources, individuals have a lot to offer their nations in terms of nation-building. There are Indigenous doctors, lawyers, academics, business owners, teachers, nurses, counsellors, trades people, hunters, fishers, elders, and even politicians who all have a role to play in building strong nations. They may have different opinions on how to rebuild their nations, but their common identity gives them all, new and old members alike, a common purpose — to improve the lives of their people, rebuild their nations, and preserve their cultures for future generations. The key connections that maintain these relations will have different meanings and levels of priority in each community. However, the goals will be similar, as Indigenous communities move from federally controlled peoples to self-determining peoples whose priority is to preserve their identity for future generations.

While a thorough consultation and information process would be necessary in each community to work out these varying priorities, and a complete community membership code or self-government citizenship code would be much larger than I can offer in this book, what follows is how I would start the discussions in my community. I will use my home community of Eel River Bar First Nation and the larger Mi'kmaq Nation as the example, and demonstrate how my family would be affected by various citizenship criteria. The three categories of criteria that I believe are most appropriate for my nation (citizenship) and community (membership) are the same and consist of the following: (1) ancestral connection (broadly defined); (2) civic loyalty or commitment to the survival of the Mi'kmaq Nation; and (3) respect for Mi'kmaq language, traditions, customs, and practices. While these categories are focused on self-government citizenship codes, they could also be applied to band membership in the interim. The criteria I will include under each category represent factors I believe are important to the Mi'kmaq Nation. One will not find any references to things like clans, houses, or hereditary chiefs that might be found in the codes of other nations. While the general categories may apply to any nation, the specific criteria and the weight each is given in determining the overall connection one has to a nation will vary with each nation.

I believe that a connection to one's ancestors is an important part of establishing citizenship in a nation, membership in a community, and for determining individual identity. However, a requirement that an applicant prove an ancestral connection to the Mi'kmaq Nation does not equate with the imposition of a certain blood quantum or fixed formula relating to remoteness or proximity of descent from one's ancestors. I view an ancestral connection as more broadly defined. Ancestry in the form of common histories, families, communities, territories, and treaties can be a great source of pride. However, ancestry can also be through birth, adoption, long-time residency, or other similar association. For example, proof of an ancestral connection to the Mi'kmaq Nation for one applicant could take the form of demonstrating familial links to citizens of the Mi'kmaq Nation directly or through its various communities all over Mi'kma'ki.[284] This might include demonstrating a familial connection to past elders, chiefs, or known Mi'kmaq families within the area. This does not mean that an individual could make an unsubstantiated claim that one of their great-grandmothers seven times removed might have looked Indian. The connection cannot be so tenuous as to be left open for abuse, but must represent a genuine familial link to the Mi'kmaq Nation through birth, adoption, or otherwise. For example, an applicant whose parents were not members of a specific Mi'kmaq band because of the *Indian Act* or past membership codes might still be able to show that their grandparents or great grandparents were members, and that they have maintained a link to the community through their family. Yet, take the example of an Acadian whose parents, grandparents, and great grandparents for four or five generations lived as Acadians, who has always identified with French language and culture, and who one day finds out that he or she has a Mi'kmaq ancestor in their family. Should such a person be considered Mi'kmaq? Assuming that the only connection this Acadian applicant had to the Mi'kmaq Nation was this ancestral connection four or five generations removed, I would say no. Otherwise, I would be basing Mi'kmaq identity solely on blood descent. Opportunistic identity claims can be weeded out using a connections methodology. There is no need to set a specific "cut-off" point in terms of descent, because it is the sum total of the applicant's connections that would be the ultimate determinant of acceptance. Of course, it would always be open to the Mi'kmaq Nation to decide if they want to include someone with tenuous connections if it felt a benefit to the nation to do so. I wouldn't recommend it if we want to maintain a strong national identity.

Another way of demonstrating an ancestral connection might be to allow spouses, male or female, who have married into our communities and have been a part of them for a substantial period of time to be considered for citizenship. I have no specific time period in mind, but a time which represents a significant connection to the community could not be reflected in a year or two. Yet, a wife or husband who has been married to a Mi'kmaq citizen for 40 years, has lived in the community, has volunteered or participated in community events, would certainly have a strong application. Other applicants may have been adopted by Mi'kmaq citizens or community members when they were young, and can therefore show an ancestral connection that way. Others may have familial connections within a specific community, may respect the traditions and customs of the Mi'kmaq, and may have always lived on traditional Mi'kmaq territory, but may not have lived on their community's reserve. I would envision that such a person would also have a strong application, because residency would be broadly defined to include traditional territory, thereby dispensing with national, provincial, or reserve boundaries. Defining residency in terms of reserve boundaries would not only incorporate the *Indian Act* into determinations of Mi'kmaq citizenship, but would also automatically disqualify the 50 per cent of Indigenous people in Canada who live off reserve. Therefore, being born within our community would include being born within any of the vast tracts of traditional territory throughout New Brunswick, Nova Scotia, Newfoundland and Labrador, Prince Edward Island, Quebec, and Maine that are Mi'kma'ki. Instead of our potential citizens being viewed as off-reserve people, they should be viewed as on-traditional-territory people. Perhaps if we change our terminology to reflect our realities rather than Canada's, we will find it easier to amend our citizenship codes to welcome home new citizens, and recognize our Mi'kmaq citizens who were always here.

The second category of criteria would involve applicants demonstrating their civic commitment or loyalty to the Mi'kmaq Nation. Commitment and loyalty is used here in the civic sense, not in the sense of supporting certain political leadership candidates, or any prohibition of public criticism of the Mi'kmaq governments, its laws, or policies. It is often the very citizens who are passionate about their nation who take the time to offer constructive criticism with a view to making their nation a better place for all its citizens. No democratic nation should want to dissuade civic participation. How, then, could civic loyalty be demonstrated in terms of an application for citizenship in the Mi'kmaq Nation? A significant way of doing this would be the very act self-identifying as a Mi'kmaq that comes with the application. While some might not see such a declaration as significant, given our colonial history which tried to make Indigenous people ashamed of who they were, such public declarations are a significant aspect of our individual and communal healing and restoration of pride. Elders, mentors, and role models who publicly declare their citizenship can only foster pride in younger generations. Therefore, an applicant who self-identifies as Mi'kmaq, has a family history of publicly identifying with the Mi'kmaq Nation, and who swears an oath of allegiance to the Mi'kmaq Nation (or some traditional method of affiliation) might meet this criterion.

Civic loyalty can be demonstrated by voting in elections, on important referendums, or on land claim, treaty, or other agreement. It is not voting in favour of an issue which demonstrates civic loyalty, but the act of voting itself. An individual citizen who cares deeply about his or her nation might vote against a certain leader or agreement. Weak applicants might be boosted by nation-based citizenship courses designed to educate current and potential applicants about the history, politics, governance structures, and laws of the Mi'kmaq, for example. Alternatively, applicants might also show their record of service to the nation, which they have accumulated through employment, volunteerism, advocacy, or other related activity or through significant contributions to the overall social well-being of their local community. Raising happy, healthy children would be a significant contribution to the overall health and well-being of the community. Similarly, elders who offer advice and guidance to younger generations perform as great a civic duty for their communities as do those who vote. The idea is not to force all citizens to demonstrate their connection to their community in the same way. There are many ways to demonstrate civic loyalty. Valuing the diverse contributions of citizens contributes to stronger communities and the Mi'kmaq Nation as a whole. Other examples could include agreeing to obey the laws, rules, and codes adopted by the Mi'kmaq Nation in relation to peace and order, distribution of resources, and taxes, or submitting to Mi'kmaq Nation jurisdiction over applicable legal matters.

The last category is characterized as a respect for the languages, traditions, customs, and practices of the Mi'kmaq. This category may sound the same as some of the band membership codes which require knowledge of specific traditions, customs, and beliefs, but there is a significant difference in what I am proposing. There is no requirement under this category for an applicant to practice Mi'kmaq beliefs, to participate in sweat lodges, or dance in powwows. However, they should have some familiarity with what the traditions, customs, practices, and beliefs are and respect them. Respect can take the form of taking time to learn the traditions, or supporting bilingual (English-Mi'kmaq or French-Mi'kmaq) signage and instruction in schools, for example. In this way, not all citizens are required to think the same way; nor are applicants required to attend traditional ceremonies instead of going to church. The Mi'kmaq Nation will have to account for the fact that many Mi'kmaq people have been converted to other belief systems, such as Catholicism, but still strongly identify with Mi'kmaq identity. These individuals have many other ways of expressing their respect of Mi'kmaq tradition, without having to physically practice it. No one would question the Mi'kmaq identity of members of the Membertou First Nation in Nova Scotia, especially after their recent Membertou 400 celebration. This celebration took the form of a large powwow in Halifax, and was organized to celebrate Grand Chief Membertou's baptism 400 years ago. There are many Mi'kmaq people who practice Catholicism but who still identify as citizens of the Mi'kmaq Nation.

I have met many Mi'kmaq people who can and cannot speak Mi'kmaq, who do and do not go to church, who like and dislike powwows. All of these people are still Mi'kmaq, but have had different life experiences and therefore express their identities in different ways. This category of respect for tradition is meant to balance the importance of tradition, customs, practices, languages, and beliefs to the maintenance and preservation of Mi'kmaq identity and culture for future generations. The Mi'kmaq Nation cannot punish its citizens for being victims of colonial and present-day interference with their identities. Respect for tradition could be shown by an individual commitment to the preservation of Mi'kmaq culture. An example of meeting this criteria would be applicants who can demonstrate that they speak the traditional Mi'kmaq language, that they are willing to learn the language, or that they will promote the language in other capacities, such as sending their children to language classes or supporting the use of Mi'kmaq language use within their communities, governments, and educations systems. Other ways of respecting Mi'kmaq traditions and practices would be through adherence to the traditional rules and laws in relation to hunting, fishing, and gathering, or contributions to give-away ceremonies or redistribution of resources that may or may not find official legislative form. This category is meant to include a wide range of factors that the Mi'kmaq Nation may find important to their survival as a nation and to make it possible for diverse citizens to meet. The key will be to encourage a great deal of flexibility in assessing applications and developing review and appeal processes so as to ensure that different ways of being Mi'kmaq are protected. At the same time, this flexibility must be balanced with core standards to ensure that applicants bringing forward tenuous or suspect claims of Mi'kmaq identity are clearly identified.

Other key aspects of the citizenship process will have to be addressed, such as the application process itself, evidentiary standards, decision-making, and appeal processes. There will initially be a two pronged process — one that determines the charter group Mi'kmaq citizens, and one that deals with how future citizenship will be determined. In my view, citizenship is a birthright which flows from generation to generation and does not require self-identification and application. I would therefore advocate that any Mi'kmaq citizenship code provide that children born or adopted to a Mi'kmaq citizen parent or parents be granted citizenship at birth. Newly approved applicants would have access to the same rights, benefits, privileges, and responsibilities as the charter group. All citizens would be treated equally.

The above review of my suggested categories of citizenship criteria demonstrates a focus on key aspects of what makes a Mi'kmaq citizen, but also incorporates enough flexibility so that applicant's for future Mi'kmaq citizenship are free to be individuals and have their own views about what makes the good life, even as they share a commitment to the preservation of their nation. No one applicant will have to demonstrate all the criteria noted above, but will be assessed based on the combination of factors which they bring forward. While applicants do not all have to have the same level or number of criteria to be accepted as citizens, they should be able to show how they meet at least some of the criteria in each category. For example, some citizens will have strong ancestral connections but may be weaker in traditional aspects, while others may have strong commitments to the Mi'kmaq Nation and lesser ancestral connections. A system will have to be developed which weighs each factor according to its priority to the nation. Applicants could then be assessed based on the overall strength of the application as compared to a pre-determined baseline. It is also important that the criteria for citizenship be publicly available, that the decision-making process be credible and fair, and that those making the decisions are representative of all who have legitimate interests in the Mi'kmaq Nation. So, one would not expect a Citizenship Committee to be made up of only status Indians who live on reserve, under the guise of using elders to make the determinations. Off-reserve band members and non-status Indians should be included in the decision-making process.

The criteria for citizenship decisions can change or evolve with the passage of time, along with the changing circumstances and priorities of the Mi'kmaq Nation. The Mi'kmaq Nation should neither be frozen in pre-contact times nor in the present. Fairness will be an essential part of the citizenship process now and in the future. Criteria which are considered important to the Mi'kmaq Nation ought to be applied equally to the charter group and new applicants for citizenship; it would be applying a double standard for the Mi'kmaq Nation to indicate that all new citizens must be fluent in the Mi'kmaq language when the majority of its current citizens are not. These are the kinds of standards that lead to arbitrary exclusions, claims of discrimination, and discontent within families and communities, and which foster ongoing, harmful divisions within the Mi'kmaq Nation. There will be inevitable growing pains, but the process can be designed to identify and eliminate obvious biases, double standards, and discrimination.

I must clarify that, in contemplating problems and offering potential solutions, I am not suggesting that the Mi'kmaq Nation or any First Nation is any more or less likely than the federal or provincial governments to enact discriminatory codes or apply them unjustly. Even a country with a solid international reputation like Canada can and does commit breaches of human rights, and therefore protections are necessary. I would expect the Mi'kmaq and other First Nations to be no more or less prone to making mistakes and violating rights, and so protections will have to be built into the processes. Especially in the area of identity and citizenship, it is often easier to identify problems than it is to offer solutions. My goal in this book is to do both. In this way, individual citizens and those who have legitimate claims to citizenship can have open, frank discussions about how to move forward.

I will conclude this chapter by using my own personal family situation as an example, to see how we might be assessed against the citizenship criteria that I have proposed. First of all, I would assume that in identifying the charter group of Mi'kmaq citizens, my family members and I would be included. In the event that we were not included and we had to apply for citizenship as new applicants, the following represents how I would envision such an analysis would take place. This may help others to assess their own situation and perhaps dissuade those with tenuous claims from applying. Despite the claims of some groups, Mi'kmaq citizenship can't be based solely on self-identification, because Mi'kmaq territories, resources, and treaties are protected exclusively for Mi'kmaq citizens. Self-identification alone would invite opportunists and those who have no connection or loyalty to the Nation. Therefore, it will be assumed that I, like any other applicant. would have to demonstrate a significant connection. By way of review, the categories and related factors that I consider important in determining citizenship in the Mi'kmaq Nation include, but are not limited to:

(1) Ancestral Connections
- Familial ties (birth, adoption, or otherwise) to elders, chiefs, or other members of local Mi'kmaq communities (on reserve or on traditional territory) within the Mi'kmaq Nation territory;
- Parent(s) or grandparent(s) who are/were community members;
- Spouses who have married into local Mi'kmaq communities and have been a part of those communities for a substantial period of time (20 years, for example);
- Adoption into the Mi'kmaq Nation in youth, by community member(s);
- Residency on traditional Mi'kmaq territory;

(2) Commitment to the Mi'kmaq Nation
- Self-identifying as Mi'kmaq;
- Familial history of identifying as Mi'kmaq;
- Official pledge/oath (or some traditional means) of commitment/loyalty to the Mi'kmaq Nation;
- Knowledge of and subscription to the aims, goals, and objectives of the Mi'kmaq Nation;
- Record of service to the Mi'kmaq Nation through volunteerism, advocacy, employment, or political and/or community activities;
- Obeying Mi'kmaq laws and submitting to the jurisdiction of the Mi'kmaq Nation, like paying taxes, or attending Mi'kmaq court;
- Participation in Mi'kmaq civic activities such as voting, consultations, surveys, and community events;
- Contributing taxes currently paid to the Canadian government to the Mi'kmaq Nation;

(3) Respect for Mi'kmaq language, traditions, customs, and practices
- Commitment to learn, maintain, and preserve Mi'kmaq culture;
- Fluency in Mi'kmaq language, willingness to learn the language, or promote the use of the language;
- Supporting use of Mi'kmaq language in school, government, and community;
- Respecting traditional and current Mi'kmaq rules regarding hunting, fishing, and gathering;
- Respecting Mi'kmaq territories, natural resources, governance structures, and other important agreements negotiated by the Mi'kmaq;
- Participating in traditional ceremonies or supporting their use in official functions like schools, government offices and celebrations. . . .

In my case, I would be able to show that my family and I meet various criteria from all three categories. For example, my children and I have a direct familial relationship to many community members, like the former Chief Louis Jerome (my great grandfather). Also, my grandmother, Margaret Jerome, and my father, Frank Palmater, were each band members of a local Mi'kmaq community — Eel River Bar First Nation. I have many aunts, uncles, nieces, nephews, and cousins who have lived on Mi'kmaq territory and/or Eel River Bar reserve their whole lives. My children and I have lived on traditional Mi'kmaq territory for the majority of our lives as well. In the second category, my children and I have always publicly identified as Mi'kmaq people, as have my brothers and sisters, my father, my grandmother, my great grandfather, and so on. We would, without hesitation, make an official commitment to the Mi'kmaq Nation and always work in furtherance of its interests. I would argue that through my years of volunteerism, advocacy, education and work, that I have a substantial record of service to the Mi'kmaq Nation specifically, and to Indigenous peoples generally, as do my children, who have been politically and socially active. In the third category, my children and I are not fluent in the Mi'kmaq language, but I have taken language courses and my children would participate in language courses made available to them. We would agree to obey all legislative and traditional laws and continue to participate in practices and ceremonies related to Mi'kmaq peoples. In many ways, my children and I have been immersed in Mi'kmaq culture, politics, and social activism since we were born. My extended family has a long history of working and volunteering in efforts to protect our lands, treaties, rights, ·and identities as Mi'kmaq people. The only difference between my family and those who live on the Eel River Bar reserve is status under the *Indian Act*. On this basis, I would assume that my family and I would meet the majority of the criteria listed, and those we do not can be linked directly to government interference with our identities.

It has been my life's work to advocate for changes that will make it possible to reunite those rightful citizens currently excluded by discriminatory *Indian Act* rules with their traditional Indigenous nations. Some might argue that I present too rosy a picture, that I have assumed that Indigenous nations will respect the rights of their citizens. I have made no such assumption, but neither have I assumed that Indigenous governments are any more likely to violate their citizens' rights than are non-Indigenous governments. That being said, all nations have to have foundational values and beliefs upon which they based their societal policies. Canada has based its society on liberal democracy, which values equality before and under the law, freedom of association and religion, and freedom of speech, and rejects unreasonable interference from government. These fundamental beliefs are incorporated in Canadian laws, policies, and decisions. Yet, Canadian governments often breach their own fundamental values and beliefs, and courts must bring governments back in line. I expect no more or less of Indigenous governments. Indigenous nations must have core fundamental beliefs and values upon which they base their laws, policies, and decisions, and sometimes they will steer off course, as any government does.

I am not saying that, once the Mi'kmaq Nation or local communities establish fair citizenship or membership codes, this will solve all social conflict in the community. There will always be political divisions, family disputes, and differences in ideologies and priorities, among other social divisions, but citizens would at least be starting from a position of equality. Individuals would have the same access to citizenship and the corresponding rights and responsibilities, whether they live on or off reserve, whether they have black hair or blonde hair, whether they dance in powwows or work in law firms, and whether they are a man or a woman. Every nation has to have core values and ideals, and I am simply advocating that my nation's core values and ideals incorporate equality among our citizens and reject the long history of externally imposed, racist ideologies about who we are as a people.

The more citizens Indigenous nations have, the more influence they can have in domestic and international forums as Indigenous peoples. It is important that the many ways of being Indigenous be protected for the benefit of Indigenous nations and for their children. Just as Indigenous nations demand the right to be self-defining, so too should Indigenous individuals have their citizenship recognized by their Indigenous nations. In this way, Indigenous nations will be able to maintain the political and social integrity of their communities in a fair and equitable manner, and thus help to rebuild their nations to their former status, while simultaneously protecting their lands, resources, and treaty rights for their heirs forever.

Beyond Blood

WHEN I STARTED MY RESEARCH FOR THIS BOOK, I had a very clear idea in my mind about what makes an Indigenous person. I felt very strongly that the determination of Indigenous identity for the purposes of land claims and treaty rights, for example, was much easier than governments were making it out to be. For the most part, I always felt that one just knew when someone was Indigenous or not. I also felt that I had better knowledge than most about the concept of Indigeneity, seeing that I had been raised in a politically active Indigenous family where the assertion, maintenance, and protection of our identity as Mi'kmaq people was the most important of all the issues we addressed. There would not have been a lawyer or professor in the world who could tell me any different. Most of my knowledge up until the writing of this book had been based on my own personal experiences gained from my family, friends, elders, mentors, my home community of Eel River Bar, my education, and my advocacy and volunteer activities with various Aboriginal organizations and First Nations.

I have also learned a great deal having worked for the federal government, especially at Justice Canada and Indian Affairs. In Halifax, I worked as legal counsel for Indian and Northern Affairs Canada (INAC). I also worked for INAC as their director of Lands and Trusts Services, and then as director of Government Relations (treaties, land claims, self-government, and economic development). More recently, in Ottawa, I worked for Justice Canada in their Aboriginal Affairs Portfolio on legal issues pertaining to Bill C-31. All these experiences have helped inform and confirm the views and opinions I have held about Indigenous identity since I was very young.

In the past, whenever I was faced with conflicting views about my identity and my place in this world, I always tried to remember the three things I knew for sure: (1) I am Mi'kmaq, (2) I come from the Mi'kmaq Nation, and (3) my purpose in this world is to make things better for future generations of Mi'kmaq. These are the three basic principles that my large extended family made sure were part of my world view. Their passion to change the world for my benefit was passed on to me so that I could do the same for my children and their children.

While this meant going through all the growing pains of understanding what this was all about, I was never unsure about who I was. I can remember endless occasions where my family challenged me to put these concepts and passions into practice, even at a young age. For example, I remember in elementary school that my older brother Nelson came to my classroom and told the teacher, in front of all of my friends, that I was not allowed to sing "O Canada" until Canada returned all the lands and resources it had stolen from us. I have to say that as a very young person, I was embarrassed and confused, especially since I was the only one of "my kind" in the class.

I did not yet know all our history and the impact that colonialism has had on our families over many generations. Similarly, when I told my older brother Frankie that the teachers had taught me that there were no treaties in the Maritimes, he lectured me for hours about our treaties, what they meant, and how important they were to our nation. He also made me promise to correct the teachers every time they tried to say otherwise. At the time, I did not even know what a treaty was, but I knew from my brother that it was important and that I had a responsibility to protect it. Therefore, without even fully understanding the complexity of the issue, I did my best. Living off reserve, I went to a school where we were the only Indigenous family, and many of the other children did not have the benefit of knowing anything about Indigenous people, except for the cowboys and Indians version they read in our school books. I cannot count how many times I was followed home by kids who would call me names and make what they must have thought were Indian war cries. To add further confusion to the matter, my mother was non-Aboriginal and did not know how to address these upsets. Her solution was to tell me to wear long socks so that no one would see the colour of my legs and not to go around telling people that I was Mi'kmaq. She had the very best of intentions because she loved us and only wanted the best for us. Unfortunately, her context for life was based on what her own parents had passed on to her, and they had significant difficulties with the fact that she had had children with a Mi'kmaq man. At various times when I was growing up, I started to wonder what being Indigenous meant if so many others appeared not to like Indigenous people.

However, those moments were countered by the times when I was surrounded by my own family and community members. These experiences reinforced the positive aspects of my identity and what it gave me in terms of a context for life. I had the benefit of a large extended family that was politically active in many Aboriginal organizations whose objectives were to combat discrimination against off-reserve Indigenous peoples, especially non-status Indians. This often meant trailing after my brothers and sisters, aunts, cousins, and in-laws to meetings, negotiations, protests, and assemblies. I did not always know what they were talking about, but I knew it had to be important because everyone at these meetings would stand up when they spoke and often yelled or cried while making their points. I always felt like I was part of something really important, and I wanted someday to be brave enough to say something really important in front of all those people. However, at the time I did not know what I should say. I had always thought of myself as a Mi'kmaq person, but in numerous meetings with governments and at various negotiations over natural resources, I heard people telling us that we were "not really Indians." We were non-status Indians and therefore did not have any "legitimate" claims on natural resources or lands. This also caused me much confusion and hurt because I had always assumed that Mi'kmaq people were Mi'kmaq regardless of where they lived, what community they came from, or what they looked like. This issue about being excluded on the basis of whether I had status or not was quite upsetting.

As I was getting older and starting to be exposed to these and other political issues, I started to understand what everyone was so passionate about at our gatherings. Try to imagine a meeting with all of your aunts, uncles, cousins, brothers, sisters, in-laws, and friends, many of whom brought babies or small children with them. These same people who passionately debated issues, sometimes at the top of their lungs, could then sit next to one another at the feast that followed. Their passion and ability to keep an open mind and forgive one another showed me how important political debate was and how important it was to ensure that everyone had a voice, regardless of whether we as individuals disagreed with those voices. The recurring theme in our meetings was that we would continue to fight for our rights and those of our children, and that no matter what the government did, they could not deny the blood that ran through our veins. I heard that phrase repeated over and over again. I was told repeatedly that the blood connection we had to our ancestors formed the very basis of our ties to our traditional communities, and so long as we had that we could never be denied our rightful identities as Mi'kmaq and Maliseet peoples. This would become a recurring theme in the years to come.

I think, best of all, was the fact that my family raised me to know who I was and to be proud of that identity, despite all the political and legal challenges that they knew I would face as I got older. My favourite time of the year when I was a child was not Christmas, but the one week out of every summer where I got to go to summer camp with all my nieces, nephews, cousins, and friends. I counted the days until we got to go to "Indian summer camp." We were taught outdoor skills, various lessons in getting along, and to be proud of who we were. Many of my family members had important roles in these summer camps, like my brother Frankie, who always took on roles that we only understood as important later in life, like his covering himself up with lily pads and pretending to be a lake monster so as to scare kids out of the deeper waters. What I liked best, though, was meal time, because all the women who cooked in the kitchen made sure to give us all lots of affection, offered comfort to anyone who was homesick, and bandaged our daily wounds. These women, like our own grandmothers, who so gently tended to our wounds during the day, were also the same politically active women who stood up at meetings and ensured that our leaders were acting in the best interests of future generations. It was not until I grew up that I realized that I had not been attending an Indian summer camp after all. It was a non-status Indian summer camp which was comprised of mainly the descendants of Indian women who had married out and lost their status (Bill C-31 women) from all different families and communities in New Brunswick. These families felt that it was important that we not lose our sense of community or our connections to our identities as Mi'kmaq and Maliseet peoples. So, even as kids, we were protected as much as possible from the assimilatory effects of government laws and policies. I had the benefit of some powerful role models, male and female, status and non-status, on and off reserve, whose collective priority was to ensure that our identities survived.

It should be no surprise, then, that I grew up staying involved in the politics related to Mi'kmaq people, and especially non-status Indians. I absorbed all those messages about the need to eliminate discrimination against non-status Indians, to overcome the imposition of foreign laws on our people, and to be proud of the blood that ran through my veins. It was on this worldview that my educational goals were based. As I started to get politically active and to exercise my voice at meetings and negotiations, I was met with numerous angry band leaders who thought I had no place at the table, first because I was a woman, and second because I was a non-status Indian. I faced similar backlash from various government officials who not only rejected non-status Indians as real Indians, but also questioned my credentials. Whether it was the federal or provincial government at the table talking about rights, they always had lawyers, scientists, or academics with doctorates backing up their positions. On the Indigenous side of the table, we had only two things: each other and the strength of our common identities. Most of the time, our side of the table knew more about the history and law than their side, but we were easily dismissed without any academic letters behind our names. Yet the negotiators on our side of the table were no less intelligent and skilled at what they did. Even today, I would pit Gary Gould, who served as president of the NBAPC for many years, against any of the lawyers working for the federal or provincial governments, and be confident that Gary would know more about the issues affecting us and how to resolve them. Gary has lived the discrimination against which we were fighting, and his passion infected those who came behind him.

The rejection of Canadian and provincial laws that were imposed upon us was a significant theme in our activities. We had never consented to the *Indian Act* and therefore, it was our view that should not apply to us. The *Indian Act* had only ever caused us pain and hardship, and was the very reason for the numerous divisions in our communities — between men and women, status and non-status, and on and off-reserve Indians. The fact that most of my extended family and families like ours either still lived off the land or, at least, supplemented their small household incomes with hunting, fishing, and gathering, also highlighted the long arm of provincial law. I cannot remember a time when my family has not been harassed by provincial enforcement officers when they hunted or fished. Members of my extended family have not only participated in protest hunts, but they continue to be stopped and charged today.[1] Most recently, my brother Nelson was stopped and charged by provincial officers as he hunted for food within Mi'kmaq territory. Though the Crown eventually dropped the charges, they had already caused much stress to my brother, and effectively prevented him from obtaining his food for the winter.

I decided to seek higher education not only to fulfill my Dad's dreams for me, but also because I grew up experiencing all the reasons such an education was necessary. By the time I got to my doctoral studies, I felt confident about what my topic would be and how I would argue it. I knew that I had to write about the struggles of non-status Indians and how to address the ongoing discrimination they face on a daily basis. My plan of action was to offer a concept of Indigeneity that ensured that non-status Indians were included in our home communities and welcomed at government negotiating tables, and that the basis of this inclusion was the fact that the blood that runs through my veins is the same which runs in the veins of status Indians who live on reserve. This solution would be bolstered by the rejection of all Canadian and provincial laws that had been imposed upon us.

Although I started this book thinking I knew what I wanted to write, reflections on my past and new historical information started to open my mind to all the other issues that affect Indigenous identity that I had not previously considered. It was quite alarming to be halfway through my doctoral program only to realize that I might have to change direction. These revelations were so significant that they changed the very basis upon which I wrote my thesis, and subsequently this book. At first this presented a huge problem for me, in that if I could no longer use blood ties to determine Indigenous identity, then I was not sure what I would use. However, it turned out that I did not have to worry so much, because all the key aspects of my Mi'kmaq identity had always been there. They were just submerged under what I thought were more important factors.

Even so, I still had a significant issue to tackle: if I had felt so strongly about my views of Indigenous being linked to blood ties, then others who may be less educated or experienced in the subject, or who had a similar upbringing where they had identified the same way I did, would also be holding on tightly to some of those same views. I had identified this as my most significant hurdle because one can win or lose arguments in court, but to advocate for a significant change in communal thinking is another process altogether. As a result, I felt that the only way to move forward was to identify the problems with some of our strongly held views about Indigenous identity and to provide an understanding of how we, as Indigenous peoples, could have held on so tightly to these views which do more harm to our people than good. I knew then that I wanted my book to be a useful tool for others to challenge the status quo and to identify what we could salvage and what should be abandoned altogether. In this regard, I had to open up myself to other teachings. My family always told me that formal education is important, but to them the education we got from our families, leaders, elders, and communities about all aspects of our people, from politics to culture, was just as important. Therefore, I had to reconsider everything I had been taught in the past in order to see where we as Indigenous peoples could go in the future.

So, I went back to the three pillars of my identity and revisited their meanings. The first pillar was based on the rights of individuals. I had always viewed the struggle with regard to a recognized legal Indigenous identity from an individual perspective. Our political struggles involved trying to combat discrimination against non-status Indians and fighting to ensure that various groups of us, like Indigenous women and their descendants, were not excluded from individual registration in the *Indian Act*. It also involved ensuring that non-status Indians were included in band membership. What I had not considered at the time was the right of Indigenous nations to determine their own identities, and, in so doing, determine who are the rightful citizens of their nations. I had seen the struggle as between individual non-status Indians and individual bands for so long that I had forgotten my earlier teachings: I am a Mi'kmaq and my nation is the Mi'kmaq Nation. From this perspective, I could see that Mi'kmaq identity is not solely determined by its collective, just as it is not solely determined by its individuals. Mi'kmaq identity is formed through the relations between individuals and the nation. This second pillar of my identity concerns the nation, which is made up of large, extended families and local communities as well as individuals. Therefore, in talking about identity rights, I came to understand that, while the Mi'kmaq Nation has the right to determine its own identity and therefore who gets to be a citizen, this right is limited and supported by the right of individuals to their identities as Mi'kmaq people and their right to belong to their nation. It also follows that, while local Mi'kmaq communities may have their own concepts about Mi'kmaq identity and who should be a band member, their ideas about identity and the right to determine band membership are limited, and supported by both the Mi'kmaq Nation and those of individual Mi'kmaq people. So, while I have abandoned the purely individual focus of Indigenous identity, it still remains an important component of it, albeit in a more relational way.

Similarly, I had definite ideas about the use of Canadian and provincial laws in determining Indigenous identity. Our identity as Mi'kmaq and other Indigenous peoples has suffered through so many assimilation policies that our nations, communities, and citizens are divided along numerous legal and political lines that we did not create. On- and off-reserve Indigenous peoples struggle in their relationships in the same way that status and non-status Indians do. My view has thus been that the external laws imposed upon us do much more harm than good and should be completely avoided. However, I have also come to see the benefit in some of the Canadian laws which are more protective in nature. For example, unlike the *Indian Act*, the *Charter of Rights and Freedoms* does not seek to assimilate Indians, ban their ceremonies, or divide nations into bands. On the contrary, the *Charter* contains the same protections and rights found in our traditional laws. It also includes special protections for Indigenous rights, so that Indigenous peoples can enjoy the good life in their nations and within the Canadian democracy. Not only should Indigenous peoples have the benefit of these rights and freedoms, but the *Charter* also makes specific allowance for an interpretation of the rights contained in it so as not to negatively affect their special Aboriginal rights. I started out with the view that no external laws should apply to Indigenous nations, but I have come to realize that certain laws resemble our own values and beliefs so closely that our traditional laws can work hand in hand with the *Charter* for the benefit of all our people. Just because the *Charter* came from Canada does not mean we should cast it aside without first assessing its potential. Just as we balanced the rights and responsibilities of our Indigenous citizens and nations in the past, we can use the *Charter* as one of many tools to help us make those same balances in the future. The *Charter,* then, can act as a mechanism to help Indigenous individuals and nations get through the difficult transitional phase of rejecting the assimilatory views of the past and moving toward our self-governing goals, as well as providing flexible ways for accommodating the diverse identities that have resulted from some of the harms, divisions, and disconnections caused by the *Indian Act* and Canada's past assimilatory policies. Just as the self-definition of an Indigenous nation is complemented and strengthened by the self-definitions of its individual citizens, so, too, can the *Charter* help reconnect individuals and nations in that self-identification process.

One of the only significant barriers to this reunification process between communal and individual conceptions of Indigenous identity is the concept that Indian blood is not only a legitimate and quantifiable criterion, but that it is the most important aspect of Indigenous identity. This brings me to the third pillar upon which I have always based my identity: the obligation I have to protect our identity for future generations. This responsibility comes into direct conflict with my previously held idea that it was the blood that runs through my veins that made me Mi'kmaq. The fact that my great grandfather was the chief of my home community, that my grandmother was a healer for my home community, and that my father was a member of that community has always assured me that I have a legitimate claim to my identity as a Mi'kmaq person. This strong familial connection is still an essential part of my identity, just not for the reasons I used to think. I have heard many Indigenous leaders and other community members say that, no matter what Canada has done to or taken away from Indigenous peoples, it can never take their bloodlines away from them. This is a powerful and significant source of identity for many Indigenous people and their communities. I, too, have struggled with the possible consequences of giving this up as the determinant of my Mi'kmaq identity. For so many years, we as Indigenous peoples — and especially non-status Indians — have looked for that critical link that proves our undeniable connection to our ancestors, our communities, and our future generations. But what is the one true connection that makes me Mi'kmaq? If I were to give up the concept that my blood determines my identity, will I still be Mi'kmaq? The fact that some people have no answer to that question is often what makes them cling so hard to blood as the ultimate determinant of identity.

As hard as it was for me to consider abandoning this concept, once I saw that it causes more harm to our identities than it does to support them, my fear started to subside. My fear completely left me when I realized that, when our ancestors spoke of the blood that runs through our veins, they were not talking about the actual blood, but were referring to our deep connections with our past through our ancestors, with our present through our families and communities, and to our future through our generations yet to come. This circle of life, within which all of us as Mi'kmaq are connected, forms the very basis of our identities. If we as individuals, families, communities, and nations looked beyond superficial measurements of blood and looked deeper at what makes those connections between individuals, their communities and nations so strong, we would see that blood is not only unnecessary as an indicator of our identities; it is completely irrelevant. My search for the one true connection that makes me Mi'kmaq was never really a search at all. All the indicators of my Mi'kmaq identity have been there all along. I had just been too affected by discriminatory laws, assimilatory policies, and racist stereotypes to be able to see through the shame and the pain to celebrate those aspects of our identities that our ancestors fought so hard to protect. I am a Mi'kmaq because I have multiple, deep-rooted connections to the Mi'kmaq Nation and no one connection defines me. My identity is the sum of all my familial connections to my home community of Eel River Bar and the larger Mi'kmaq Nation; the history, values, and beliefs that I share in common with other Mi'kmaq people; my connection to our traditional territories upon which I have lived the majority of my life; and my deep sense of commitment and responsibility to the Mi'kmaq Nation to protect our treaties. No amount of Indian blood could either reinforce or destroy those connections. Had I been adopted into the Mi'kmaq community, I would still have all these connections. Had both of my parents been Mi'kmaq, I would still have all these connections. Identity is formed in part by one's parents, extended families, and community as well as one's own personal journey of discovery. I started out this journey as a Mi'kmaq person and I have ended it more confident of my Mi'kmaq identity than I could have imagined. Even more important, to me, is that my views about Mi'kmaq identity, which are based on my ancestral connections, will also ensure that this rich identity will be available for my children and their children for generations to come.

Getting to this stage took many years of questioning the world around me. This book reflects my journey and how my own opinions have changed. I set out wanting to demonstrate that excluding non-status Indians was wrong, and, in supporting those arguments, I have discovered how inextricably entwined the concepts of Indigenous identity and belonging truly are. Indigenous individuals and communities rely on each other to support, protect, and reinforce each other's identities. My review of how Indigenous identity came to be legislated and why identity is so important for Indigenous peoples, is an important background to understanding how Indigenous identity was changed and how some of those changes (like status) are so ingrained that they seem to have always been part of Indigenous identity. Only in exposing the hidden dangers of how we construct our otherness or difference is it possible to undo those factors which hurt our identities rather than enrich them. Through my research, I came to realize that a balancing of interests between the right of individuals to belong and the right to be self-defining as a nation is necessary. By acknowledging both the positive and problematic aspects of how we identify ourselves, we can start undoing the harms that negatively affect our identities, while fostering those key aspects of our identities with our families and communities.

In the Introduction, I introduced my personal family history and the specific identity issues which affect my family. It was important to me that a real life example be evaluated against the legal analysis and theory that was to follow in subsequent chapters. My great-grandfather, Louis Jerome, was one of the first chiefs of our home community, Eel River Bar First Nation. It was his daughter (my grandmother) Margaret Jerome, who married a non-Indian man and gave birth to my father Frank Palmater. My father also parented with a non-Indian woman, and I was born. As a result, when the Bill C-31 amendments were made to the *Indian Act*, my grandmother was deemed to have been a section 6(1)(c) Indian, my father a section 6(2) Indian, and I and my children are all considered non-status Indians. My father eventually gained band membership in Eel River Bar, but their membership code does not allow me or my children to be members because of our lack of status. Therefore, we are excluded from participating in our band's governance, land claims, and both federal and band-related programs and services. We are also not invited to cultural gatherings, included in consultation meetings or information sessions, and have lacked equal access to our communal elders and leaders. We are denied both our individual identities and the communal identities that come with band membership. While I have used my family as an example, there are many more families just like mine that suffer from the same type of exclusions. It was for this reason that the first chapter highlighted the legal, political, and historical context behind these present-day identity issues. While this will change for me with Bill C-3, it won't for my children.

In Chapter 1, I provided a detailed background on how Indigenous peoples became so divided politically, socially, and legally. The long process of controlling Indigenous identity, dividing Indigenous individuals from their communities and Indigenous communities from their nations, was part of Canada's original assimilation plans. Present-day Aboriginal organizations are divided among which legal sub-group of Aboriginal peoples they represent. For example, the Assembly of First Nations (AFN) represents status Indians through their band chiefs, while the Congress of Aboriginal Peoples (CAP) represents status Indians who live off-reserve, non-status Indians, and Métis. Even the Métis are generally divided between those represented by CAP, those represented by the Métis National Council (MNC), and those in the Métis Settlements in Alberta. The long history of assimilatory laws and policies in Canada have also left Indigenous nations divided into smaller bands, and Indigenous individuals divided into those with or without status and membership and even along gender lines. While Canada has since acknowledged that reliance on those assimilatory views to establish Indigenous policy was wrong, it has not taken steps to amend the *Indian Act* or its related policies that still continue with the old objective of assimilation. Chapter 1 also provided an overview of the development of Indian legislation over the years, especially in regard to individual and communal identities. The preference for Indians that descend from the male Indian blood line has been part of Indian legislation for decades, and is incorporated into the most recent *Indian Act*. Even today, Indian status is solely determined by Canada, and factors as the largest determinant of individual and communal Aboriginal identity. The second generation cut-off rule in the registration provisions, together with often high rates of out-marriage for most bands, amounts to a disappearing formula for Indians, and disproportionately affects the descendants of Indian women who married out. Numerous demographic studies indicate that Indians and their home communities are facing legislative extinction within several generations as a result. Band membership codes that have blood quantum or two-parent rules will bring their communities' population decline even faster. My band is among those that have dismal population forecasts, owing to their current membership code, which relies on entitlement to status under the *Act*.[2] My children cannot be members of our own community, which, for Eel River Bar, represents a lost generation of members who could be contributing to their government and acting alongside other band members to bring about positive changes for the band. They are excluding their youth and future citizens.

While Chapter 1 laid out the politics surrounding Indigenous identity, the history of Canada's legislative control over various definitions of status and membership, and the grim population forecasts awaiting bands if nothing is done to change the situation, Chapter 2 asked a more basic question: why is Indigenous identity important? Canadians live in a modern liberal democracy based on the principle of equality. Some commentators have suggested that Indigenous peoples should just assimilate into the majority culture and assume the majority identity.[3] Some even suggest that, since urbanism is inevitable and urbanism equates with loss of identity, that the assimilation of Indigenous peoples is inevitable.[4] These same commentators seem to suggest that equality among citizens means sameness. But I argued that equality can also mean difference in treatment and the protection of difference. The Supreme Court of Canada has recognized that Indigenous peoples were the original inhabitants of this land, with their own governments, laws, traditions, and ways of life.[5] Section 35 of the *Constitution Act, 1982* recognizes this fact and protects all Aboriginal and treaty rights, including land claims and modern agreements.[6] Indigenous peoples have resisted decades of assimilatory laws and policies, and, while they have suffered a great deal of harm, they have also demonstrated that preservation of their culture is part of the good life for Indigenous peoples, and access to this identity and culture is part of their substantive equality.

In Chapter 2, I argued that Indigenous nations have a constitutional right to be self-defining and to determine their own citizenship. It is not the proper function of the Canadian government to make decisions for Indigenous peoples and their nations about how to determine either individual or communal identities, be it through registration provisions, band membership codes, or rigidly defined self-government citizenship codes. I further argued that there is no right which is more integral to an Indigenous nation than its ability to be self-defining, and, therefore, to have the ability to determine its own citizenship criteria. However, there are no governments, including Indigenous governments, which are all-powerful, and thus their rights and powers are limited by the rights of others. The right of an Indigenous nation to determine its own citizenship is tempered by other rights such as section 35(4) which guarantees the exercise of Indigenous and treaty rights equally as between male and female persons.[7] These rights are also limited and supported by the *Charter*. Framing the debate in terms of individual rights versus communal rights, or Indigenous women versus their communities, detracts from addressing the potentially beneficial application of the *Charter*, which offers a way to balance the rights of citizens and their governments in a way that can preserve their identities rather than harm them, as the *Indian Act* does. The main argument in this chapter — that Indigenous nations have a right to determine their own citizenship — is balanced by the following chapter, which highlights the rights of citizens to belong.

In Chapter 3, I argued that individual Indigenous peoples have a right to belong to their nations, and to be legally recognized as Indians. The right of individual Mi'kmaq to belong to their nation means that they cannot be unfairly excluded from their home communities on discriminatory grounds such as registration status, gender, blood quantum or proximity or remoteness of descent from their Indigenous ancestors. When First Nations or self-governing Indigenous nations rely on status as the criterion for belonging, they end up incorporating the discrimination in the registration provisions as part of their identity. The *McIvor* case has exhausted all domestic legal avenues, and the growing level of dissatisfaction with Canada's policy and legislative response has resulted in an application being made to the international human rights tribunal. Even if a satisfactory legislative remedy is found to address the gender discrimination within the *Indian Act*, it still would not address the second generation cut-off rule, which amounts to racial discrimination on the analogous grounds of blood quantum/descent; gender-neutral discrimination on the basis of blood is still discrimination. My grandmother was an Indian woman who married out, and therefore my children and I are affected by the residual sex discrimination that was not addressed in the Bill C-31 amendments. However, we are also negatively affected by the second generation cut-off rule, which denies me and my children status under the *Act* and membership in our home band. This chapter concludes with a discussion about possible remedies that are meant to be an interim solution to address discrimination in the *Act* so that reliance on it in the future for band membership codes or self-government agreements will not incorporate the same discrimination.

In Chapter 4, I argued that Indigenous communities must look seriously at the principles upon which they base their identities and rules for communal belonging, so that they do not perpetuate the same racist criteria that have been imposed on them for so long. Included in this chapter is a discussion of how important factors in determining identity have been interpreted in ways that harm Aboriginal peoples. A comparison is made between ancestry versus blood quantum, and connection versus tradition, in determining identity. I also argued that any rules which were established should be interpreted with a view to including citizens rather than excluding them. So much damage has been caused by the *Indian Act*, residential schools, and forced relocations that the benefit of the doubt ought to be given to those who have a weaker connection than others to their communities. Chapter 4 continues the discussion about remedies, but in the form of long-term remedies that would be found in self-government agreements. After a review of the types of band membership codes that currently exist, I highlighted some of the key problem areas in those codes. For example, if status is the determining criterion for membership under a code, this could result in the unfair exclusion of an applicant for membership whose lack of status might be the result of residual discrimination in the *Indian Act*. I argued that the same problem occurs for self-government agreements which rely on band lists or status lists to determine the charter group and future members. If self-government agreements merely incorporate the discrimination found in either status or membership, then they only serve to perpetuate the status quo.

My proposed solutions offer flexible categories of criteria that balance the need to maintain the culture for future generations with some allowance for historical factors which may have unfairly prejudiced some applicants for citizenship. It also builds on my arguments in the preceding chapters that the discrimination within the status provisions must be remedied first in order to prevent these longstanding inequities being incorporated into band membership codes and self-government agreements. This chapter also reviewed the suggestions by other commentators who offered principles to address some of these problems in the future. For example, Cornet argues that the dismantling of status might be possible if we relied on band membership codes in the interim. However, as I pointed out, most of the bands in Canada do not have their own codes and rely on status to determine membership. Even among those that do have their own codes, many are fraught with the same discriminatory provisions that can be found in the *Act*. Lawrence suggests that perhaps a reconstitution of the old confederacies would rid us of the need for the *Indian Act* and band membership codes, but given the reluctance of First Nations bands to reconstitute themselves into nations as suggested by the Royal Commission on Aboriginal Peoples in 1996, it is hard to imagine that the reconstitution of multiple nations into confederacies would happen any quicker, if at all. Borrows, on the other hand, offers general principles on which Indigenous nations might base their citizenship codes. Those principles specifically exclude criteria like blood quantum, and would allow non-Indigenous people to become citizens. He does not indicate how these principles might be applied practically, or how to address the matter in the interim. My solutions build on the positive ideas and critiques of these commentators, all of whom have significant expertise in their respective fields.

My contributions to solutions for the future deal with all aspects of the problem in the context of registration, band membership, and both current and future self-government agreements. We cannot rely on band membership agreements to replace the registration provisions of the *Indian Act* if they themselves are based on the *Act* or incorporate their own discriminatory provisions. Similarly, we cannot rely on current or self-government agreements if they, in turn, rely on their previous band membership lists that were determined either by problematic membership codes or on the *Indian Act*'s membership provisions.

The inequities that remain in the registration provisions and membership codes have to be addressed in the interim, as we will be relying on these provisions for some time, and to ensure that long-term solutions are not tainted with discrimination. The criteria that I suggested were meant for practical application, as opposed to some of the more theoretical ideas suggested by some commentators. As a result, although significant community consultations are always required, my suggestions could be the framework or starting point for discussion. While some may argue that my suggestions for criteria may open up citizenship too widely, I believe that flexibility is necessary to address some of the discrimination issues that exist within the *Act,* band membership codes, and current self-government agreements. In the end, nation-building has far more to gain from over-inclusiveness, which will help protect the identity of Indigenous peoples, rather than over-exclusiveness, which can only serve to extinguish it. That being said, in order to protect Indigenous identity, this flexibility must be balanced with protections for nations against illegitimate claims.

This book does not represent a complete review of the issues affecting Indigenous identity in Canada. Many of the issues raised are so complex that to deal with them all would have made the book much longer. For example, I could only deal with certain types of discrimination claims regarding the status provisions of the *Indian Act*. I had no space to deal with Canada's exercise of its section 91(24) jurisdiction in the *Constitution Act, 1867*, except to argue that determining individual or communal identity for Indigenous peoples is well beyond its scope. This topic would be an excellent project for future research, especially given the upcoming challenge to this section by the Congress of Aboriginal Peoples in the *Daniels* case.[8] In addition to the federal jurisdictional issue, there are many other issues that are worthy of separate research. For example, specific Indigenous nations may also have treaties that could support claims that Indigenous nations have the right to determine their own citizens, or even claims by individuals that they have the right to belong. I know that the Mi'kmaq are signatories to several treaties that protect the treaty rights of their heirs and heirs forever. How this may assist with identity and belonging claims would make a worthy legal or historical research project. Similarly, arguments that were raised in *McIvor* but not addressed here relate to the potential of international legal instruments to assist status and non-status Indians in their efforts to rid the *Indian Act* of discriminatory distinctions between individuals based on sex or blood quantum. Lovelace's victory, together with relevant international laws, may well support international options.[9] In the same vein, comprehensive international comparisons between different Indigenous groups are a particular interest of mine. I would be interested in knowing how the Maori in New Zealand, the Aborigines in Australia, or Native Americans have addressed these issues of identity and belonging, and what they view as options for the future. Lessons learned in Indigenous communities around the world would be useful for domestic consideration.

International research and the potential for international human rights claims in this regard would be a relevant undertaking for what is happening here in Canada. However, what has been missing on the domestic scene is involvement by the Canadian Human Rights Commission (CHRC). It was in June 2008 that section 67 of the *Canadian Human Rights Act* was repealed and replaced with provisions allowing individual Indigenous peoples to bring claims against their bands and/or Canada for breaching their human rights.[10] While claims can now be brought against Canada, Indigenous people have to wait until June 2011 to bring claims against their bands. Given that the CHRC represents uncharted territory for most Indigenous peoples, communities, and organizations, research in the area of domestic human rights might be a timely undertaking, especially in the context of *Indian Act* discrimination. Having worked for a provincial human rights commission, I am aware that claims such as these are not within provincial jurisdiction, and have traditionally been referred to the CHRC, even if the CHRC could not previously deal with them. I imagine that a significant amount of research would benefit this area of the law.

I think the project that most interests me is an opportunity to undertake a complete membership review in a First Nation, such as my home community of Eel River Bar. Being involved in community based membership consultations, going through the whole process of determining the community's priorities, and trying to bring about consensus would bring a whole new dynamic to the legal research that I have completed to date. Getting input from the youth, elders, past and current community leaders, and various role models both inside and outside the community would be an incredible source of information and a valuable tool for both researcher and First Nation. A project like this could also assist a community in its efforts to draft a code that truly represents who they are. Future projects might even include assisting communities to determine how they might tie their local community codes into that of a future nation-based citizenship code that may be promulgated by the larger Indigenous nation to which they belong. For example, a future membership code so constructed by Eel River Bar may also provide a good example for how the Mi'kmaq Nation may want to construct its nation-based code.

Canada has made a promise to Indigenous peoples in section 35 to protect our cultures so that we could leave thriving communities to our future generations. However, we as Indigenous peoples cannot rely solely on that promise to get us there. We have our own responsibilities — as individuals, families, communities, and nations — to do whatever it takes to preserve our identity and culture for our children's children seven generations into the future. If we do any less, we dishonour all the suffering experienced by our families and all the hard work done by our ancestors to ensure that our cultures, lands, treaties, and communities would be protected. It has been a long journey for me to discover that our identities should not be tied to racist concepts like blood. At times, this left me feeling uncertain about my own identity. However, having reflected on the teachings that I have had over the years, I discovered that the principles underlying my Mi'kmaq identity had always been there. We as Mi'kmaq people never had an identity based on racial concepts like blood quantum, nor has any other Indigenous nation. Part of the legacy of the assimilatory laws and policies that have been imposed on our people is that we have come to believe some of these racial characterisations of ourselves. I owe it to those who have asked me to use my education for the benefit of my family and community — like my father — and those who need my protection — like my children — to ensure that we are no longer left out. We who have been labelled "non-status" are not asking to be welcomed as newcomers into our communities. We were always here, living on our traditional territories and fighting for the rights of future generations, status and non-status alike. We have always been Mi'kmaq, and if I have any say in the matter, the Mi'kmaq Nation, with us included, will always be here for future generations.

Comparing the status of my grandmother's line to my family's line had she been a grandfather

Pre-1985 Our grandmother, Margaret Jerome's line	Bill C-31 Our grandmother, Margaret Jerome's line	Bill C-3 Our grandmother, Margaret Jerome's line	Bill C-3 If our grandmother had been a grandfather
Margaret Jerome marries a non-Indian –> loses status; her husband does not gain status.	Margaret Jerome regains status under s. 6(1)(c).	Margaret Jerone still has s. 6(1)(c) status.	Grandfather Jerome marries a non-Indian –> he and she have status pre-1985, s. 6(1)(a) status after Bill C-31, and s. 6(1)(a) status with Bill C-3.
Frank Palmater (our father) has no status.	Frank Palmater gets status under s. 6(2).	Frank Palmater to gain s. 6(1)(c.1) status.	Frank Palmater would have had s. 6(1)(a) status.
Nelson Palmater* (Frank's son, my brother), born pre-1985, has no status.	Nelson Palmater, born pre-1985, still has no status.	Nelson Palmater, born pre-1985, to gain s. 6(2) status.	Nelson Palmater, born pre-1985, would have had s. 6(1)(a) status.
Jeremiah Palmater (Nelson's son), born post-1985, has no status.	Jeremiah Palmater still has no status	Jeremiah Palmater will still not have status.	Jeremiah Palmater would have had s. 6(2) status.

* I use my brother Nelson as an example because he has the least complicated fact scenario: he was born post-1951 and pre-1985 to a legally married father and mother.

Notes

URLs for websites conatined in this book are accurate to 2010 to the best of the author's knowledge. Documents which may no longer be available on the Indian and Northern Affairs Canada (INAC) website can be found at: www.indigenousnationhood.com/identity/membership/codes.html.

Notes to the Introduction

1   Indian Claims Commission, "Eel River Bar First Nation Inquiry: Eel River Dam Claim," Indian Claims: www.indianclaims.ca/pdf/EelRiverEng.pdf, at 6.

2   Indian and Northern Affairs Canada, "Eel River Bar First Nation": www.ainc-inac.gc.ca/at/mp/pg8_e.html.

3   B. LeCouffe, *One in Brotherhood: The Labillois and Related Families* (unpublished manuscript in the possession of the author; Moncton, 1989), p. 24. This book is a genealogy compiled by one of the sisters of the local church who recorded the information from church records, vital statistics, and news articles in relation to the Labillois family, who are related to my family, the Jeromes.

4   Margaret and William were married Sept. 5, 1912. INAC, however, reported their marriage taking place on June 7, 1910. Frank Palmater was born April 8, 1914, and passed away Sept. 17, 2000.

5   Nation Council of Veterans Association Canada, "Submission: Canada's Aboriginal War Veterans" (2006): www.waramps.ca/news/abvet/pdf/06-06-28.pdf. See also National Aboriginal Veterans Association, "NAVA News": www.abo-peoples.org/Vets/AbVets.pdf.

6   *Indian Act*, R.S.C. 1985, c. I-5.

7   See Mikmawey, Cape Breton University, "Mi'kmaq Resource Centre," Treaties: http://mikmawey.uccb.ns.ca/treaties.html. Some of the treaties signed by the Mi'kmaq which our elders always referred to are the treaties of 1725, 1749, 1752, and 1760-61.

8   *Indian Act, supra* note 6 at ss.6-11.

9   In my own letter from INAC denying me status as an Indian dated April 9, 2009, INAC specifically refers me to the letter they sent my father dated Sept. 6, 1990, which explained to him that his children were not entitled to status.

10   *McIvor* v. *Canada* [2009] 2 C.N.L.R. 236 (BCCA).

11   Bill C-31, *Indian Act*, R.S.C. 1985, c. I-5, as amended by R.S.C. 1985, c.2 (1st Supp.).

12   *R.* v. *Fowler* (1993), 134 N.B.R. (2d) 361. My two brothers-in-law participated in this protest hunt and won their case. My brother Nelson was recently arrested for hunting, and brought to court in 2008 but later had all the charges dropped.

13   I use the term "Aboriginal" in the constitutional sense, meaning Indian, Inuit, and Métis, whereas "Indigenous" means First Peoples — Mi'kmaq, Mohawk, etc.

14   *Constitution Act, 1982*, being Schedule B to the *Canada Act, 1982* (U.K.), 1982, c.11. *Constitution Act, 1867* (U.K.), 30 & 31 Vict., c.3 [*Constitution Act, 1867*].

15 *Indian Act, supra* note 6 at s.4.

16 *Ibid.* at s.4.1.

17 *Daniels* v. *Canada (Minister of Indian Affairs and Northern Development)* [2002] F.C.J. No. 391 (QL).

18 *Indian Act, supra* note 6 at s.4(1). *Reference re Whether the term "Indians" in s.91(24) of the B.N.A. Act 1867, includes Eskimo Inhabitants of Quebec,* [1939] S.C.R. 104.

19 *Constitution Act, 1982,* being Schedule B to the *Canada Act, 1982* (U.K.), 1982, c.11. at s.35.

20 Assembly of First Nations and Indian and Northern Affairs, Joint Technical Committee, "First Nations Registration (Status) and Membership Research Report": www.afn.ca/misc/mrp.pdf.

21 *McIvor, supra* note 10. *Daniels, supra* note 17.

22 *McIvor, supra* note 10.

23 *Sandra Lovelace* v. *Canada,* Communication No. R.6/24, U.N. Doc. Supp. No. 40 (A/36/40) at 166 (1981). In this case the issue related to a denial of access to Lovelace's culture by means of barring her residency rights on her reserve as she had lost her status through marriage. As a result, Canada was found to be in violation of article 27 of the *International Covenant on Civil and Political Rights,* 16 Dec. 1966, CAN. T.S. 1976 No. 47 (entry into force 23 March 1976; in force for Canada, 19 Aug. 1976), which provides as follows: "In those States in which ethnic, religious or linguistic minorities exist, persons belonging to such minorities shall not be denied the right, in community with the other members of their group, to enjoy their own culture, to profess and practise their own religion, or to use their own language."

24 *Corbiere* v. *Canada* (Minister of Indian and Northern Affairs) [1999] 2 S.C.R. 203.

25 Congress of Aboriginal Peoples, "Justice is Equality: Post-Corbiere Report": www.abo-peoples.org/policy/Justice_Is_Equality_PostCorbierejuly08.pdf.

Notes to Chapter One

1 National Archives of Canada, Record Group 10, Vol. 6810, file 470-2-3, Vol. 7, pp. 55 (L-3) and 63 (N-3). Scott was the Deputy Superintendant of Indian and Northern Affairs from 1913 to 1932.

2 Right Honourable Prime Minister Stephen Harper, Statements by Ministers, "Statement of Apology to Former Students of Indian Residential Schools" (11 June 2008): www.ainc-inac.gc.ca/ai/rqpi/apo/pmsh-eng.asp.

3 *Indian Act,* R.S.C. 1985 c. I-5.

4 *McIvor* v. *Canada (Registrar, Indian and Northern Affairs)* [2007] 3 C.N.L.R. 72 (BCSC), [2009] 2 C.N.L.R. 236 (BCCA), [2009] S.C.C.A. No.234 (SCC).

5 S. Clatworthy, *Reassessing the Population Impacts of* Bill C-31 (Winnipeg: Four Directions Project Consultants), 2001: www.ainc-inac.gc.ca/pr/ra/rpi/rpi_e.pdf. S. Clatworthy, *Revised Population Scenarios Concerning the Population Implications of Section 6 of the Indian Act* (Winnipeg: Four Directions Consulting Group, 1994). S. Clatworthy and A. Smith,

Population Implications of the 1985 Amendments to the Indian Act: Final Report, (Winnipeg: Four Directions Consulting Group, 1992). S. Clatworthy, Bill C-31, *Indian Registration and First Nations Membership* (Winnipeg: Four Directions Consulting Group, 2001).

6   See, generally, Royal Commission on Aboriginal Peoples, *Report of the Royal Commission on Aboriginal Peoples*, Vols. 1-5 (Ottawa: Minister of Supply and Services Canada, 1996). In the second volume of the *RCAP Report* at 166, 234-235, RCAP explains that the right of self-government belongs to Aboriginal nations as opposed to individual bands.

7   Indian and Northern Affairs Canada, "Highlights from the *Report of the Royal Commission on Aboriginal Peoples*: People to People, Nation to Nation": www.ainc-inac.gc.ca/ap/pubs/rpt/rpt-eng.asp, at "Renewal and Renegotiation."

8   *Ibid.* at "Politics of Domination and Assimilation."

9   *McIvor, supra* note 4.

10 *Ibid.*; *Indian Act, 1985, supra* note 3, s.6(1)(a), (c).

11 *McIvor, supra* note 4.

12 P. Palmater, "Presentation to the Standing Committee on Aboriginal Affairs and Northern Development (AANO) Re: Bill C-3 *Gender Equity in Indian Registration Act*": www.nonstatusindian.com/docs/Presentation_to_Standing_Committee.pdf.

13 *Indian Act, supra note 3* at s.6-7.

14 *Canadian Charter of Rights and Freedoms*, Part I of the *Constitution Act, 1982*, being Schedule B to the *Canada Act 1982* (U.K.), 1982, c.11, at s.15.

15 *Indian Act*, R.S.C. 1951, c.149.

16 M. Boldt, *Surviving as Indians: The Challenge of Self-Government* (Toronto: University of Toronto Press, 1993), p. 206; T. Isaac, *Pre-1868 Legislation Concerning Indians: A Selected and Indexed Collection* (Saskatoon: University of Saskatchewan Native Law Centre, 1993); S. Venne, *Indian Acts and Amendments 1868-1975: An Indexed Collection* (Saskatoon: University of Saskatchewan Native Law Centre, 1981); Z. Wilson (Ed.), *The Indian Acts and Amendments 1970-1993: An Indexed Collection* (Saskatoon: University of Saskatchewan Native Law Centre, 1993).

17 See, generally, B. Lawrence, *"Real" Indians and Others: Mixed Blood Urban Native Peoples and Indigenous Nationhood* (Lincoln: University of Nebraska Press, 2004).

18 Canada's Apology, *supra* note 2.

19 Métis National Council, "National Definition of Métis": www.metisnation.ca/who/definition.html. While the MNC requires that their members be distinct from other Aboriginal peoples — presumably Indians and Inuit — other Métis communities and organizations are specific about whether status Indians can be part of their organization. See, for example, Metis Settlements General Council and the Government of Alberta, "Metis Settlements Act": www.canlii.org/en/ab/laws/stat/rsa-2000-c-m-14/latest/rsa-2000-c-m-14.html, at s.75. This section provides that status Indians and Inuit who are registered in land claims cannot be members. Some notable exceptions are children who were raised in the settlement area or whose parents were settlement members.

20 *Constitution Act, 1982*, being Schedule B to the *Canada Act 1982* (U.K.), 1982, c.11.

21 *Constitution Act, 1867,* (U.K.) 30-31 Vict., c.3, reprinted in R.S.C. 1985, App. II, No.5, at s.91(24).

22 *Indian Act, supra note 3* at s.2.

23 Indian and Northern Affairs Canada, "Non-Status Indians": www.ainc-inac.gc.ca/ap/nsi/index-eng.asp. The term "non-status Indian" "refers to people who identify themselves as Indians but who are not entitled to registration on the Indian Register pursuant to the Indian Act."

24 Those individuals (mostly women and their descendants) who are reinstated as Indians pursuant to the Bill C-31 amendments to the *Indian Act* are referred to as Bill C-31 reinstatees.

25 National Centre for First Nations Governance, "Memorandum on Indian Status and Band Membership": www.fngovernance.org/toolkit/Institutions/Transparency_and_Fairness/CitizenshipCodes/MemoIndianStatusBandMembershipTitle.pdf, at 3.

26 Indian and Northern Affairs Canada, "Frequently Asked Questions About Aboriginal Peoples": www.ainc-inac.gc.ca/ai/mr/is/info125-eng.asp, at 1.

27 *Indian Act, supra* note 3 at s.4.1. In situations where non-status Indians are band members, only certain sections of the *Act* will apply to them.

28 *Ibid.* at 3.

29 O. Dickason, *Canada's First Nations: A History of Founding Peoples from Earliest Times,* 3rd ed. (Don Mills: Oxford University Press, 2002), pp. 352-353.

30 Métis National Council, "Who are the Métis?": www.metisnation.ca/who/definition.html.

31 Government of Alberta, Métis Settlements Act, 2009: www.qp.alberta.ca/574.cfm?page=m14.cfm&leg_type=Acts&isbncln=9780779743704 at s.1(j).

32 *R. v. Powley* [2003] 2 S.C.R. 207, at para. 30.

33 *Indian Act, supra* note 3 at 2.

34 *Reference re Whether the term "Indians" in s.91(24) of the B.N.A. Act 1867, includes Eskimo Inhabitants of Quebec,* [1939] S.C.R. 104.

35 Inuit Tapiriit Kanatami, "Inuit Statistical Profile: 2008": www.itk.ca/sites/default/files/InuitStatisticalProfile2008.pdf.

36 *Who are th Métis? supra* note 30 at xiv-xv.

37 *RCAP Report,* Vol. 2, Part 1, *supra* note 6 at 107.

38 *Ibid.*

39 *Indian Act, supra* note 3 at s.2.(1).

40 INAC, *supra* note 26 at 2.

41 Canadian Heritage, "History of Bilingualism in Canada": www.pch.gc.ca/pgm/lo-ol/bllng/hist-eng.cfm. at 1-3.

42   See, generally, T. Flanagan, *First Nations? Second Thoughts* (Montreal: McGill-Queen's University Press, 2000); G. Gibson, *A New Look at Canadian Indian Policy: Respect the Collective – Promote the Individual* (Vancouver: Fraser Institute, 2009).

43   *Ibid.* See also D. Gibson, "Rights shouldn't depend on race" (*Edmonton Journal*, 2 Feb. 2009).

44   Flanagan, *supra* note 42.

45   *Ibid.*

46   *RCAP Report*, Vol. 1, *supra* note 6 at 36.

47   *Ibid.* at 37.

48   *Ibid.* at 38.

49   *Ibid.*

50   *Ibid.*

51   *Ibid.* at 38-39.

52   *Ibid.* at 39.

53   *Indian Act, supra* note 3 at ss.6, 7, 11.

54   *Indian Act, 1951, supra* note 15 at ss.5-14.

55   *An Act for the better protection of the Lands and Property of the Indians in Lower Canada*, S. Prov. C 1850, c.42.

56   *An Act to repeal in part and to amend an Act, intitled, An Act for the better protection of the Lands and property of the Indians in Lower Canada*, S. Prov. C. 1851, c.59 at s. II.

57   *An Act to encourage the gradual Civilization of the Indian tribes in this Province, and to amend the Laws respecting Indians*, S. Prov. C. 1857, c.26.

58   *An Act respecting Indians and Indian Lands*, C.S.L.C. 1861, c.14 at s.3.

59   *Ibid.* at ss.12-13.

60   *Ibid.* at s.11.

61   *An Act providing for the organisation of the Department of the Secretary of State of Canada, and for the management of Indian and Ordnance Lands* (22 May 1868) at s.15.

62   *An Act for the gradual enfranchisement of Indians, the better management of Indian affairs, and to extend the provisions of the Act 31st Victoria, Chapter 42.* S.C. 1869, c.6 (32-33 Vict.).

63   *Ibid.* at s.1.

64   W. Cornet, "Aboriginality: Legal Foundations, Past Trends, Future Prospects," in J. Magnet and D. Dorey (Eds.), *Aboriginal Rights Litigation* (Markham: LexisNexis, 2003) at 125.

65   *An Act for the gradual enfranchisement of Indians, supra* note 62 at s.4.

66   *An Act to amend and consolidate the laws respecting Indians*, S.C. 1876, c.18 (39 Vict).

67   *Ibid.* at s.3.

68 *Ibid.* at ss.4 and 2, respectively.

69 *Ibid.* at ss.11, 61 and 64.

70 *Ibid.* at s.86.

71 *An Act Respecting Indians*, R.S.C. 1906, c.81 at ss.12, 14.

72 *An Act Respecting Indians*, R.S.C. 1927, c.98 at s.16.

73 *An Act Respecting Indians*, S.C. 1951, c.29 at ss.5- 6.

74 *Ibid.* at ss.7-8.

75 *Ibid.* at ss.10-15.

76 *Ibid.* at s.14.

77 *Lovelace* v. *Canada*, Communication No. R.6/24, U.N. Doc. Supp. No.40 (A/36/40) at 166 (1981).

78 *RCAP Report*, Vol. 1, *supra* note 6 at 306: "Thus, the post-1985 status rules continue to discriminate as the pre-1985 rules did, except that the discriminatory effects are postponed until the subsequent generations."

79 J. Fiske and E. George, *Seeking Alternatives to Bill C-31: From Cultural Trauma to Cultural Revitalization through Customary Law* (Ottawa: Status of Women, 2006).

80 *McIvor* v. *Canada* (3-4 Oct. 2008) (Factum of the Respondent, Sharon McIvor).

81 *Population Implications, supra* note 5 at 54.

82 *McIvor*, appeal, *supra* note 4.

83 *Population Implications,* supra note 5 at 54.

84 P. Paul, "Bill C-31: The Trojan Horse: An Analysis of the Social, Economic and Political Reaction of First Nations People as a Result of Bill C-31." Master's thesis, University of New Brunswick, 1990, at 105.

85 *Ibid.* at 106.

86 *RCAP Report*, Vol. 1, *supra* note 6 at 304.

87 *Ibid.* at 305.

88 *Ibid.* at 304.

89 *Ibid.* at 307.

90 *McIvor* v. *Canada* (3-4 Oct. 2008, BCCA) (Factum of the Appellant, Canada) at para.12. *Population Implications, supra* note 5; *Revised Population Scenarios, supra* note 5; *Indian Registration and Membership, supra* note 5; *Reassessing Population Impacts, supra* note 5; S. Clatworthy, *Paternal Identity and Entitlement to Indian Registration: The Manitoba Context* (Winnipeg: Four Directions Consulting Group, 2001); S. Clatworthy, *First Nation Affiliation Among Registered Indians Residing in Select Urban Areas* (Winnipeg: Four Directions Project Consultants, 2000); S. Clatworthy, *Factors Contributing to Unstated Paternity* (Winnipeg: Four Directions Project Consultants, 2003).

91 *McIvor* v. *Canada Factum, ibid.* at v.

92 *McIvor* v. *Canada Factum, ibid.* at para. 96.

93 Memorandum to Cabinet, 9 Feb. 1984; Memorandum to Cabinet, 10 May 1984; Record of Cabinet decision, 29 May 1984.

94 *Population Implications, supra* note 5, *Revised Population Scenarios, supra* note 5, *Indian Registration and Membership, supra* note 5, *Paternal Identity and Registration, supra* note 91, *First Nation Affiliations, supra* note 90, *Unstated Paternity, supra* note 90, *Reassessing Population Implications, supra* note 5; *Founding Peoples, supra* note 29.

95 *Population Implications, supra* note 5 at viii.

96 *Founding Peoples, supra* note 29 at 9. See also *RCAP Report*, Vol. 1, *supra* note 6 at 13.

97 *RCAP Report, Vol. 1, supra* note 6 at 13.

98 Statistics Canada, "2001 Census: Aboriginal peoples of Canada," www12.statcan.ca/english/census01/Products/Analytic/companion/abor/canada.cfm. Statistics Canada qualified the reliability of its data: "Undercoverage in the 2001 Census was considerably higher among Aboriginal people than among other segments of the population due to the fact that enumeration was not permitted, or was interrupted before it could be completed, on 30 Indian reserves and settlements. These geographic areas are called incompletely enumerated Indian reserves and settlements."

99 Statistics Canada, "2006 Census: Aboriginal Peoples in Canada in 2006: Inuit, Métis and First Nations, 2006 Census," www12.statcan.ca/census-recensement/2006/as-sa/97-558/p2-eng.cfm. In the 1996, 2001, and 2006 Census, respectively, the identified Aboriginal population increased from 2.8 per cent of the Canadian population to 3.3 per cent and then 3.8 per cent. They also noted that undercoverage of Indian reserves had dropped from 30 reserves in 2001 to 22 reserves in 2006.

100 J. Magnet, "Who Are the Aboriginal Peoples of Canada?" in J. Magnet, D. Dorey (Eds.), *Aboriginal Rights Litigation* (Markham: LexisNexis, 2003), 23 at 79.

101 P. Paul, *The Politics of Legislated Identity: The Effect of Section 6(2) of the Indian Act in the Atlantic Provinces* (Nova Scotia: Atlantic Policy Congress of First Nations Chiefs Secretariat, 1999) at 1.

102 *Population Implications, supra* note 5.

103 *Ibid.* at ii.

104 *Ibid.* at 36.

105 *Ibid.* at iii.

106 *Ibid.* at v.

107 *Ibid.* at 49.

108 *Reassessing Population Impacts, supra* note 5.

109 *Ibid.* at viii.

110 *Ibid.*

111 *Indian Registration and Membership, supra* note 5.

112 *Ibid.* at 16.

113 *Ibid.* at 7-9. Clatworthy explains that as of December 31, 2002, there were actually 241 First Nations that had band membership codes, but one First Nation was previously identified in error and 6 First Nations in the Yukon and 2 First Nations (the Nisga'a communities) all have self-government agreements. In addition, only 212 First Nations responded to his survey for this study and thus the data is based on the 212 First Nations of the 232 that were known to have band membership codes as of December 31, 2002. At that time, there were a total of 609 First Nations, 19 of which had self-government agreements.

114 *Ibid.* at 9.

115 *Ibid.*

116 *Ibid.* at 11.

117 *Ibid.* at 41

118 *Ibid.* at 19.

119 *Ibid.* at 64.

120 *Population Implications, supra* note 5 at 71.

121 *Ibid.*

Notes to Chapter Two

1 S. Imai, "Aboriginal Rights: Disincentives to Negotiate: *Mitchell* v. *M.N.R.*'s Potential Effect on Dispute Resolution" (2002) 22 Windsor Y.B. Access Just. 309 (QL) at 3. Imai calls for a more collaborative relationship between the Crown and Aboriginal peoples that is based on good faith and give and take: "While judicial support for negotiated settlements is very strong, court decisions have not always helped to create appropriate conditions for productive negotiations. Some decisions have had the effect of discouraging the parties from returning to the negotiating table or have encouraged negotiations over the wrong issues." At page 7 Imai explains how they adopt a "winner take all" strategy and wait for litigation to resolve their mutual issues, instead of negotiating.

2 *R.* v. *Marshall; R.* v. *Bernard* [2005] 2 S.C.R. 220.

3 *Sharon McIvor* v. *Canada (The Registrar, Indian and Northern Affairs Canada)*, [2009] 2 C.N.L.R. 236 (BCCA).

4 A few of the cases currently before the courts include: *Brenda Pauline Sanderson* v. *The Attorney General of Canada* [Re-Re-Re-Amended Statement of Claim] (Winnipeg Queen's Bench, File No. CI 03-01-32940); *Nathan McGillivary acting as Guardian ad Litem of Dakota Erin McGillivary, an infant under the age of 18 years, Diana Lynn McGillivary, Diane Lehmann-Ballantyne, and The Opaskwayak Cree Nation* v. *Her Majesty the Queen* [Re (x5) Amended Statement of Claim] (Fed. Ct. File No. T-1975-93); *Sawridge Band* v. *Canada*, [1995] 4 C.N.L.R. 121 (FCTD).

5 A. Long and K. Chiste, "Indian Governments and the Canadian Charter of Rights and Freedoms," *American Indian Culture and Research Journal*, Vol. 18, No. 2 (1994) at 96.

6 *The Canadian Encyclopedia*, 2nd ed., s. v. "liberalism."

7   This number is a rough estimate based on the fact that, statistically, over half the total Aboriginal population lives off reserve, and we would have to subtract all the Bill C-31 reinstatees, non-traditionalists, and so on.

8   J. Fiske and E. George, *Seeking Alternatives to Bill C-31: From Cultural Trauma to Cultural Revitalization through Customary Law* (Ottawa: Status of Women Canada, 2006).

9   G. Alfred, *Heeding the Voices of Our Ancestors: Kahnawake Mohawk Politics and the Rise of Native Nationalism* (Toronto: Oxford University Press, 1990).

10 P. Macklem, *Indigenous Difference and the Constitution of Canada* (Toronto: University of Toronto Press, 2001) at 47.

11 *Ibid.* at 48.

12 *Ibid.* at 54-55.

13 *Ibid.* at 75.

14 *Ibid.* at 66-69.

15 *Ibid.* at 76-79.

16 *Ibid.* at 121.

17 *Ibid.* at 136.

18 *R. v. Sparrow,* [1990] 1 S.C.R. 1075; *R. v. Van der Peet,* [1996] 2 S.C.R. 507; *R. v. Simon,* [1985] 2 S.C.R. 387; *R. v. Marshall,* [1999] 3 S.C.R. 456 (*Marshall 1*); *R. v. Marshall,* [1999] 3 S.C.R. 533 (*Marshall 2*); *Delgamuuwk v. B.C.,* [1997] 3 S.C.R. 1010; *R. v. Sappier, R. v. Gray,* [2006] 2 S.C.R. 686 (*Sappier and Gray*).

19 *Indigenous Difference, supra* note 10 at 70.

20 *Heeding the Voices, supra* note 9 at 172.

21 T. Schouls, *Aboriginal Identity, Pluralist Theory, and the Politics of Self-Government* (Vancouver: UBC Press, 2003) at 119.

22 *Ibid.*

23 *Ibid.* at 129.

24 *Ibid.* at 131.

25 *Ibid.*

26 *Ibid.* at 120.

27 W. Kymlicka, *Multicultural Citizenship* (New York: Oxford University Press, 1995) at 2.

28 *Ibid.* at 79. While this quote refers to the American notion of the status of Indian tribes, the historical and political factors that led to their status as "domestic dependent nations" are largely applicable in the Canadian context.

29 *Ibid.* at 76.

30 *Cultural Trauma, supra* note 8.

31 *Multicultural Citizenship, supra* note 27 at 36-37.

32 *Ibid.* at 32-33.

33 *Ibid.* at 38.

34 *Ibid.* at 36-45.

35 A. Cairns, *Citizens Plus: Aboriginal Peoples and the Canadian State* (Vancouver: UBC Press, 1999) at 84-85.

36 *Ibid.* at 100.

37 *Ibid.* at 93-104.

38 *Ibid.* at 114.

39 *Ibid.* at 130.

40 *Ibid.* at 145, 152.

41 *Ibid.* at 211.

42 *Ibid.* at 131.

43 T. Flanagan, *First Nations? Second Thoughts* (Montreal: McGill-Queen's University Press, 2000) at 196.

44 *Ibid.* at 194.

45 *Ibid.* at 195.

46 *Ibid.* at 22.

47 *Ibid.* at 21.

48 M. MacDonald, "The Man Behind Stephen Harper": www.walrusmagazine.com/articles/the-man-behind-stephen-harper-tom-flanagan/.

49 G. Gibson, *A New Look at Canadian Indian Policy: Respect the Collective – Promote the Individual* (Vancouver: Fraser Institute, 2009) [*Indian Policy*].

50 F. Widdowson, A. Howard, *Disrobing the Aboriginal Industry: The Deception Behind Indigenous Cultural Preservation* (Montreal: McGill-Queen's University Press, 2008).

51 *Ibid.* at 7, 161.

52 *Ibid.* at 9.

53 *Multicultural Citizenship, supra* note 27 at 60-68.

54 *Ibid.* at 70-73.

55 *Ibid.* at 65.

56 *Ibid.* at 53.

57 *Ibid.*

58 *Citizens Plus, supra* note 35 at 152-153.

59 *Sparrow, supra* note 18 at para. 27.

60 *Indigenous Difference, supra* note 10 at 169-170.

61 *Aboriginal Identity, supra* note 21 at 160.

62 *Ibid.* at 172.

63 *Multicultural Citizenship, supra* note 27 at 103.

64 A. Gutmann, "Introduction," in A. Gutmann (Ed.), *Multiculturalism: Examining the Politics of Recognition* (Princeton: Princeton University Press, 1994) at 5.

65 *Ibid.* at 8.

66 *Ibid.* at 12.

67 C. Taylor, "The Politics of Recognition," in A. Gutmann (Ed.), *Multiculturalism: Examining the Politics of Recognition* (Princeton: Princeton University Press, 1994) at 25.

68 *Ibid.* at 36.

69 M. Minow, *Making All the Difference: Inclusion, Exclusion and American Law* (New York: Cornell University Press, 1990) at 20.

70 *Ibid.* at 25.

71 *Ibid.* at 30.

72 *Ibid.* at 29.

73 *Ibid.* at 27.

74 A. Gutmann, *Identity in Democracy* (Princeton: Princeton University Press, 2003) at 42.

75 *Multicultural Citizenship, supra* note 27 at 83.

76 *Sparrow, supra* note 18. When I speak about Aboriginal rights cases, unless otherwise noted, I am referring to Aboriginal rights in general and not treaty rights.

77 *Ibid.; Van der Peet, supra* note 18; *R. v. Gladstone* [1996] 2 S.C.R. 723; *R. v. NTC Smokehouse,* [1996] 2 S.C.R. 672 (these latter three cases are often referred to as the "*Van der Peet* trilogy," as the decisions from the Supreme Court of Canada came out at the same time); *Sappier and Gray, supra* note 18.

78 *Marshall 1, supra* note 18; *Marshall 2, supra* note 18; *Delgamuukw, supra* note 18. Other cases have equally important contributions to the law in this area: *Mitchell* v. *Canada (Minister of National Revenue — M.N.R.)* [2001] 1 S.C.R. 911; *R. v. Adams,* [1996] 3 S.C.R. 101; and *R. v. Coté,* [1996] 3 S.C.R. 139. Just as the *Van der Peet* trilogy refers to three cases, *Adams and Coté* are often referred to together.

79 *R. v. Powley,* [2003] 2 S.C.R. 207; *Van der Peet, supra* note 18 at para. 46.

80 By non-gathering-related claims, I mean practices, customs, or traditions that do not fall within the usual hunting and fishing activities or the gathering of wood categories, for example.

81 *R. v. Pamajewon,* [1996] 2 S.C.R. 821; *Corbiere* v. *Canada* [1999] 2 S.C.R. 203; *Lovelace* v. *Ontario,* [2000] 1 S.C.R. 950 (these cases deal, in part, with self-government, political rights [elections], and identity and discrimination, respectively); *McIvor* v. *Canada (Registrar, Indian and Northern Affairs),* [2009] S.C.C.A. No. 234 (Sharon McIvor's application to appeal to the Supreme Court of Canada was denied); *Sawridge, supra* note 4.

82 Assembly of First Nations, "Elections and Leadership Selection and First Nations Citizenship, Membership and Registration (Status)": www.afn.ca/misc/Policy-Updates.pdf at 3.

83 *Indian Act*, R.S.C. 1985, c. I-5 at s.10. Section 10 of the *Indian Act* allows bands to assume control of their own band membership subject to conditions.

84 Assembly of First Nations, "Our Nations, Our Governments: Choosing Our Own Paths: Report of the Joint Committee of Chiefs and Advisors on the Recognition and Implementation of First Nations Governments: Executive Summary": www.afn.ca/cmslib/general/Executive-Summary.pdf at 5.

85 See, for example, *Treaty or Articles of Peace and Friendship Renewed*, 1752. The relevant portion of the Treaty stated who the parties to the Treaty were and provided that it was between His Majesty in the old territories of Nova Scotia (also called Acadie) and "Major Jean Baptiste Cope chief Sachem of the Tribe of Mick Mack Indians, inhabiting the eastern Coast of the said Province, and Andrew Hadley Martin, Gabriel Martin and Francis Jeremiah members & Delegates of the Said Tribe, for themselves and their said Tribe and their heirs and the heirs of their heirs forever."

86 *Constitution Act, 1982*, being Schedule B to the *Canada Act 1982* (U.K.), 1982, c.11 at s.35.

87 *Calder et al* v. *Attorney-General of British Columbia*, [1973] S.C.R. 313 at para. 328. The Supreme Court of Canada held: "Although I think that it is clear that Indian title in British Columbia cannot owe its origin to the Proclamation of 1763, the fact is that when the settlers came, the Indians were there, organized in societies and occupying the land as their forefathers had done for centuries."

88 *Van der Peet, supra* note 18 at para. 28.

89 *Ibid.* at para. 5.

90 *Ibid.* at para. 30.

91 *Ibid.* at para. 31.

92 *Sparrow, supra* note 18 at para. 1.

93 *Ibid.* at para. 23. The Court further clarified that "extinguished rights are not revived by the *Constitution Act, 1982*."

94 *Ibid.* at paras. 24-27. More specifically, the court cited with approval academic commentary and explained that the word "'existing' means 'unextinguished' rather than exercisable at a certain time in history."

95 *Ibid.* at para. 53.

96 *Ibid.* at para. 62.

97 *Ibid.* at para. 59.

98 *Ibid.* at para. 57.

99 *Ibid.* at para. 58.

100 *Ibid.* at para. 56.

101 *Ibid.* at para. 68.

102 *Ibid.* at para. 70.

103 *Ibid.* at paras. 71-75.

104   *Ibid.* at para. 75.

105   *Ibid.* at para. 82.

106   *Van der Peet, supra* note 18, *Gladstone, supra* note 77, *Smokehouse, supra* note 77.

107   *Van der Peet, supra* note 18 at para. 1.

108   *Ibid.* at para. 3.

109   *Ibid.* at paras. 17-21.

110   *Ibid.* at para. 20.

111   *Ibid.* at para. 46. However, an important clarification was made by the Court in *Delga-muuwk, supra* note 18 at para. 126. The court characterized the "integral to distinctive culture" test as including not only Aboriginal practices but also their laws.

112   *Van der Peet, supra* note 18 at para. 48.

113   *Ibid.* at para. 49. The Court did go on to state in para. 49 that the Aboriginal perspective "must be framed in terms cognizable to the Canadian legal and constitutional structure."

114   *Ibid.* at para. 51.

115   *Ibid.* at para. 55.

116   *Ibid.* at para. 60.

117   *Ibid.* at para. 68.

118   *Ibid.* at para. 69.

119   *Ibid.* at para. 70.

120   *Ibid.* at para. 71.

121   *Ibid.* at para. 73.

122   *Ibid.* at para. 74.

123   *Ibid.* at para. 91.

124   *Gladstone, supra* note 77 at paras. 1, 85-86.

125   *Ibid.* at para. 30.

126   *Sparrow, supra* note 18 at para. 78.

127   *Gladstone, supra* note 77 at para. 24.

128   *Ibid.* at para. 63.

129   *Sappier and Gray, supra* note 18.

130   *Ibid.* at para. 72.

131   *Ibid.* at para. 22.

132   *Ibid.* at para. 24. The use of the word "domestic" in this case means that the Aboriginal right has no commercial dimension.

133   *Ibid.* at paras. 40-41.

134 *Ibid.* at para. 41.

135 *Ibid.* at para. 49.

136 L. Dufraimont, "From Regulation to Recolonization: Justifiable Infringement of Aboriginal Rights at the Supreme Court of Canada" (2000) 58 U.T. Fac. L. Rev. 1, paras. 1-12; *Delgamuukw, supra* note 18 at para. 165.

137 *Van der Peet, supra* note 18 at para. 315, as cited by Dufraimont in Justifiable Infringement, *ibid.* at para. 15.

138 Justifiable Infringement, *supra* note 136 at para. 23.

139 *Ibid.*

140 K. McNeil, *Defining Aboriginal Title in the 90s: Has the Supreme Court Got it Right?* (Toronto: Robarts Centre for Canadian Studies, 1998) at 19.

141 *Ibid.* at 20.

142 K. McNeil, "We must pay to reconcile aboriginal and private property" (2008) 27 Lawyers Weekly no. 45 at 1 (QL); *Tsilhqot'in Nation v. British Columbia* [2008] 1 C.N.L.R. 112.

143 Reconcile, *supra* note 142 at 3.

144 K. McNeil, "Aboriginal Title and the Supreme Court: What's Happening?" (2006) 69 Sask. L. Rev. 282 (QL) at paras. 44-45; *Marshall and Bernard, supra* note 2.

145 K. McNeil, "Reconciliation and the Supreme Court: The Opposing Views of Chief Justices Lamer and McLachlin" (2003) 2 Indigenous L.J. 1.

146 *Ibid.* at para. 10 (footnote removed).

147 *Ibid.* at para. 16.

148 *Ibid.* at para. 34.

149 J. Borrows and L. Rotman, "The *Sui Generis* Nature of Aboriginal Rights: Does it Make a Difference" (1997) 36 Alta. L. Rev. 9 (QL) at 3.

150 *Ibid.* at 15.

151 *Ibid.* at 16.

152 *Ibid.* at 17, citing K. McNeil, "The Meaning of Aboriginal Title" in M. Asch (Ed.), *Aboriginal and Treaty Rights in Canada: Essays on Law, Equality, and Respect for Difference* (Vancouver: UBC Press, 1997) 135 at 152.

153 *Ibid.*

154 See, for example, B. Slattery, "Making Sense of Aboriginal and Treaty Rights" (2000) 79 Can. Bar. Rev. 196; "The Organic Constitution: Aboriginal Peoples and the Evolution of Canada" (1996) 34 Osgoode Hall L.J. 101; "First Nations and the Constitution: A Question of Trust" (1992) 71 Can. Bar. Rev. 261.

155 B. Slattery, "The Generative Structure of Aboriginal Rights" (2007) 38 Supreme Court Law Review 595 at 1.

156 *Ibid.* at 2.

157 *Ibid.*

158 *Ibid.* at 3.

159 *Ibid.* at 2.

160 *Ibid.* at 3.

161 *Ibid.*

162 *Delgamuukw, supra* note 18 at para. 127.

163 *Sappier and Gray, supra* note 18 at para. 33.

164 *Powley, supra* note 79 at para. 17.

165 *Ibid.* at para. 37.

166 *Ibid.* at para. 13.

167 *Ibid.*

168 *Canadian Human Rights Act*, R.S.C. 2008, c.30. Section 67, which provided immunity from claims of discrimination to both the federal government and First Nations (bands) for decisions or actions made pursuant to the *Indian Act, 1985*, was repealed with the coming into force of this *Act*. Claims can now be brought against the federal government; however, claims cannot be brought against bands until June 2011.

169 Indian and Northern Affairs Canada, "The Government of Canada's Approach to Implementation of the Inherent Right and Negotiation of Aboriginal Self-Government" (1995): www.ainc-inac.gc.ca/al/ldc/ccl/pubs/sg/sg-eng.asp#inhrsg.

170 *Ibid.*

171 *Sparrow, supra* note 18 at para. 24.

172 *Ibid.* at para. 38.

173 *Ibid.* at para. 35.

174 *Ibid.* at para. 36.

175 *Powley, supra* note 79.

176 Royal Commission on Aboriginal Peoples, *Report of the Royal Commission on Aboriginal Peoples* (Ottawa: Ministry of Supply and Services, 1996) Vol. 2: *Restructuring the Relationship*, Part 1 at p. 217.

177 *Van der Peet, supra* note 18.

178 Our Nations Summary, *supra* note 84 at p. 5. See also Assembly of First Nations, "Our Nations Our Governments: Choosing Our Own Paths: Joint Committee of Chiefs and Advisors on the Recognition and Implementation of First Nations Governments: Final Report": www.afn.ca/cmslib/general/FNG%20report_Eng%20final.pdf at p. 21.

179 Our Nations Report, *ibid.*

180 *Ibid.* at 23.

181 Assembly of First Nations, "Remarks to the House of Commons Standing Committee on Aboriginal Peoples and Northern Development: April 13, 2010": www.afn.ca/misc/RC-WR.pdf at 3-4.

182 Chiefs in Ontario, "Bill C-3 and the Indigenous Right to Identity: April 20, 2010": www.afn.ca/misc/CIO.pdf at 1-3.

183 Union of British Columbia Indian Chiefs, "Response to Bill C-3 Gender Equity in Indian Registration Act": www.afn.ca/misc/UBCC-C3.pdf.

184 *Van der Peet, supra* note 18 at para. 65.

185 *Sappier and Gray, supra* note 18 at para. 44.

186 *Powley, supra* note 79 at para. 14.

187 *Ibid.* at para. 17.

188 *Ibid.* at para. 13.

189 *Van der Peet, supra* note 18 at para. 74.

190 *Delgamuukw, supra* note 18 at para. 128.

191 *Ibid.* at para. 132.

192 *Sparrow, supra* note 18 at para. 62.

193 *Delgamuukw, supra* note 18 at para. 112.

194 *Sparrow, supra* note 18 at para. 71.

195 *Ibid.* at para. 62.

196 P. Palmater, "Presentation to the Standing Committee on Aboriginal Affairs and Northern Development re: Bill C-3, *Gender equity in Indian Registration Act*": www.nonstatusindian.com/docs/Presentation_to_Standing_Committee.pdf; Six Nations of the Grand River, "Presentation to the Standing Committee on Aboriginal Affairs and Northern Development": www.afn.ca/misc/Six-Nations-C3.pdf; Chiefs in Ontario, "Bill C-3 and the Indigenous Right to Identity": www.afn.ca/misc/CIO.pdf at 1-3; Union of British Columbia Indian Chiefs, "Response to Bill C-3 Gender Equity in Indian Registration Act": www.afn.ca/misc/UBCC-C3.pdf; Assembly of First Nations, "Remarks," *supra* note 181 at 3-4; S. McIvor and G. Brodsky, "Equal Registration Status for Aboriginal Women and their Descendants: Sharon McIvor's Comments on Bill C-3, An Act to promote gender equity in Indian registration by responding to the Court of Appeal for British Columbia decision in McIvor v. Canada (Registrar of Indian and Northern Affairs)": Submission to the Standing Committee on Aboriginal Affairs and Northern Development (April 13, 2010).

197 *Haida Nation* v. *British Columbia (Minister of Forests)* [2004] 3 S.C.R. 511 at paras. 57-59; *Taku River Tlingit First Nation* v. *British Columbia (Project Assessment Director)* [2004] 3 S.C.R. 550.

198 *Canadian Charter of Rights and Freedoms*, Part I of the *Constitution Act, 1982*, being Schedule B to the *Canada Act 1982* (U.K.), 1982, c.11.

199 T. Isaac, "Individual versus Collective Rights: Aboriginal People and the Significance of *Thomas* v. *Norris*: Case Comment" (1992) 21 Ma. L.J. 618.

200 *Charter, supra* note 198 at s.32.

201 B. Morse, "Twenty Years of Charter Protection: The Status of Aboriginal Peoples under the Canadian Charter of Rights and Freedoms," in *The Symposium: 20 Years Under the Charter* (2002) 21 Windsor Y.B. Access Just. 385 at 386.

202 *Charter, supra* note 198 at s.25.

203 Charter Protection, *supra* note 201 at 386.

204 *RCAP Report*, Vol. 2, Part 1, *supra* note 176 at 227.

205 *CHRA, supra* note 168 at ss. 1.1-4 of the *Related Provisions.*

206 Indian and Northern Affairs Canada, "Standing Committee on Aboriginal Affairs and Northern Development (AANO) Evidence": www2.parl.gc.ca/content/hoc/Committee/403/AANO/Evidence/EV4408689/AANOEV07-E.PDF.

207 Canadian Human Rights Commission, "Standing Committee on Aboriginal Affairs and Northern Development (AANO) Evidence": www2.parl.gc.ca/content/hoc/Committee/403/AANO/Evidence/EV4460730/AANOEV11-E.PDF at 4.

208 *RCAP Report,* Vol. 2, Part 1, *supra* note 176 at 229.

209 *Ibid.* at 230.

210 *Ibid.* at 231.

211 *Ibid.* at 234.

212 INAC, "The Government of Canada's Approach to Implementation of the Inherent Right and Negotiation of Aboriginal Self-Government" (1995): www.ainc-inac.gc.ca/al/ldc/ccl/pubs/sg/sg-eng.asp#inhrsg.

213 *Ibid.*

214 *Ibid.*

215 *The Canadian Encyclopedia,* 2nd ed., s. v. "Charlottetown Accord."

216 Charter Protection, *supra* note 201 at 386.

217 Assembly of First Nations, "Proposed Framework to Advance the Recognition and Implementation of First Nation Governments" (Ottawa: AFN, 2005) 13.

218 Charter Protection, *supra* note 201 at 386.

219 J. Borrows, "Contemporary Traditional Equality: The Effect of the Charter on First Nations Politics," in D. Scheidermen and K. Sutherland (Eds.), *Charting the Consequences: The Impact of Charter Rights on Canadian Law and Politics* (Toronto: University of Toronto Press, 1997), pp. 173-174.

220 Native Women's Association of Canada, "Aboriginal Women, Self-Government, and the Canadian Charter of Rights and Freedoms" (Ottawa: NWAC, 1991).

221 *Ibid.*

222 *Ibid.* at 7.

223 Traditional Equality, *supra* note 219 at 172-175.

224 *Ibid.*

225 K. McNeil, "Aboriginal Governments and the Charter: Lessons from the United States" (2002) 17 Canadian Journal of Law and Society 73.

226 *Ibid.* at 73-74.

227 *Ibid.* at 100.

228 M. Boldt and J. A. Long, "Tribal Philosophies and the Canadian Charter of Rights and Freedoms," in M. Boldt and J. A. Long (Eds.), *The Quest for Justice: Aboriginal Peoples and Aboriginal Rights* (Toronto: University of Toronto Press, 1985) at 165.

229 Aboriginal Governments and the Charter, *supra* note 225 at 101-102.

230 *Ibid.* at 103.

231 Tribal Philosophies, *supra* note 228 at 169.

232 *Ibid.* at 172.

233 *Ibid.* at 174.

234 *Ibid.* at 172.

235 *Ibid.* at 177.

236 M. E. Turpel, "Aboriginal Peoples and the Canadian Charter: Interpretive Monopolies, Cultural Differences" (1989-90) 6 CHRYB 3 at 4, 16.

237 *Ibid.* at 25.

238 *Ibid.* at 42.

239 Indian Governments, *supra* note 5 at 112.

240 Aboriginal Peoples and the Charter, *supra* note 236 at 44.

241 *Ibid.*

242 *Ibid.* at 103.

243 *Ibid.*

244 Tribal Philosophies, *supra* note 228 at 178.

245 Indian Governments, *supra* note 5 at 114.

246 *Ibid.* at 113.

247 *Ibid.* at 115.

248 P. Hogg and M. Turpel, "Implementing Aboriginal Self-Government: Constitutional and Jurisdictional Issues" (1995) 74 Can. Bar. Rev. 187 at 215.

249 *Ibid.*

250 *Ibid.*

251 *Ibid.* at 216.

252 *RCAP Report*, Vol. 2, part 1, *supra* note 176 at 233.

253 *Ibid.*

254 *Indigenous Difference, supra* note 10 at 195.

255 *Ibid.* at 209.

256 Traditional Equality, *supra* note 219 at 170-171.

257 *Ibid.* at 170.

258 *Ibid.* at 171.

259 *Ibid.; Sui Generis* Nature of Aboriginal Rights, *supra* note 149 at 11-12.

260 Traditional Equality, *supra* note 219 at 174.

261 *Ibid.* at 183.

262 *Ibid.* at 170.

263 *Ibid.* at 183.

264 T. Nahanee, "Aboriginal Women and Self-Government" in M.A. Jackson and N.K. Bancks, (Eds.), *Ten Years Later: The Charter and Equality for Women* (Vancouver: Simon Fraser University, 1996) 27 at 28. See also S. McIvor, "Self-Government and Aboriginal Women," in *ibid.*, 77 at 84.

265 *Scrimbitt* v. *Sakimay Indian Band Council*, [2000] 1 C.N.L.R. 205.

266 *Ibid.* at 221.

267 *Ibid.* at 222.

268 *Ibid.* at 226.

269 *Six Nations of the Grand River Band* v. *Henderson*, [1997] 1 C.N.L.R. 202.

270 *Ibid.*

271 *Ibid.*

272 INAC, "Frequently Asked Questions: Aboriginal Self-Government": www.ainc-inac.gc.ca/ai/mr/nr/s-d2004/02551dbk-eng.asp.

273 *Yukon First Nations Self-Government Act*, S.C. 1994, c.35.

274 Canada, *Agreement Between the Inuit of the Nunavut Settlement Area and Her Majesty the Queen in Right of Canada*: www.nonstatusindian.com/docs/selfgovern/Nunavut_Agreement.pdf.

275 Canada, *Land Claims and Self-Government Agreement among the Tlicho and the Government of the Northwest Territories and the Government of Canada*: www.nonstatusindian.com/docs/selfgovern/Tlicho_SG_and_LC_Agreement.pdf.

276 Canada, *Land Claims Agreement Between the Inuit of Labrador and Her Majesty the Queen in Right of Newfoundland and Labrador and Her Majesty the Queen in Right of Canada*: www.nonstatusindian.com/docs/selfgovern/LIA_Land_Claim_Agreement.pdf at ss.2.15.1, 2.18.

277 *United Nations Declaration on the Rights of Indigenous Peoples*, UNGA, 62nd Sess. UN Doc. A/RES/61/295 (13 Sept. 2007).

278 CTV News, "Atleo calls for end of Indian Act within five years" (July 20, 2010): www.ctv.ca/CTVNews/Canada/20100720/atleo-indian-act-100720/.

279 At the time of writing, non-Aboriginal spouses of Mohawk band members at Kahnawake have been issued eviction notices, and some have already been forced to leave.

Notes to Chapter Three

1   *Lavell* v. *Canada (Attorney General)*; *Isaac* v. *Bedard* (1974) S.C.R. 1349. This case involved two separate appeals that were heard together.

2   *Sandra Lovelace* v. *Canada*, Communication No. 24/1977 (6 June 1983), U.N. Doc. Supp. No. 40 (A/38/40).

3   *Indian Act*, R.S.C. 1951, c.149 at s.12(1)(b).

4   *Ibid.* at s.12(1)(a)(iv).

5   *McIvor* v. *Canada (Registrar of Indian and Northern Affairs)*, [2009] 2 C.N.L.R. 236.

6   *Gehl* v. *Canada*, [2002] 4 C.N.L.R. 115 (Ont. CA), [2002] 4 C.N.L.R. 108 (Ont. Sup. Ct. Jus.). Gehl has since amended her claim to include a constitutional challenge to the Indian Act registration scheme as per the judgement on appeal. *Perron* v. *Canada (Attorney General)*, [2003] 3 C.N.L.R. 198. As per the court's decision, Connie Perron has amended her pleadings to include the constitutional challenge to the registration provisions of the Indian Act, while certain other portions of the claim were struck down. *Sanderson* v. *Canada*, [2003] M.J. No. 87 (Man. CA). Brenda Sanderson has also amended her pleadings. See *Sanderson* v. *Canada* (Winnipeg Queen's Bench, 31 August 2007, File No. CI 03-01-32940) (Re-Re-Re Amended Statement of Claim of the plaintiff, Brenda Pauline Sanderson).

7   Turtle Island Native Network News, "Assembly of Manitoba Chiefs — Womens [sic] Issues: Annual Report August 2003: Bill C-31": http://turtleisland.org/news/news-c31.htm.

8   Assembly of First Nations, "Remarks to the House of Commons Standing Committee on Aboriginal Peoples and Northern Development April 13, 2010: Bill C-3: *Gender Equity in Indian Registration Act*": www.afn.ca/misc/RC-WR.pdf; Six Nations, "Six Nations of the Grand River Presentation to the Standing Committee on Aboriginal Affairs and Northern Development (AANO) and C-3 *An Act to Promote Gender Equity in Indian Registration*" (Ottawa: April 20, 2010); Chiefs of Ontario, "Bill C-3 and the Indigenous Right to Identity" (Ottawa: April 20, 2010); P. Palmater, "Presentation to the Standing Committee on Aboriginal Affairs and Northern Development (AANO) Re: Bill C-3 – *Gender Equity in Indian Registration Act*" (Ottawa: April 20, 2010).

9   *Lovelace, supra* note 2; *International Covenant on Civil and Political Rights*, 16 Dec. 1966, CAN. T.S. 1976 No. 47 (entry into force 23 March 1976; in force for Canada, 19 Aug. 1976) at art. 27.

10   *Indian Act, 1951, supra* note 3.

11   *Canadian Charter of Rights and Freedoms*, Part I of the *Constitution Act, 1982*, being Schedule B to the *Canada Act 1982* (UK), 1982, c.11.

12   *McIvor, supra* note 5 at para. 123.

13 *McIvor v. Canada (Registrar, Indian and Northern Affairs)*, [2007] 3 C.N.L.R. 72 at para. 73.

14 *Corbiere v. Canada (Minister of Indian and Northern Affairs)*, [1999] 2 S.C.R. 203.

15 Aboriginal Justice Implementation Commission, *Report of the Aboriginal Justice Inquiry of Manitoba* (Nov. 1999): www.ajic.mb.ca/volume.html.

16 *Ibid.* at Chap. 1, n.p.

17 *Ibid.* at Chap. 5, n.p.

18 *Ibid.*

19 *Ibid.*

20 M. Furi and J. Wherrett, Parliamentary Information and Research Service, Library of Parliament, "Indian Status and Band Membership Issues" (Feb. 1996, revised Feb. 2003): www2.parl.gc.ca/Content/LOP/ResearchPublications/bp410-e.htm at "Continuing Inequities in Legislation."

21 *Indian Act*, R.S.C. 1985, c. I-5 at ss.6(1), 6(2).

22 *McIvor, supra* note 5 at para. 43.

23 Indian Status Issues, *supra* note 20.

24 P. Paul, "The Politics of Legislated Identity: The Effect of Section 6(2) of the Indian Act in the Atlantic Provinces" (Nova Scotia: Atlantic Policy Congress of First Nations Chiefs Secretariat, 1999).

25 *Aboriginal Justice Inquiry, supra* note 15 at Chap. 5.

26 W. Cornet, "Aboriginality: Legal Foundations, Past Trends, Future Prospects," in J. Magnet and D. Dorey (Eds.), *Aboriginal Rights Litigation* (Markham: LexisNexis Canada, 2003); B. Lawrence, *"Real" Indians and Others: Mixed Blood Urban Native Peoples and Indigenous Nationhood* (Lincoln: University of Nebraska Press, 2004).

27 J. Fiske and E. George, "Final Report: Seeking Alternatives to Bill C-31: From Cultural Trauma to Cultural Revitalization through Customary Law" (Paper presented to the Bill C-31 and First Nation Membership Pre-Conference Workshop, March 2006) at 1.

28 Native Women's Association of Canada, "Aboriginal Women and Unstated Paternity: An Issue Paper: Prepared for the National Aboriginal Women's Summit" (20-22 June 2007) at 2.

29 *Ibid.*

30 M. Mann, "Indian Registration: Unrecognized and Unstated Paternity" (Paper presented to the Bill C-31 and First Nation Membership Pre-Conference Workshop, March 2006) at v.

31 *Ibid.*

32 *Ibid.*

33 *Ibid.*

34 *Ibid.* at preface.

35 *Ibid.* at 6.

36 Indian Status Issues, *supra* note 20 at "Continuing Inequities in Legislation."

37 Native Women's Association of Canada, "Guide to Bill C-31: 1986: An Explanation of the 1985 Amendments to the Indian Act," at 23.

38 *Ibid.* at 14.

39 J. Teillet, "Métis Law Summary 2004": www.metisnation.ca/rights/download/MLS-2004.pdf at 5.

40 "Fifth Report of the Standing Committee on Aboriginal Affairs and Northern Development on consideration of the implementation of the Act to Amend the Indian Act as passed by the House of Commons on June 12, 1985, Minutes of Proceedings and Evidence of the Standing Committee on Aboriginal Affairs and Northern Development," 2nd sess. 33rd Parl., issue no. 46.

41 *Real Indians and Others, supra* note 26 at 69.

42 *McIvor, supra* note 5 at para. 129.

43 J. Magnet, *et al.*, " 'Arbitrary, Anachronistic and Harsh': Constitutional Jurisdiction in Relation to Non-Status Indians and Metis," in J. Magnet and D. Dorey (Eds.), *Legal Aspects of Aboriginal Business Development* (Markham: LexisNexis, 2005) at 171.

44 L. Gilbert, *Entitlement to Indian Status and Membership Codes in Canada* (Toronto: Thomson Canada, 1996) at 12.

45 Note to Minister (Jan. 11, 1985), as quoted in *McIvor v. Canada* (3-4 Oct. 2008, BCCA) (Factum of the Intervener, Abenakis) at para. 109.

46 C. MacIntosh, "From Judging Culture to Taxing 'Indians': Tracing the Legal Discourse of the 'Indian Mode of Life'" (2009) 47 Osgoode Hall L.J. 399 at 3, 6, and 7.

47 *Charter, supra* note 11, s. 15.

48 *Andrews v. Law Society of British Columbia*, [1989] 1 S.C.R. 143.

49 *Law v. Canada (Minister of Employment and Immigration)*, [1999] 1 S.C.R. 497.

50 *R. v. Kapp*, [2008] 2 S.C.R. 483.

51 *Ibid.* at paras. 21-24.

52 *Ermineskin Indian Band and Nation v. Canada*, [2009] 2 C.N.L.R. 102.

53 *Andrews, supra* note 48 at para. 2. The act referred to was the *Barristers and Solicitors Act*, R.S.B.C. 1979, c. 26.

54 *Ibid.* at para. 25.

55 *Ibid.*

56 *Ibid.* at para. 38.

57 *Ibid.*

58 *Ibid.* at para. 59.

59 *Ibid.* at para. 37.

60   *Ibid.* at para. 46. See also *Law, supra* note 49 at para. 23 which summarizes the test laid out in Andrews.

61   *Andrews, supra* note 48 at paras. 50-52; *R. v. Oakes,* [1986] 1 S.C.R. 103.

62   *Oakes, ibid.* at para. 67.

63   *Ibid.* as cited in *Andrews, supra* note 48 at paras. 8-10.

64   *Andrews, supra* note 48 at para. 51.

65   *R. v. Edward Books and Art Ltd.,* [1986] 2 S.C.R. 713 at p. 768, as cited in *Andrews, supra* note 48 at para. 11.

66   *Oakes, supra* note 61 at paras. 69-71.

67   *Andrews, supra* note 48 at para. 10.

68   *Law, supra* note 49 at para. 31.

69   *Kapp, supra* note 50 at para. 14.

70   *Ibid.* at para. 25.

71   *Ibid.* at para. 37.

72   *Ibid.*

73   *Hodge* v. *Canada (Minister of Human Resources Development),* [2004] 3 S.C.R. 357 at para. 23.

74   *McIvor* trial, *supra* note 13 at paras. 123-125.

75   *Ibid.* at paras. 126-143

76   *Corbiere, supra* note 14 at para. 4.

77   *Report of the Royal Commission on Aboriginal Peoples,* Vols. 1-5 (Ottawa: Minister of Supply and Services Canada, 1996); P. Palmater, "An Empty Shell of a Treaty Promise: *R. v. Marshall* and the Rights of Non-Status Indians" (2000) 23 Dal. L.J. 102; A. Sterritt, "Racialization of Poverty: Indigenous Women, the Indian Act and Systemic Oppression: Reasons for Resistance" (Vancouver: Vancouver's Status of Women's Racialization of Poverty Project, 2007): www.vsw.ca/Documents/IndigenousWomen_DEC2007FINAL.pdf; Human Rights Committee, "Concluding Observations of the Human Rights Committee: Canada: 2/11/2005": www.treatycouncil.org/PDFs/Concluding_observations_Canada_HRC.pdf; M. Cannon, "Revisiting Histories of Gender-Based Exclusion and the New Politics of Indian Identity" (Vancouver: National Centre for First Nations Governance, 2008): www.fngovernance.org/research/martin_cannon.pdf.

78   S. Clatworthy, "Bill C-31, Indian Registration and First Nations Membership" (Winnipeg: Four Directions Consulting Group, 2001) at 15.

79   *Lovelace* v. *Ontario,* [2001] 1 S.C.R. 950 at para. 70.

80   *Corbiere, supra* note 14.

81   *Ibid.* at para. 13.

82   *Ibid.* at para. 15.

83   *Constable Darrel Bruno* v. *Canada (Attorney General, Royal Canadian Mounted Police Grievance Reviewer)* (2006) FC 462.

84   Indian Mode of Life, *supra* note 46 at para. 82.

85   Memorandum to Cabinet (10 May 1984), Record of Cabinet Decision (29 May 1984), Memorandum to Cabinet (9 February 1984), as cited in *McIvor* v. *Canada* (3-4 Oct. 2008, BCCA) (Factum of the Intervener, Abenakis) at paras. 4-9.

86   Cabinet MC 1984, *ibid.* at paras. 4-9.

87   *Real Indians and others, supra* note 26 at 55.

88   *McIvor* v. *Canada* (3-4 Oct. 2008, BCCA) (Factum of the Appellant, Canada) at para. 97: "Section 6(1)(a) preserved rights acquired under the prior Indian Acts. And ss.6(1)(f) and 6(2) ensures those registered have sufficient genealogical proximity to the historical 'Indian' population." See also paras. 12, 64, 65, 84, 108, 110, 118; *McIvor* trial, *supra* note 13 at paras. 309, 313.

89   *Ibid.* at para.12.

90   *McIvor* trial, *supra* note 13; *McIvor, supra* note 5.

91   *R.* v. *Sappier, R.* v. *Gray,* [2006] 2 S.C.R. 686 at para. 46.

92   *Corbiere, supra* note 14 at para. 18.

93   *Ibid.* at para.17

94   *Ibid.*

95   *Report of the Royal Commission on Aboriginal Peoples,* Vol. 1. (Ottawa: Supply and Services Canada, 1996) at 521.

96   *Ibid.* at 525.

97   SCAAND Report on C-31, supra note 40 at 40.

98   M. Cannon, "First Nations Citizenship, Bill C-31, and the Accommodation of Sex Discrimination Policy" (Paper presented to the Bill C-31 and First Nation Membership Pre-Conference Workshop, March 2006) at 20.

99   *McIvor* trial, *supra* note 13 at paras. 313-314.

100 *McIvor, ibid.* at para. 112.

101 *Supra* note 5 at para. 124.

102 *McIvor-Canada* factum, *supra* note 88 at para. 96.

103 *McIvor* trial, *supra* note 13 at para. 312; *McIvor, supra* note 5 at para. 123. Only five objectives were accepted by the appeal court, and genealogical proximity was not one of them.

104 *Lovelace, supra* note 79 at para. 69.

105 T. Isaac and M. Maloughney, "Dually Disadvantaged and Historically Forgotten? Aboriginal Women and the Inherent Right of Self-Government" (1992) 21 Man L Rev 453; *McIvor* trial, *supra* note 13 at para. 87; *Corbiere, supra* note 14.

106 *Corbiere, supra* note 14 at para. 21.

107 *Ibid.* at para. 21.

108 First Nations Citizenship, supra note 98 at 20.

109 *Lovelace,* supra note 79 at para. 70.

110 *Charter, supra* note 11 at s.1: "The *Canadian Charter of Rights and Freedoms* guarantees the rights and freedoms set out in it subject only to such reasonable limits prescribed by law as can be demonstrably justified in a free and democratic society."

111 *Schachter v. Canada,* [1992] 2 S.C.R. 679 at para. 25.

112 *Ibid.* at para. 79.

113 *Corbiere, supra* note 14 at para. 126 (the SCC suspended its declaration of invalidity for 18 months); *McIvor, supra* note 5 at para. 166 (the BCCA suspended its judgement for 12 months).

114 *R. v. Powley,* [2003] 2 S.C.R. 207.

115 *Ibid.* at para. 49.

116 *Corbiere, supra* note 14 at para.21.

117 Arbitrary, Anachronistic and Harsh, *supra* note 43 at 175.

118 *Ibid.* at 174.

119 *Ibid.* at 175.

120 *Ibid.*

121 Associate Deputy Minister Drummie, "Removing Discrimination from the Indian Act: January 11, 1985," as cited by the First Nations Leadership Council (FNLC) in *McIvor v. Canada,* (Vancouver: Court of Appeal of British Columbia, July 4, 2008) (Factum of the Intervener, First Nations Leadership Council).

122 *Schachter, supra* note 111 at para. 63.

123 *Ibid.* at para. 41: "Perhaps in some cases s. 15 does simply require relative equality and is just as satisfied with equal graveyards as equal vineyards, as it has sometimes been put. Yet the nullification of benefits to single mothers does not sit well with the overall purpose of s. 15 of the Charter and for s. 15 to have such a result clearly amounts to 'equality with a vengeance,' as LEAF, one of the interveners in this case, has suggested. While s. 15 may not absolutely require that benefits be available to single mothers, surely it at least encourages such action to relieve the disadvantaged position of persons in those circumstances."

124 *Constitution Act, 1982 supra* note 11 at s.52.(1): "The Constitution of Canada is the supreme law of Canada, and any law that is inconsistent with the provisions of the Constitution is, to the extent of the inconsistency, of no force and effect."

125 "Michel Band History": www.michelfirstnation.net/our-story.html. See also Michel First Nation, "An Opportunity to Amend the Indian Act": www.michelfirstnation.net/an-opportunity-to-amend-the-indian-act.html.

126 See, generally, S. Clatworthy and A. Smith, "Population Implications of the 1985 Amendments to the Indian Act: Final Report" (Winnipeg: Four Directions Consulting Group, 1992); S. Clatworthy, "Reassessing the Population Impacts of Bill C-31" (Winnipeg: Four Directions Project Consultants, 2001); S. Clatworthy, "Implications of First Nations Demography: Final Report" (Winnipeg: INAC, 2004); S. Clatworthy, "Indian Registration, Membership and Population Change in First Nation Communities" (Winnipeg: INAC, 2005).

127 Native Women's Association of Canada, "Aboriginal Women's Rights are Human Rights": http://action.web.ca/home/narcc/attach/AboriginalWomensRightsAreHumanRights.pdf at 29.

128 AFN-INAC Joint Technical Working Group, "First Nations Registration (Status) and Membership Research Report: July 2008": www.afn.ca/misc/mrp.pdf at 6-7.

129 *Ibid.* at 14.

130 Aboriginal Justice Implementation Commission, *The Report of the Aboriginal Justice Inquiry of Manitoba* (Nov. 1999): www.ajic.mb.ca/volume.html at Chap. 5.

131 Indian and Northern Affairs Canada, "Backgrounder: Labrador Innu Registration and Band Creation": www.ainc-inac.gc.ca/ai/scr/at/irp/bkg-eng.asp.

132 M. Hanrahan, "The Lasting Breach: The Omission of Aboriginal People From the Terms of Union Between Newfoundland and Canada and its Ongoing Impacts" (Newfoundland: Royal Commission on Renewing and Strengthening Our Place in Canada, 2003): www.exec.gov.nl.ca/royalcomm/research/pdf/Hanrahan.pdf. See also "About Miawpukek": www.mfngov.ca/about.html; and "Agreement in Principle: For the Recognition of the Qalipu Mi'kmaq First Nation Band": http://qalipu.com/message.html.

133 Indian and Northern Affairs Canada, "Labrador Innu — Chronology of Events": www.ainc-inac.gc.ca/ai/scr/at/irp/coe-eng.asp at 3.

134 C. Backhouse and D. McRae, *Report to the Canadian Human Rights Commission on the Treatment of the Innu of Labrador by the Government of Canada* (Ottawa: CHRC, 2002): www.chrc-ccdp.ca/pdf/reports/InnuReport2002.pdf.

135 *Ibid.* at 58.

136 Innu Chronology, *supra* note 133; Mushuau Innu First Nation Band Order, P.C. 2002-1948, SOR/2002-415, C. Gaz. 2002, Vol. 136, No. 25; Sheshatshiu Innu First Nation Band Order, P.C. 2002-1947, SOR/2002-424, C. Gaz. 2002, Vol. 136. No.25. The date of both OICs was Nov. 21, 2002.

137 See Indian and Northern Affairs Canada, "Backgrounder: Miawpukek First Nation Land Transfer Agreement" (Ottawa: INAC, 2005): www.ainc-inac.gc.ca/nr/prs/j-a2005/02634bbk_e.html; Indian and Northern Affairs Canada, "News Release: Self-Government Framework Agreement and Land Transfer Agreement for Miawpukek First Nation" (Ottawa: INAC, 2005): www.ainc-inac.gc.ca/nr/prs/j-a2005/2-02634_e.html; Miawpukek Band Order, P.C. 1989-2206, SOR/89-533, 2 Nov. 1989; Department of Justice Canada: http://lois.justice.gc.ca/en/I-5/SOR-89-533/139499.html.

138 Miawpukek Backgrounder, *supra* note 137 at 1. While the reserve is commonly referred to as Miawpukek, the official name is *Aosamiaji'jij Miawpukek Mi'kmawey Mawi'omi* Reserve, which means "too small Conne River Reserve."

139 Miawpukek News, *supra* note 137.

140 Federation of Newfoundland Indians, "Registration and Recognition for Mi'kmaq of Newfoundland" (St. George's: FNI, 2006): www.fni.nf.ca/news/Negoations%20Newletter.pdf at 1. In this newsletter, the president of the FNI, Brendan Sheppard updates his members on the process of the negotiations: "[T]here is no guarantee that negotiations will result in a successful conclusion (i.e. status and recognition), however we are closer now than ever before in the history of this organization. The Federal Government has certainly maintained their promise to work with the FNI to settle this issue outside of court and negotiations are proceeding well."

141 Canadian Heritage, "News Release: Government of Canada Supports Federation of Newfoundland Indians" (Corner Brook: Canadian Heritage, 2005).

142 *Innu Report 2002*, *supra* note 134 at 23.

143 Sharon McIvor, "Sharon McIvor's Response to the August 2009 Proposal of Indian and Northern Affairs Canada to Amend the 1985 Indian Act," (6 Oct. 2009) at 4.

144 *McIvor*, *supra* note 5 at para.1.

145 *McIvor* trial, *supra* note 13 at para. 1; *McIvor*, *supra* note 5 at para. 43

146 *McIvor* trial, *supra* note 13 at para. 4.

147 *Ibid.* at para. 6.

148 *Ibid.* at para. 7.

149 *Ibid.* at para. 32

150 *Ibid.* at para. 73

151 *Ibid.* at para. 126.

152 *Ibid.* at para. 134.

153 *Ibid.* at paras. 176-178.

154 *Ibid.* at para. 193.

155 *Ibid.* at paras. 179, 186

156 *Ibid.* at para. 7.

157 *Ibid.* at paras. 73, 198.

158 *McIvor*, *supra* note 5 at para. 71.

159 *Ibid.* at para. 73.

160 *McIvor* trial, *supra* note 13 at para. 199.

161 *Ibid.* at para. 211.

162 *Ibid.* at para. 213.

163 *Ibid.* See also: *Andrews, supra* note 48, referring to *Bliss* v. *Canada* (Attorney General), [1979] 1 S.C.R. 183.

164 *McIvor* trial, *supra* note 13 at para. 217.

165 *McIvor, supra* note 5 at para. 74.

166 *Ibid.* at para. 77.

167 *Ibid.* at paras. 78, 82.

168 *McIvor* trial, *supra* note 13 at para. 237.

169 *Ibid.* at paras. 239-240.

170 *Ibid.* at paras. 87-88.

171 *Ibid.* at para. 92. See also paras. 95-100: The court agreed that Benner was analogous, but did not agree that matrilineal/patrilineal descent was an analogous ground.

172 *Ibid.* at para. 262.

173 *Ibid.* at para. 268.

174 *McIvor, supra* note 5 at para. 111.

175 *McIvor* trial, *supra* note 13 at para. 269.

176 *Ibid.* at para. 271.

177 *McIvor, supra* note 5 at para. 123.

178 *McIvor* trial, *supra* note 13 at paras. 310-319; *ibid.* at para. 124.

179 *McIvor* trial, *supra* note 13 at paras. 309-314.

180 *McIvor, supra* note 5 at para. 123.

181 *Ibid.* at paras. 130-132.

182 *McIvor* trial, *supra* note 13 at para. 323.

183 *McIvor, supra* note 5 at para. 133.

184 *McIvor* trial, *supra* note 13 at para. 328.

185 *McIvor, supra* note 5 at para. 134.

186 *McIvor* trial, *supra* note 13 at paras. 329-332.

187 *Ibid.* at paras. 331-333.

188 *McIvor, supra* note 5 at paras. 140-145.

189 *McIvor* trial, *supra* note 13 at para. 340.

190 *McIvor, supra* note 5 at paras. 145, 150.

191 *McIvor* v. *Canada* (2007) No. A941142. Order of Justice Ross dated June 8, 2007.

192 *McIvor, supra* note 5 at para. 154.

193 *Ibid.* at para. 166.

194 *McIvor* v. *Canada*, [2009] S.C.C.A. No. 234.

195 Neil Haesler, "Aboriginal woman takes status battle to the UN" (Saskatoon StarPhoenix, Nov. 13, 2010), at C8.

196 "Discussion Paper on Needed Changes to the Indian Act Affecting Indian Registration and Band Membership, McIvor v. Canada": www.ainc-inac.gc.ca/br/is/bll/exp/dpnc-eng.asp.

197 Bill C-3: *An Act to promote gender equity in Indian registration by responding to the Court of Appeal for British Columbia decision in McIvor v. Canada (Registrar of Indian and Northern Affairs)* (First Reading March 11, 2010) (short title: *Gender Equity in Indian Registration Act*): www.ainc-inac.gc.ca/br/is/bll/index-eng.asp.

198 INAC, "How Do the New Legislative Changes to the *Indian Act* Affect Me?": www.ainc-inac.gc.ca/br/is/neir-eng.pdf.

199 P. Palmater, "Presentation to the Standing Committee on Aboriginal Affairs and Northern Development (AAON) Re: Bill C-3 — *Gender Equity in Indian Registration Act*" (Ottawa: April 20, 2010).

200 Assembly of First Nations, "Remarks to the House of Commons Standing Committee on Aboriginal Peoples and Northern Development April 13, 2010: Bill C-3: *Gender Equity in Indian Registration Act*": www.nonstatusindian.com/docs/aaon-submit/AFN.pdf; Six Nations, "Six Nations of the Grand River Presentation to the Standing Committee on Aboriginal Affairs and Northern Development (AANO) and C-3: *An Act to Promote Gender Equity in Indian Registration*" (Ottawa: April 20, 2010); Palmater submission, *supra* note 199.

201 Palmater submission, *supra* note 199 at 7, 8.

202 Palmater submission, *supra* note 199; Sharon McIvor and Gwen Brodsky, "Equal Registration Status For Aboriginal Women and Their Descendants: Sharon McIvor's Comments on Bill C-3, An Act to promote gender equity in Indian registration by responding to the Court of Appeal for British Columbia decision in McIvor v. Canada (Registrar of Indian and Northern Affairs)": Submission to the Standing Committee on Aboriginal Affairs and Northern Development (Ottawa: April 13, 2010).

203 *Gehl, supra* note 6; *Perron, supra* note 6; *Sanderson, supra* note 6; *Nathan McGillivary et al. v. Her Majesty the Queen* (File No. T-1975-93) (Re 5x Amended Statement of Claim of the Plaintiff). It will depend on whether these cases move forward and if any or all of these cases specifically argue the second generation cut-off rule.

Notes to Chapter Four

1 *Indian Act*, R.S.C. 1985, c. I-5 at s.4, which provides: "A reference in this Act to an Indian does not include any person of the race of Aborigines commonly referred to as Inuit."

2 *Indian Act*, R.S.C. 1985, c.I-5, as am. by R.S.C. 1985, c.2 (1st Supp.) (Bill C-31).

3 *Indian Act, supra* note 1 at ss.6-11.

4 S. Clatworthy, "Indian Registration, Membership and Population Change in First Nations Communities" (Ottawa: INAC, 2005) at 7; Indian and Northern Affairs Canada: www.ainc-inac.gc.ca/ap/fn/index-eng.asp.

5 P. Macklem, *Indigenous Difference and the Constitution of Canada* (Toronto: University of Toronto Press, 2001) at 230.

6 *Indian Act, supra* note 1 at ss.8, 9.

7 R. Soonias, "Membership — Indian Status," *Saskatchewan Indian* (1978) Vol. 8, No. 2 at 2.

8 *Indian Act, supra* note 1 at s.11. (1) (a)-(d).

9 Indian Registration and Membership, *supra* note 4 at 11-12.

10 *Ibid.* at 19.

11 *Ibid.* at 2.

12 *Ibid.* at 11-12.

13 *Ibid.* at 16.

14 *Ibid.* at 15.

15 *Sawridge Band* v. *Canada*, [1997] F.C.J. No. 794 (FCA), [1995] 4 C.N.L.R. 121 (FCTD). Native Council of Canada, "Comment: Bill C-31": www.ammsa.com/classroom/CLASSiC-31.html. The NCC explains that the Sawridge band, which is worth between $14 and $100 million dollars, is fighting the reinstatement of Indian women to their band membership list. This litigation was commenced by Chief Walter Twinn, who claimed the case was about where to draw the line and who does the drawing, while at the same time indicating that it was not sexist or racist. The Chief's wife, Catherine Twinn, was their legal counsel and stated that they did not want off-reserve people to be band members as they could possibly "unite" and would have the power to vote. Two other Alberta bands, the Sarcee and the Ermineskin, also challenged Bill C-31.

16 Indian Registration and Membership, *supra* note 4 at 17. Clatworthy studied 609 First Nations. He noted that 19 First Nations had their own rules under self-government arrangements at the time that were not included in his statistics. Some of the First Nations had approved codes and some did not. He also advised that while some were following their codes, some were not. For the purposes of the above statistics, he refers to 593 First Nations.

17 *Ibid.* at 21-22.

18 *Ibid.* at 22-23.

19 *Ibid.* at 26.

20 *Ibid.* at 30.

21 *Ibid.*

22 *Ibid.* at 41.

23 E. Asante, "Negotiating Identity: Aboriginal Women and the Politics of Self-Government" (2005) 25 Can. J. N. Stud. (Issue 1) 1 at 5, 16. Asante argues that the degree to which Aboriginal peoples can access their culture and identify with Aboriginal identity is related to socio-economic factors such as whether they live on reserve, their level of education, and income levels.

24 Indian Registration and Membership, *supra* note 4 at 7-15. Clatworthy notes that there exist 70 sets of non-approved band membership rules, 8 of which are currently under review by INAC.

25 *Ibid.* at 9.

26 S. Clatworthy and A. Smith, "Population Implications of the 1985 Amendments to the *Indian Act*: Final Report," (Ottawa: Assembly of First Nations, 1992).

27 *Ibid.* at iii.

28 *St. Basile Indian Reserve Membership Code and Rules* (Ottawa: INAC, 2007) at ss.5-8.

29 *McIvor* v. *Canada* (3-4 Oct. 2008, BCCA) (Factum of the Appellant, Canada).

30 *St. Basile Membership Code, supra* note 28 at s.3.(2) defines the original families as: "Bernard, Cimon, Francis and Wallace, as was recorded in 1952 by the Government."

31 *Ibid.*

32 S. Clatworthy, "Reassessing the Population Impacts of Bill C-31" (Winnipeg: Four Directions Project Consultants, 2001) at 6.

33 Population Implications, *supra* note 26 at 94.

34 *Ibid.*

35 Tseshaht First Nations, "We Are the Tseshaht": www.tseshaht.com/?page=1>. The Tseshaht First Nation is one of 14 Nations that are part of the Nuu-chah-nulth Tribal Council. Their band is located on West Vancouver Island in British Columbia.

36 Population Implications, *supra* note 26 at 104.

37 *Ibid.* Clatworthy explains: "In contrast with the population entitled to registration, the population eligible for membership in Sheshaht would experience growth throughout most of the projection time frame and eventually stabilize at a level roughly 2.2 times larger in size than at present."

38 Indian and Northern Affairs Canada, "Registered Population: Madawaska Maliseet": http://sdiprod2.inac.gc.ca/FNProfiles/FNProfiles_GeneralInformation.asp?BAND_NUMBER=6&BAND_NAME=Madawaska+Maliseet+First+Nation.

39 As with all these codes, it is not known how they are enforced in reality. For example, in Eel River Bar it is not known if a single mother who was also a band member could register her child if she did not acknowledge the name of the father.

40 Population Implications, *supra* note 26 at 83.

41 *Ibid.*

42 *Ibid.* at 120.

43 *Ibid.*

44 *Ibid.* The out-marriage rate for Golden Lake's off-reserve population is over 65 per cent.

45 Indian and Northern Affairs Canada, "Registered Indian Population: Eel River Bar First Nation": <http://sdiprod2.inac.gc.ca/FNProfiles/FNProfiles_GeneralInformation.asp? BAND_NUMBER=8&BAND_NAME=Eel+River+Bar+First+Nation. See also Indian and Northern Affairs Canada, "Registered Indian Population: Algonquians of Pikwakanagan": http://sdiprod2.inac.gc.ca/FNProfiles/FNProfiles_GeneralInformation.asp?BAND _NUMBER=163&BAND_NAME=Algonquins+of+Pikwakanagan.

46 Wasauksing First Nation: http://firstnation.ca/wasauksing.

47 *Parry Island Citizenship Code* (Ottawa: INAC, 2007) at ss.2, 3.

48 *Ibid.* at s.16. In the code, the term "citizen" is defined as "band member." Therefore, their citizenship code is really their band membership code.

49 *Ibid.* at ss.10-13.

50 *Ibid.* at ss.13-14.

51 *Ibid.* at s.15.

52 Population Implications, *supra* note 26 at 89.

53 *Ibid.* at 89.

54 *Ibid.* at 111-112.

55 *Ibid.* at 112.

56 *Ibid.*

57 *Ibid.*

58 *Ibid.* at 94. See also Indian and Northern Affairs Canada, "Registered Population: Wahta Mohawks": http://sdiprod2.inac.gc.ca/FNProfiles/FNProfiles_GeneralInformation.asp? BAND_NUMBER=134&BAND_NAME=Wahta+Mohawk.

59 Aboriginal Canada Portal, "Connectivity Profile: Wasauksing First Nation": www.aborigi nalcanada.gc.ca/abdt/apps/connectivitysurvey.nsf/vAllCProfile_en/363.htm.

60 Population Implications, *supra* note 26 at 87.

61 *Ibid.*

62 *Ibid.*

63 *Ibid.* at 99.

64 *Ibid.*

65 *Ibid.*

66 *Ibid.* at 87 and 91.

67 *Ibid.*

68 *Ibid.* at 88.

69 Indian and Northern Affairs Canada, "Registered Population: Mowachaht/Muchalaht": http://sdiprod2.inac.gc.ca/FNProfiles/FNProfiles_GeneralInformation.asp?BAND_ NUMBER=630&BAND_NAME=Mowachaht/Muchalaht.

70 *Mowachaht Membership Rules* (Ottawa: INAC, 2007) at preamble.

71 *Ibid.* at s.4.

72 Population Implications, *supra* note 26 at 88, 103.

73 *Mowachaht Membership Rules, supra* note 70 at s.6(1).

74 *Ibid.* at s.6(2).

75 *Ibid.* at s.7.

76 *Ibid.* at s.7.3(c). Only those who reside on reserve are entitled to be part of the band's membership committee.

77 Population Implications, *supra* note 26 at 86. See also *Ehattesaht Tribe Membership Rule* (Ottawa: INAC, 2007) at 6.

78 Indian and Northern Affairs Canada, "General Information: Registered Population: Ehattesaht": http://sdiprod2.inac.gc.ca/FNProfiles/FNProfiles_GeneralInformation.asp? BAND_NUMBER=634&BAND_NAME=Ehattesaht.

79 *Ehattesaht Membership Rule, supra* note 77 at 1.

80 *Ibid.*

81 *Ibid.*

82 Population Implications, *supra* note 26 at 83, 103.

83 *Ehattesaht Membership Rule, supra* note 77 at s.4.

84 *Ibid.* at s.4(f).

85 *Ibid.* at ss.5(a) and 3(i).

86 *Ibid.* at s.7(a)(ii).

87 *Ibid.* at s.7(o).

88 *Sandra Lovelace* v. *Canada*, Communication No. R.6/24, U.N. Doc. Supp. No. 40 (A/36/ 40) at 166 (1981). *Lavell* v. *Canada (Attorney General); Isaac* v. *Bedard* (1974) S.C.R. 1349.

89 *Constitution Act, 1982*, being Schedule B to the *Canada Act, 1982* (UK), 1982, c.11.

90 Indian and Northern Affairs Canada, "General Information: Matsqui First Nation": http://sdiprod2.inac.gc.ca/FNProfiles/FNProfiles_GeneralInformation.asp?BAND_ NUMBER=565&BAND_NAME=Matsqui.

91 *Matsqui Band Membership Code* (Ottawa: INAC, 2007) at 2 (preamble).

92 *Ibid.* at ss.3,4.

93 *Ibid.* at ss.5,6.

94 *Ibid.* at s.12(4).

95 *Corbiere* v. *Canada (Minister of Indian and Northern Affairs)* [1999] 2 S.C.R. 203; *Canadian Charter of Rights and Freedoms*, Part I of the Constitution Act, 1982, being Schedule B to the Canada Act 1982 (U.K.), 1982, c.11 at s.15.

96 The band referred to here is to be differentiated from the Sucker Creek band of Ojibways on Manitoulin Island.

97 Population Implications, *supra* note 26 at 91, 111.

98 *Ibid.*

99 *Sucker Creek Band Membership Code* (Ottawa: INAC, 2007) at Part 1, ss.1,5.

100 *Ibid.* at Part 1, s.6.

101 *Ibid.* at Part 3, s.3-5.

102 *Ibid.* at Part 4, s.2(b).

103 *Ibid.* at Part 4, s.2(c),(d).

104 *Ibid.* at Part 4, s.3.

105 Population Implications, *supra* note 26 at 112.

106 Registration and Membership, *supra* note 4 at 9. Clatworthy indicated that when he followed up with First Nations on the current status of band membership codes, some bands indicated that they were not using their codes to determine membership. Some indicated that they had instituted a moratorium on membership altogether.

107 See Indian and Northern Affairs Canada, "Federal Policy Guide: Aboriginal Self-Government: The Government of Canada's Approach to the Implementation of the Inherent Right and the Negotiation of Aboriginal Self-Government": http://dsp-psd.pwgsc.gc.ca/Collection-R/LoPBdP/CIR/962-e.htm.

108 Indian and Northern Affairs Canada, "Agreements": www.ainc-inac.gc.ca/pr/agr/index_e.html#Self-GovernmentAgreements.

109 *Ibid.*

110 Inherent Right Policy, *supra* note 107.

111 M. Hurley and J. Wherrett, "*The Report of the Royal Commission on Aboriginal Peoples*": www.parl.gc.ca/content/LOP/ResearchPublications/prb9924-e.htm at 1.

112 *Ibid.*

113 In Dec. 1998, the United Nations Committee on Economic, Social and Cultural Rights viewed "with concern the direct connection between Aboriginal economic marginalization and the ongoing dispossession of Aboriginal people from their lands, as recognized by RCAP," and expressed its "concern that the recommendations of RCAP have not yet been implemented, in spite of the urgency of the situation." In April 1999, the United Nations Human Rights Committee also expressed concern that Canada had "not yet implemented the recommendations of the [RCAP]," and recommended "that decisive and urgent action be taken towards the full implementation of the RCAP recommendations on land and resource allocation." In its 1999 Annual Report, the Canadian Human Rights Commission "reiterate[d] the view expressed in previous annual reports that the government's response to the 1996 report of the [RCAP] has been slow."

114 Report of Rodolfo Stavenhagen, Special Rapporteur on the situation of human rights and fundamental freedoms of indigenous people — Mission to Canada, CHR 61st, UN ESC, 2005, UN Doc, E/CN.4/2005/88/ADD.3.

115 *Ibid.* at 21. (para. 85).

116 *Ibid.* at 23, 24. (paras. 105, 107).

117 *Report of the Royal Commission on Aboriginal Peoples*, Vol. 2: Restructuring the Relationship: Part 1 (Ottawa: Minister of Supply and Services, 1996) at 87.

118 *Ibid.; Royal Proclamation, 1763,* R.S.C., 1985, App. II, No.1.

119 *RCAP Report*, Vol. 2, Part 1, *supra* note 117 at 88.

120 *Ibid.*

121 *Ibid.* at 89.

122 *Ibid.* at 106, 140.

123 *Ibid.* at 140.

124 *Ibid.*

125 *Ibid.* at 140-141.

126 *Ibid.* at 160-163.

127 *Ibid.*

128 *Ibid.* at 166.

129 *Ibid.* at 168.

130 *Ibid.* at 179.

131 *Ibid.* at 183.

132 *Ibid.* at 215.

133 *Ibid.* at 218.

134 Inherent right policy, *supra* note 107. See also *RCAP Report*, Vol. 2, Part 1, *supra* note 117 at 221.

135 *RCAP Report*, Vol. 2, Part 1, *supra* note 117 at 237.

136 *Ibid.*

137 *Ibid.* at 237-238.

138 *Ibid.* at 240.

139 *Ibid.* at 251-252.

140 *Ibid.* at 251.

141 Indian and Northern Affairs Canada, "Umbrella Final Agreement Between the Government of Canada, the Council for Yukon Indians and the Government of the Yukon": www.ainc-inac.gc.ca/pr/agr/umb/index_e.html.

142 See *RCAP Report*, Vol. 1, *supra* note 117. The RCAP started in 1991 but was not published until 1996. See also Inherent Right Policy, *supra* note 107. The federal government's Inherent Right Policy was released in 1996.

143 Indian and Northern Affairs Canada, "Council for Yukon Indians Sign Umbrella Final Agreement / Four Yukon First Nations Sign Land Claim and Self-Government Agreements": www.ainc-inac.gc.ca/pr/agr/ykn/1-9325_e.html.

144 *Ibid.*

145 Council of Yukon First Nations, "Our Nations": www.cyfn.ca/ournations.

146 *Yukon Agreement Highlights, supra* note 143; see also *ibid.*

147 Westbank First Nation, "Community Profile": www.wfn.ca/profile.asp. The Okanagan Nation is also referred to as *syilx.*

148 Indian and Northern Affairs Canada, *Westbank First Nation Self-Government Agreement*: www.ainc-inac.gc.ca/al/ldc/ccl/fagr/wfn/wfn-eng.asp.

149 Ministry of Aboriginal Relations and Reconciliation, "Westbank First Nation": www.gov.bc.ca/arr/firstnation/westbank/default.html.

150 *Ibid.*

151 *Westbank First Nation Constitution: Consolidated Version: Including amendments approved by Referendum, July 19, 2007*: www.wfn.ca/pdf/070719wfn_constitution_revision_final.pdf.

152 *Ibid.* at s. 7.3.

153 Indian and Northern Affairs Canada, *Nisga'a Final Agreement*: http://www.ainc-inac.gc.ca/al/ldc/ccl/fagr/nsga/nis/nis-eng.asp.

154 *Ibid.* at s.8-10.

155 *Nisga'a Agreement, supra* note 153 at Chap. 20, s.1.

156 *Constitution Act, 1982, supra* note 89 at s.35(3),(4).

157 *Sahtu Dene and Métis Comprehensive Land Claims*: www.ainc-inac.gc.ca/al/ldc/ccl/fagr/sahtu/sahmet/sahmet-eng.pdf; *Gwich'in Comprehensive Land Claim Agreement*: www.gwichin.nt.ca/LCA.

158 *Ibid.* at s.4.

159 *Ibid.* at s.4.2.2(a).

160 *Ibid.* at s.4.2.2(b) for both agreements.

161 See, generally, M. Chandler and C. Lalonde, "Cultural Continuity as a Protective Factor against Suicide in First Nations Youth," in Government of Canada, *Horizons Policy Research Initiatives: Hope or Heartbreak: Aboriginal Youth and Canada's Future* (Ottawa: Policy Research Initiative, 2008) Vol. 10, No.1: www.policyresearch.gc.ca/doclib/Horizons_Vol10Num1_final_e.pdf.

162 Statistics Canada, "Aboriginal Peoples in Canada in 2006: Inuit, Métis and First Nations, 2006 Census": www12.statcan.ca/english/census06/analysis/aboriginal/pdf/97-558-XIE2006001.pdf at 14.

163 *Ibid.* at "Highlights."

164 J. Steffler, "Aboriginal Peoples: A Young Population for Years to Come," in *Hope or Heartbreak, supra* note 161 at 19.

165 M. Brant Castellano, "Reflections on Identity and Empowerment: Recurring Themes in the Discourse on and with Aboriginal Youth" in *ibid.* at 7.

166 *Ibid.* at 8.

167 *Ibid.*

168 *Ibid.* at 12.

169 See, generally, Suicide in First Nations Youth, *supra* note 161.

170 *Ibid.* at 68.

171 *Ibid.* at 70.

172 *Ibid.* at 71. "Clearly, the 'epidemic' of youth suicides regularly reported in the popular press is not a 'First Nations' epidemic, but a tragedy suffered by some communities and not others."

173 *Ibid.*

174 *Ibid.*

175 *Ibid.* at 72.

176 V. Gideon et al, "First Nations Youth Health: Recognizing the Challenges, Recognizing the Potential," in *Hope or Heartbreak, supra* note 161 at 85.

177 *Ibid.*

178 Royal Canadian Mounted Police, "Criminal Intelligence: The Aboriginal Youth Cohort: A Discussion Paper on Future Consequences" (Ottawa: RCMP, 2007) at 5-6. This paper was obtained through an ATIP request in 2008.

179 T. Schouls, *Aboriginal Identity, Pluralist Theory, and the Politics of Self-Government* (Vancouver: UBC Press, 2003) at 120-122.

180 *R. v. Van der Peet*, [1996] 2 S.C.R. 507 at para. 30.

181 *Indigenous Difference, supra* note 5 at 9, 48.

182 *R. v. Powley* [2003] 2 S.C.R. 207 at para. 32.

183 *Ibid.*

184 T. Flanagan, *First Nations? Second Thoughts* (Montreal: McGill-Queen's University Press, 2000) at 21.

185 *Ibid.* at 22.

186 A. Cairns, *Citizens Plus: Aboriginal Peoples and The Canadian State* (Vancouver: UBC Press, 1999) at 153.

187 *Ibid.* at 45.

188 C. MacIntosh, "From Judging Culture to Taxing 'Indians': Tracing the Legal Discourse of the 'Indian Mode of Life'" (2009) 47 Osgoode Hall L.J. 399.

189 *Indigenous Difference, supra* note 5 at 75.

190 *Ibid.* at 71-75.

191 *Ibid.* at 54-55.

192 *Ibid.* at 169-70.

193   *Ibid.* at 53, 124.

194   *Ibid.* at 125.

195   J. Borrows, "'Landed' Citizenship: Narratives of Aboriginal Political Participation," in W. Kymlicka and W. Norman (Eds.), *Citizenship in Diverse Societies* (New York: Oxford University Press, 2000) at 326.

196   *Indigenous Difference, supra* note 5, Landed Citizenship, *supra* note 195.

197   Landed Citizenship, *supra* note 195 at 329.

198   *Ibid.* at 330. Borrows reminds readers that one in every two Aboriginal people marries a non-Aboriginal person.

199   S. Grammond, *Identity Captured by Law: Membership in Canada's Indigenous Peoples and Linguistic Minorities* (Montreal: McGill Queen's University Press, 2009) at 7-8.

200   G. Alfred, *Heeding the Voices of Our Ancestors: Kahnawake Mohawk Politics and the Rise of Native Nationalism* (Toronto: Oxford University Press, 1990) at 73-75.

201   W. Kymlicka, *Multicultural Citizenship: A Liberal Theory of Minority Rights* (New York: Oxford University Press, 1995) at 10.

202   *Ibid.* at 23.

203   *Ibid.*

204   *Ibid.* at 105.

205   K. Clark, "The Blood Quantum and Indian Identification" (2004) 2 *Dartmouth College Undergraduate Journal of Law* (Issue 2) 40 at 41.

206   *Ibid.*

207   B. Lawrence, *"Real" Indians and Others: Mixed Blood Urban Native Peoples and Indigenous Nationhood* (Lincoln: University of Nebraska Press, 2004) at 40.

208   *Ibid.* at 40-41.

209   Blood Quantum, *supra* note 205.

210   Population Implications, *supra* note 26.

211   Cited in *RCAP Report*, Vol. 1, *supra* note 142 at 183.

212   C. Schick, et al (Eds.), *Contesting Fundamentalisms* (Halifax: Fernwood Publishing, 2004).

213   *Aboriginal Identity, supra* note 179 at 154.

214   *Ibid.* at 155.

215   *Ibid.*

216   *Ibid.* at 155-156.

217   J. Borrows, "Contemporary Traditional Equality: The Effect of the Charter on First Nations Politics," in D. Scheidermen and K. Sutherland (Eds.), *Charting the Consequences: The Impact of Charter Rights on Canadian Law and Politics* (Toronto: University of Toronto Press, 1997) 169 at 183.

218 *Aboriginal Identity, supra* note 179 at 158.

219 *Ibid.* at 159.

220 *Ibid.* at 162.

221 Contemporary Traditional Equality, *supra* note 217 at 174.

222 *Ibid.* at 175.

223 Negotiating Identity, *supra* note 23 at 3.

224 *Ibid.* at 13-14.

225 M. Minow, "Identities" (1991) 3 Yale J. L. Hum. 97 at 116.

226 Prime Minister Stephen Harper, "Statements by Ministers: Apology to Former Students of Indian Residential Schools" (11 June 2008): www.ainc-inac.gc.ca/ai/rqpi/apo/pmsh-eng.asp.

227 F. Lomayesva, "Indian Identity — Post Indian Reflections" (1999) 35 Tulsa L.J. 63 at 64.

228 *Ibid.* at 65.

229 *Ibid.* at 66.

230 *Ibid.* at 67.

231 Blood Quantum, *supra* note 205 at 42.

232 J. Nickel, "The Value of Cultural Belonging: Expanding Kymlicka's Theory" (1995) 33/4 Dialogue 635 at 639.

233 C. Helin, *Dances with Dependency: Out of Poverty Through Self-Reliance*, 2nd Ed. (Woodland Hills, CA: Ravencrest Publishing, 2008) at 108.

234 2006 Census, *supra* note 162 at 6.

235 M. Morris, "Voices of Aboriginal Youth Today: Keeping Aboriginal Languages Alive for Future Generations," in *Hope or Heartbreak, supra* note 161 at 60.

236 Negotiating Identity, *supra* note 23 at 21, 23.

237 *United Nations Declaration on the Rights of Indigenous Peoples*, UNGA, 62nd Sess. UN Doc. A/RES/61/295 (13 Sept. 2007).

238 Negotiating Identity, *supra* note 23 at 6-7, 8-12.

239 Statistics Canada, "Canada's Ethnocultural Mosaic, 2006 Census": www12.statcan.ca/english/census06/analysis/ethnicorigin/pdf/97-562-XIE2006001.pdf at 11.

240 *Ibid.*

241 Landed Citizenship, *supra* note 195 at 330.

242 *Ibid.* at 339-340.

243 *Ibid.* at 340.

244 W. Cornet, "Aboriginality: Legal Foundations, Past Trends, Future Prospects," in J. Magnet and D. Dorey (Eds.), *Aboriginal Rights Litigation* (Markham: LexisNexis Canada, 2003) at 141.

245 *Real" Indians and Others, supra* note 207 at 245.

246 *Ibid.* at 242.

247 E. Garroutte, *Real Indians: Identity and the Survival of Native America* (Los Angeles: University of California Press, 2003).

248 *Ibid.* at 78.

249 *Ibid.* at 81.

250 *Ibid.* at 135.

251 Indian Identity, *supra* note 227 at 64.

252 *Ibid.* at 72.

253 *Aboriginal Identity, supra* note 179 at 120.

254 Membership Department, Mohawk Council of Kahnawa'ke, "A Review of the Kahnawa'ke Membership Law": www.kahnawake.com/org/docs/MembershipReport.pdf.

255 M. Patriquin, "Inside the Kahnawake Evictions," *Macleans Magazine*: www2.macleans.ca/2010/02/10/inside-the-kahnawake-evictions; CBC News, "Kahnawake issues 2nd eviction notice": www.cbc.ca/canada/montreal/story/2010/02/11/kahnawake-evicts-non-native-residents.html.

256 Kahnawa'ke Membership Report, *supra* note 255.

257 *Heeding the Voices, supra* note 200 at 2.

258 *Ibid.* at 163.

259 *Ibid.* at Executive Summary.

260 *Ibid.*

261 *Ibid.* at 10.

262 *Ibid.*

263 *Ibid.* at 7.

264 *Ibid.*

265 *Ibid.* at 3.

266 *Ibid.* at 12.

267 *Ibid.*

268 *Ibid.*

269 *Ibid.*

270 *Ibid.*

271 *Ibid.*

272 *Ibid.* at 18, 19.

273 New Brunswick Aboriginal Peoples Council: www.nbapc.org/. See also Congress of Aboriginal Peoples, "Overview": www.abo-peoples.org/about/overview.html.

274 *Ibid.* See the "Terms and Conditions" under the section entitled "Membership." The base criteria for membership (in addition to living off reserve in New Brunswick for 6 months and filling out the form), one must "be a descendant of a verified and known Aboriginal person since July 1, 1867." See also *The New Brunswick Aboriginal Peoples Council Constitution and By-Laws* (Fredericton: NBAPC, Feb. 19, 2008) at s.1.

275 *NBAPC Constitution, supra* note 274 at s.1. (iv).

276 Interview with Frank Palmater, former president, director, and member of the NBAPC Membership Committee (July 2010). Correspondence between Palmater and the NBAPC indicates that these issues have been raised both at committee and with executive, but to date the practice remains unchanged.

277 *NBAPC Constitution, supra* note 275 at 2.

278 This example refers to the situation where a non-Aboriginal woman married a status Indian man pre-1985 and gained status as an Indian. This circumstance is compared to a non-Aboriginal woman who married a non-status Indian man. Post 1985, the non-Aboriginal spouse of the Indian man can have membership in the NBAPC, but the non-Aboriginal spouse of the non-status Indian cannot.

279 Despite the fact that off-reserve band members won the right to vote in *Corbiere, supra* note 95, many bands subsequently enacted election codes that continued to exclude off-reserve band members from voting.

280 The New Brunswick Aboriginal Peoples Council Constitution and By-Laws (Fredericton: NBAPC, July 4, 2006), taken from the 36th Annual General Meeting Docket.

281 *Ibid.* at s.1.G.

282 *Ibid.* at s. 11.A., 1.C. Notice of annual AGMs were given to members in good standing only, defined as full members. This was interpreted by NBAPC as meaning only resident members.

283 Cape Breton University, "The Mi'kmaq": http://mikmawey.uccb.ns.ca/mikmaq.html. Mi'kma'ki is Mi'kmaq territory which is comprised of seven districts throughout eastern Canada and Maine.

Notes to the Conclusion

1 See *R.* v. *Fowler* (1993), 134 N.B.R. (2d) 361.

2 *Eel River Band Membership Rules* (Ottawa: INAC, 2007).

3 T. Flanagan, *First Nations? Second Thoughts* (Montreal: McGill-Queen's University Press, 2000); G. Gibson, *A New Look at Canadian Indian Policy: Respect the Collective – Promote the Individual* (Vancouver: Fraser Institute, 2009); F. Widdowson and A. Howard, *Disrobing the Aboriginal Industry: The Deception Behind Indigenous Cultural Preservation* (Montreal: McGill-Queen's University Press, 2008).

4 A. Cairns, *Citizens Plus: Aboriginal Peoples and the Canadian State* (Vancouver: UBC Press, 1999).

5 *R.* v. *Van der Peet*, [1996] 2 S.C.R. 507.

6 *Constitution Act, 1982*, being Schedule B to the *Canada Act, 1982* (U.K.), 1982, c.11.

7   *Ibid.* at s.35(4).

8   *Congress of Aboriginal Peoples* v. *Canada (Minister of Indian Affairs and Northern Development, Attorney General)* (14 Dec. 1999) T-2172-99 (Fed. Ct.) (Statement of Claim, Plaintiffs). The Congress of Aboriginal Peoples argues that non-status Indians and Métis peoples should fall under the definition of the term "Indian" within section 91(24) of the *Constitution Act, 1867.* They further argue that Canada has an obligation to include non-status Indians and Métis peoples in consultations and negotiations on a wide range of issues that affect Aboriginal peoples.

9   *Sandra Lovelace* v. *Canada*, Communication No. R.6/24, U.N. Doc. Supp. No. 40 (A/36/40) at 166 (1981).

10 *Canadian Human Rights Act*, S.C. 2008, c.30.

Index

BC Supreme Court (BCSC): *see McIvor*

Bernard 74

Bill C-3: *Gender Equity in Indian Registration Act* 25, 28-29, 31-32, 43, 46, 51, 53, 78, 84-85, 87, 90, 138-40, 220

Bill C-31 as ameliorative legislation 136; to address discrimination under *Indian Act* s.12(1)(b) *which see*; objectives of 103, 119, 122, 123-24, 133, 136-37, 140; reinstatement under, *which see*

Bliss 134

blood quantum/ descent-based criteria for determining Indigeneity 19-20, 24, 26, 28-32, 41, 44, 50-52, 57, 81, 105-06, 108-09, 111-13, 115, 117-24, 128, 132, 140-41, 168-74, 178-84, 189, 193-202, 220-224, 226; with band membership codes 150-64

Borrows, John 93-97, 181-82.186, 191-92, 223

boundaries to identity 24, 59-60

British North America Act, 1867 7

Cairns, Alan 61-63, 180

Calder 68

Canadian Charter of Rights and Freedoms 85-93, 93-100; between individuals and governments, not private parties 85-86, 94; "cultural authority" of 91, 92, 97; discrimination 25, 113; exemption 91-92, 93, 96; Indigenous people to enjoy protection of 87, 96-100; Indigenous objections to 86-87, 88-91, 93; *section 1* 96, 122, 133;

section 15 32, 95, 112, 114-16, 124-25, 128, 142, 172; *section 24* 125; *section 25* 86-87, 92, 160, 173; *section 28* 173; *section 33* "notwithstanding" clause 87

Canadian Human Rights Act (CHRA) 76, 96; *section 67* repealed 86-87, 89, 98, 225

Canadian Human Rights Commission (CHRC) 76, 87, 102, 129-30, 142, 225

Canadian Human Rights Tribunal (CHRT) 76, 87

Cannon, M 121

Carcross/Tagish 164, 170

caste-like social structures under *Indian Act* 53

census data 48, 191

Charlottetown Accord 88

Chiefs in Ontario (CIO) 79

"Citizens Plus" 61

classes of Indians 40, 44, 45, 101, 126, 148

Clatworthy, Stewart 44, 47, 49-52, 116, 147, 149-51, 154, 155, 156-57

collective: identity 36, 58, 60, 67, 82-83, 167-68, 176, 191, 216; nature of nationhood claims 61-62, 67, 90-92, 142; rights 60, 169, 185

colonialism 38, 47, 55, 59, 94, 148, 175-76, 185, 189-90, 185-96, 204, 205, 212; effects of colonial government 14, 23, 30, 32, 38, 54, 89, 144

common law 68, 74, 84, 118

perpetuating racist concepts 19-20, 28-29, 40, 44, 99, 143-48, 173, 176, 178, 195, 198-99

Membertou First Nation 205

Métis 33, 37, 125-26, 144, 165-66, 179, 220;
definition 34-35;
"distinctive culture" test 67, 75-76, 78, 81-82;
outside *Indian Act* 21, 39, 144;
rights 84, 90;
"scrip takers" 21, 103, 128-10;
survival through constitutional protection 75, 81-82

Métis National Council (MNC) 34-35, 90, 220

Métis Settlements Grand Council (Alberta) 35, 144, 220

Miawpukek (Conne River) 129-31

Michel First Nation 128, 129, 131

Mill, John Stuart 63

Minow, Martha 66, 186

mixed marriage: moratorium on 182, 195-96

modern treaties 25, 30, 79, 164, 170, 173, 174

nation-building 26, 37, 55, 66-67, 97, 141-42, 175, 191, 201;
rebuilding 54, 78, 175-76, 185, 188-89

"Native American" 35, 65

Labrador Metis Association 130

Native Council of Canada: now CAP, *which see.*

Native Women's Association of Canada (NWAC) 89, 106;
calling for repeal of s.67 of CHRA 89, 128

New Brunswick Aboriginal Peoples Council (NBAPC) 198-99

Nisga'a 164, 172-73

non-status Indians 20-22, 28, 43-96, 101, 105, 111, 120, 129-30, 149, 177-79, 206;
and the *Charter* 111;
definitions 34-36;
disadvantaged 116, 120, 123-24, 124-28, 130, 145, 150, 177-78;
excluded from membership 22, 25-26, 42, 98, 103-04, 110, 115, 120-22, 127.143, 152, 155, 168, 174, 187, 195

Nunavut Settlement Agreement 96

Oakes 113-14, 122

off-reserve organizations 34, 53, 57, 83, 87, 89-90, 198, 220

off-reserve Indigenous people 13, 53, 82-83, 123, 125, 189-90;
and *Charter* 96, 118;
excluded 22, 116, 120, 123, 199, 203-04;
population numbers 130, 149-50, 156, 157, 158, 159-60, 161

one-parent descent rules 50-52, 124.138, 141-42, 151-52, 154-55, 158, 162-63, 169

one-quarter blood rule (Bill C-31) 29, 32, 41, 105, 115, 118-20, 122, 124, 128-29, 140-41, 174, 176

oppression 65

"original" group (often referred to as full status Indians) 43;

DR. PAMELA PALMATER is a Mi'kmaq lawyer from the Eel River Bar First Nation in northern New Brunswick. She has two children, Mitchell and Jeremy, and a large extended family. Currently, she holds the position of Associate Professor and Chair in Indigenous Governance in the Department of Politics and Public Administration at Ryerson University.

Pamela has worked for the federal government on Indigenous legal and governance issues, and has held several director positions at Indian and Northern Affairs Canada.

She completed her doctorate in the Science of Law at Dalhousie University Law School in 2009. She holds a Master of Laws from Dalhousie University in Aboriginal Law, a Bachelor of Laws from the University of New Brunswick, and a BA with a double major in Native Studies and History from St. Thomas University in New Brunswick.

She has published articles related to Aboriginal and treaty rights and has her own website dedicated to these issues. She has specialized in Indigenous identity issues, which include Indian status, band membership, and self-government citizenship and traditional Indigenous citizenship.

She is active in the Indigenous community, volunteering as a board member of Native Child and Family Services Toronto as well as ongoing work with First Nations in Ontario. She regularly appears as a commentator on APTN and has appeared before the House and Senate as an expert witness on legislation affecting Indigenous peoples.